THE NEW
NATIVE GARDEN
Designing with Australian Plants

THE NEW NATIVE GARDEN
Designing with Australian Plants

Paul Urquhart

Photography: Leigh Clapp

CONTENTS

INTRODUCTION 6

ABOUT AUSTRALIAN PLANTS 8
The beginnings 1788–1888 • The birth of nationalism

BUILDING A GARDEN 14
Starting to design • Design principles • Getting started • Planning • Soil preparation • Choosing plants

THE LIVING PALETTE 32
Colour • Reds and pinks • Blues and mauves • Silver • Green • Creams and whites • Copper tones • Yellow and orange • Texture and touch

GARDEN STYLES 50
The Australian landscape • 'Seamless transition' and the wild garden • Naturalistic gardens: bush and rainforest • Cottage gardens • Formal gardens • Contemporary and urban interpretations • Urban and courtyard gardens • Style and climate • Blended or tapestry gardens

GARDEN DESIGNS AND PLANS 86
A meadow garden • A cottage border • A rock lily garden • A stroll garden • A gravel 'beach' • A raised garden • A bog garden • A green woodland • Formal garden ideas • A contemporary formal garden • A naturalistic courtyard • A rainforest garden

DESIGN DETAILS 136
Access routes • On the edge • Pool planting • Design principles in action • Groves • Kids' gardens • Garden art • Water • Seating and outdoor living • Containers

ATTRACTING WILDLIFE 166
Possums, lizards and frogs • Butterfly gardens • Creating habitats for birds

PLANT SELECTION 174
Trees • Shrubs • Accent plants • Perennials • Climbers • Groundcovers • Grasses and grass-like plants

GARDEN CARE 194
Planting techniques • Planting the arid garden • Fertilising • Pruning techniques • Mulching • Low water use • Propagation • Pests and diseases

RESOURCE LIST 215
PICTURE CREDITS 217
INDEX 218

INTRODUCTION

In the past fifty years we have learned a lot about the characteristics of native plants. We know that they have adapted to low-fertility soils, that many are phosphorus-intolerant, that fire and seasonal rains play a significant part in their germination. We have learned new methods of propagation and we understand the peculiar cultivation needs of various species. There are now more cultivars than ever in nurseries and the range of new horticultural varieties is growing daily. The getting-to-know-you phase of native gardening is coming to an end.

Now it's time to use native plants as part of a 'designed' garden, not just as an imitation of natural bush. What makes this book different is the emphasis on design. Until now, Australian plants have been viewed as 'specimens'. Some writers have seen them as botanical oddities, others as collectibles.

The reaction to native plants has a lot to do with recent gardening fashions. In the 1990s, nothing polarised gardeners as much as the pros and cons of Australia's plants. Simply mentioning 'native' evoked a negative reaction ranging from dismissal to revulsion. A small minority took the other extreme with a purist zeal that condemned all exotic planting. Now it seems the wheel has come full circle, with Australian plants set to ride a new wave of popularity, but this time as legitimate garden subjects better adapted to our climate and conditions than the majority of those plants already common in our gardens. This signals a new-found maturity in garden design and understanding.

Australian plants are popular. Grevilleas, bottlebrush and many other groundcover plants, all 'Australian' plants, are bought and planted in their hundreds of thousands each year, but for some reason 'native' still has a negative connotation.

What this seems to indicate is that we can place too much emphasis on origin and too little on what makes a good garden or a good garden plant.

Attractive flowers, growth habit, plants that do the job and are easy to grow — these are the criteria gardeners consciously or unconsciously apply when searching through the nursery. Blending native with exotic is the way most of us use our native plant material, and this is the way of the future. Yet there is little in the literature showing how to do this well. This book addresses this need.

In the 1970s, natives were proclaimed as the 'no maintenance' alternative. Australian plants were sold to non-gardeners as the garden you have when you don't like gardening, rather like a catchy advertising slogan for a non-alcoholic drink at the time. It caught on. No one mentioned how straggly and untidy they become when not trained, so they grew … and grew … and grew. Eventually they either died or were pulled out and replaced. It was no wonder the reaction, when it came, latched onto pretty cottage colour.

In the 1980s, the cottage garden filled with exotics was popular. The truth is the same as it ever was. Modern cottage gardens have little to do with the traditional cottage garden, and native plants can be as labour-intensive as any other.

In the 1990s, another reaction saw the colourful exuberance of the cottage garden replaced by the order of the boxed hedge; green and more green. Both are a reaction to and the antithesis of the native garden of the 1970s.

Garden styles come full circle, and it was only with the rise of interest in the Mediterranean garden with its sturdy, dry-looking grey tones, that natives began to be reconsidered. The rising popularity of the tropical garden, and in particular the Balinese style, allowed our rainforest plants access to the public consciousness too. Both developments offer us tremendous scope for developing native gardens with style.

Our approach in this book is to look at Australian plants from the point of view of how they fit into an overall garden setting. By concentrating on style and design concepts such as mass, texture, shape and foliage we hope to dispel common misconceptions about the 'bush' garden. The native garden does not have to be alien and uninviting, made up of clumps of ill-kempt, hard-to-grow plants that scratch and bite.

Styles other than the traditional are possible. For every exotic plant used in our gardens there is probably a native that will do much the same job. Often they are better adapted to our conditions. This book opens up a whole new world of blending natives with exotics to create new and exciting gardens with style and an authentic Australian ambience even though the plants used may be from many lands. And isn't that what Australia is all about!

about AUSTRALIAN Plants

The New Native Garden

ABOVE

Yellow Box (*Eucalyptus melliodora*).

OPPOSITE

Europeans' first real encounter with Australian flora was around the shores of Sydney Harbour. Most gardens have been designed with this look in mind ever since. *Angophora costata* is the dominant tree.

THE BEGINNINGS — 1788-1888

Imagine the fear and trepidation of white settlers when they first alighted on the Australian mainland. What did they find? Soil so poor it slipped through their fingers like sand, for that was all it was. No cultivated crops or plants likely to sustain life, a dry, desiccated land of thorny, hard and woody plants, all grey and glaucous, a landscape devoid of the green fields and soft leaves they were familiar with. Here was a harsh, unforgiving land of rocky outcrops and hard, tough trees that had to be cleared to make way for houses, farms, streets and towns.

This was how it was for more than a century. The cultivation of native plants was rarely attempted. Some, such as acacias and eucalypts, were left as a backdrop to house and garden, but mostly native trees and scrub were obstacles to be removed for crops and stock. Even in the suburbs, this attitude still persists today as land is cleared for housing blocks in an ever-expanding sprawl.

Some of the early chroniclers, however, wrote favourably of their impressions of the Hawkesbury sandstone flora. Watkin Tench, a young marine captain on the First Fleet, wrote of what is thought to be a tea-tree in June 1788:

> *In those places where trees are scarce a variety of flowering shrubs abound, most of them entirely new to a European and surpassing in beauty, fragrance and number, all I ever saw in an uncultivated state. Among these, a tall shrub bearing an elegant white flower which smell like English May is particularly delightful and perfumes the air to a great distance.*[1]

Later, in 1791, he wrote of the heathland between the Hawkesbury and Botany Bay:

> *The grass ... does not overspread the land in a continued sward, but arises in small detached tufts, growing every way about three inches apart, the intermediate space being bare; though the heads of the grass are often so luxuriant as to hide all deficiency on the surface. The rare and beautiful native flowering shrubs, which abound in every part, deserve the highest admiration and panegyric.*[2]

Other records, gleaned from letters, journals and diaries, tell of colonists captivated by the native plants found in that first settlement around Port Jackson. The flowers were often picked as nosegays or wildflower posies. Some intrepid gardeners tried (mostly unsuccessfully) to transplant perennials and shrubs from the bush to their humble cottage gardens. But the plants they favoured were delicate things such as flannel flowers, waratahs and the fragrant boronia, the native rose of the Sydney region. Even now, these are plants for the specialist native gardener. Little wonder they met with failure.

Herein lies the root cause of the unpopularity of native plants. They were alien and they were hard to grow. Their cultivation and propagation required specialised skills and techniques as yet unknown. Most settlers had enough trouble simply staying alive, and anyway, there were millions of acres of these lovely but unknown plants. They put on a pretty show each spring and it was easy to pick a few from an as-yet-untouched patch of ground. What did it matter if every skerrick of native vegetation was cleared from a few acres? Out in the vast wilderness there were plenty more of these plants, so clearing continued unabated.

Gardens were also a luxury, and the availability of water governed the practice of gardening. Making a garden was a tough job. The ground was thin and hard to work. When the summer sun sucked all the moisture from the surface, it set like concrete. The lack of organic matter in the soil also made tilling difficult.

The botanists 'back home', though, were having a field day. Sir Joseph Banks and his team of collectors had marvelled at the prospect of a complete continent of unknown plants. Banks' interest in Australian plants resulted from his position on the Cook expedition. He was fortunate to be embarking on a career in botany when the science was growing. These were heady days for botany.

Banks became George III's horticultural adviser in 1771. The king bought Kew House the following year and Banks became Director of the Royal Botanical Gardens in 1773. Several expeditions to the New World followed. Later the Royal Horticultural Society was founded in 1804. The Linnaean system of nomenclature was also in its infancy.

It was in response to this interest of botanists and the general sense of inquiry in this new age of scientific discovery that Governor King in 1800 established the Horticultural Gardens at Government House at Parramatta, with the help of the botanist George Caley. It included many plants collected in the early voyages of discovery, all as new to botany as they were to horticulture.

Some indigenous plants such as the wattles were retained though relegated to a secondary position outside the boundaries of the main garden. A Russian visitor quoted in Beatrice Bligh's gardening history *Cherish the Earth* describing the gardens at Government House at Parramatta wrote this of the acacias in the grounds in Governor Macquarie's day:

Along the hedges surrounding the garden masses of yellow downy Mimosa flowers are growing. These trees contribute greatly to the beauty of the garden ... [3]

By the 1830s there were agricultural and horticultural societies to further the knowledge of gardening. Thomas Shepherd was the first professional landscape designer to visit and work in the colony. In 1834 he was commissioned to deliver a series of lectures during the rule of Governor Darling. Shepherd was horrified by the wholesale destruction of the native flora around homesteads and selections. He castigated the colonists in the lecture series published posthumously:

When you, gentlemen, first go to your estates your ground was well furnished with beautiful shrubs. You ignorantly set the murderous hoe and grubbing axe to work to destroy them, and the ground that had been full of luxurious verdure was laid bare and desolate ... No person of taste

who has seen the rocks which border the shore of Port Jackson, and the beautiful trees, flowering shrubs, rock lilies and other plants growing there indigenous in masses and groups, unequalled by the art of man, must but admire them. No rocky scene in England or Scotland can be compared with it. Extensive parks may therefore be made in the first style of magnificence here at a comparative trifling expense when contrasted with the large sums of money which have been expended on similar objects in Britain.[4]

But all was not so forlorn, according to Beatrice Bligh. In the Illawarra region south of Sydney, native cabbage tree palms, acacias and eucalypts were already being incorporated into gardens. Gardening was easier here due to a mild and warm climate with plentiful rainfall. Camden was settled early by John Macarthur, a gardening pioneer. The Monaro district around Goulburn and Braidwood was explored in 1820 and gardens soon sprang up near homesteads. Kurrajongs were included in gardens with imported trees, following the popular style of the day — the landscape park. In England at this time Humphrey Repton was the leading exponent of this style, which had been started by Capability Brown. Many wealthy settlers had no doubt been influenced by his ideas.

Dr George Bennett, a naturalist, wrote of his observations in the 1830s in his *Gatherings of a Naturalist* (London 1860), that many indigenous plants, such as the New South Wales Christmas bush *(Ceratopetalum gummiferum)*, became favoured ornamentals in Sydney gardens:

The elegant tree named Christmas tree ... is preserved on all the grounds. It is used like Holly in England as a decoration. This pretty tree ... formerly grew in the vicinity of Sydney in abundance; but, owing to persons, at Christmas, cutting down entire trees, the owners of the land stopped the destruction — this succeeded in preserving this handsome tree, and it is growing plentifully at the present time in the grounds about Darling Point and Lower South Head Road.[5]

In the 1840s, the colonies' gardens followed in the English landscape tradition. This was a style for the wealthy. The rise of a landed gentry class, the squatters and free settlers and the colonies' dependence on wool made this possible. Gardens were still limited to stations on good land with a plentiful and regular supply of water. Architecture was borrowed from the Indian bungalow style, with long wide verandahs and high-pitched roofs designed to keep the house as cool as possible in summer. It was a simple style and the gardens were built to match. Native vegetation was confined to shade trees and background fill-in, it was never the main game.

The 1850s and 60s were the decades of gold-generated wealth, and ostentation came to gardens and houses. Repton had earlier reintroduced the idea of the terrace garden to house the growing collections of plants and horticultural oddities that were sweeping into English gardens. It marked a slow restoration of the formal and Renaissance styles that had been swept away by Brown decades before. By the early Victorian period, it found favour with fashionable colonial gardeners. It was not uncommon to find a small formal garden surrounding the homestead and a wilder 'park', including natives, outside the boundaries. Gardens in the ensuing decades, the high Victorian period, became even more elaborate. Some of Australia's oldest surviving gardens date from this period, but none could be considered 'native'.

BELOW
Grey spider flower (*Grevillea buxifolia*) and bacon-and-eggs (*Dillwynia sericea*) in spring.

THE BIRTH OF NATIONALISM

Australia's first century of European settlement was one of discovery, and as with all pioneer cultures, the refinements of horticulture, architecture and art were to come much later. It wasn't until late in the nineteenth century that an appreciation of the Australian landscape began to filter into the collective consciousness. Artists such as Tom Roberts, Arthur Streeton, Charles McCubbin and others painted pastoral scenes of artists and settlers in the bush in the 1880s and 1890s.

At the same time other artisans were busily reproducing tree ferns in silver, and waratahs in wallpaper friezes. The age of nationalism had arrived. In Europe, nationalist movements had been strong since the middle of the century; by the later two decades, similar nationalist sentiment was rampant throughout the New World, particularly in the USA.

While Australian plants featured in the decorative arts, not many were used in gardens — a few rainforest trees only were used. When the Chilean monkey puzzle trees were an oddity in Europe, we took to our indigenous members of the araucaria family. Kauri, bunya and hoop pines popped up in public parks and some large estate gardens, as did the almost native Norfolk Island pine. Cabbage tree palms and Moreton Bay figs also appeared as street and park trees.

Gardens took a backseat from the outbreak of the First World War to the cessation of the second. There were more important issues to deal with. War, depression and rearmament dominated intellectual thought and again the struggle to survive overtook the luxuries of life.

The Romance of Edna Walling
This period produced one notable gardener: Edna Walling. There was a limited understanding of design in the Australia of the early twentieth century. In the scheme of things, Walling was a big fish in a small pond.
Walling's designs were popular among a certain echelon, garden design being a luxury in those days, and her impact on the gardening public as a whole was limited. Her lasting influence came about more through her writing, in particular as gardening editor of *Australian Home Beautiful* from 1926 to 1950. Her influence had a geographical limitation too. Her work was largely, but not exclusively, restricted to Melbourne and some cooler areas of southern New South Wales.

She has, however, captured the imagination of a few scholars anxious to learn more about her advanced ideas in those lean years. As such she stands out as a beacon. Though not responsible for the birth of an 'Australian style' as some have claimed, she did not operate in a design vacuum either. Influenced by the most respected English designer of the time, Gertrude Jekyll, and probably by the work of Beatrix Farrand, one of the first successful American female landscape architects. Farrand was the hand behind the design of the famous Dumbarton Oaks garden in Washington DC.

Walling began to include a few native plants in her designs only in the latter part of her career. By the 1950s, she was extolling the virtues of Australian plants in her books. She wrote lovingly of many: *Boronia*, *Grevillea*, *Eriostemon*, all common in gardens now, and a few which still are not: *Callitris*, *Calytrix* and *Olearia* (particularly *O. phlogopappa*).

Beyond Walling
Although there was little development in garden design in the period following the Second World War, there was a quiet revolution taking place in the concept of 'the garden' and outdoor living. The influence of the California lifestyle snowballed around this time. We adopted both the look and the lifestyle.

The Society for Growing Australian Plants was founded in 1958. Native plants have ridden a roller-coaster of concurrent popularity and apathy. Through the 1980s and 1990s an argument has raged in landscape architecture about 'Australian style'. Some purists have maintained that an 'Australian' garden must be composed of indigenous plants. Others, in the true tradition of the cultural cringe, were contemptuous of the merest possibility of the concept of an 'Australian garden'.

If we are ever to develop a truly 'Australian' style, the elements would be the same as those that distinguish other distinct styles around the world. The first feature is the use of art and decorative elements that are distinguishable as Australian. Second, we should use plants to reflect the character of the overall landscape. Australia is a diverse continent with many climates and different terrains. We need to come to terms with our regional climates and conditions, but not necessarily using exclusively native plants. In every region of the continent, climate is the determining factor. Using native plants is one way to revel in these differences.

building a GARDEN

STARTING TO DESIGN

Building a garden is an enjoyable pastime. A garden performs a host of functions. It's a haven from the busy working week, a place for relaxation and a social forum for entertaining friends, family and neighbours.

The worth of a garden is determined by atmosphere, mood, charm and attention to detail. It is these subjective, indeterminate things that can make your garden appealing, relaxing and beautiful.

Romance is a product of design, whether intentional or unintentional. The placement of trees, the position of paths, the features, the drift of views, the form of shrubs, whether they are billowing, or tightly controlled, all blend to create an ambience inviting us to stroll, sit or admire.

Planning and design go together, as the song says, 'like a horse and carriage'. A well-drawn plan is useful, but well before you get to that stage there are three simple steps that can make all the difference. First, formulate a 'big picture' view of the garden and how it may be used; second, take breathing space after your initial considerations, and lastly, re-assess all your options.

FORMULATE THE 'BIG PICTURE'

Starting any new garden requires an all-encompassing concept — the 'big picture' — that ties together all the elements you want from a garden. Without this overall view a garden can become a mess of unconnected features, unpleasant to look at and uncomfortable to be in. It would be a mistake to make a blanket declaration that you always need a fully drawn-up plan. Some of the loveliest gardens have grown like Topsy. In almost all cases, though, you will find that a great deal of thought has been given to placement and the way the different elements are blended. Undertaking some form of planning process, even if only a rough sketch, is essential so that ultimately, everything works together in harmony.

TAKE A BREATHER

Develop this 'big picture' view and then leave yourself some breathing space. It's a mistake to rush out and tackle the 'instant garden'. Let ideas percolate through your mind for a few weeks, even months, while you price landscape materials and get quotes. Problems will inevitably show up and you will need time to solve them. Never rush garden design — there is always a better idea just around the corner.

CONSIDER YOUR OPTIONS

Design problems may present themselves and leave you stumped for an answer. You may find there are gaps and inconsistencies in your plan that require solutions. Here you should consider whether professional advice could solve them most effectively. Sometimes it is cheaper and more efficient to call in a professional garden designer. Most will give you a working plan that you can do yourself in stages. Certainly the hard work of measuring and drawing a plan may be best left to a garden designer. Any good designer will discuss your own ideas, suggest options and help you make decisions. Very often they will think of entirely new solutions which would have otherwise eluded you.

OTHER CONSIDERATIONS

Getting started is often the hardest part of any creative exercise. Once that initial hurdle is overcome, ideas, problems and solutions will present themselves. Eventually everything seems to fall into place. Here are a few things to get you started.

First, consider mood. Ask yourself, 'What atmosphere do I want to create?' Mood is closely allied to style. Some styles seem to lift the soul more than others, and since this is very much dependent on the individual, you alone can decide. The soaring lushness of the rainforest, the floral carpet of the coastal heath, the wildflower wonderland of carpeting annuals, the simplicity of the stylised desert — these are some ideas and atmospheres you could consider.

Your lifestyle and the use you will make of the garden are also important. The notion of a garden changes with each decade. Australian gardens are outdoor living spaces much more than gardens in Europe and parts of North America. When the American architect, Thomas Church, first proposed the concept of outdoor living in the design of his Californian gardens, it was seen as revolutionary. Yet it has entered the Australian psyche and now is part and parcel of every garden design.

Issues such as this will inevitably arise in your discussions with your garden designer, family and friends. The best advice is to think deeply about the role of a garden in your life *before* you do any work in it. And the easiest way to do that is to sit down and make a simple 'wish' list of what you would like in a garden. The next few pages provide the basics for designing a garden, from the indeterminate principles of design to technical considerations. But never forget the need for enjoyment.

Building a Garden

There are four elements to the design process:
1. How you intend to use the garden
2. Understanding the principles of design
3. Gaining new technical skills in measuring and plotting points
4. Applying the information and ideas you now have.

PREVIOUS PAGES

Pages 14–15: The natural bushland often resembles a natural cottage garden in spring. What seems to be a haphazard arrangement of plants endlessly and randomly repeated is actually well planned and carefully placed. Designer Roger Stone has achieved the natural effect with low shrubs, perennials and hard landscaping.

BELOW

Start with the big picture. Fill a rainforest garden with plants that look the part. Oliver's sassafras (*Cinnamonum oliveri*) is a preferred foodplant for the blue triangle butterfly, which also feeds on the weedy camphor laurel.

DESIGN PRINCIPLES

FORM, STRUCTURE AND FUNCTION
Elements of garden design

Design principles are nothing more than tricks of the trade. They are the means by which you can make a good garden a great garden, creating harmony and restfulness. They make small spaces appear bigger, narrow spaces appear wider and unpleasant views palatable.

Design always throws up problems needing solutions. Rather than being intimidating, design principles help us find practical options. Observing gardens that are successful, and analysing why they are, presents us with general principles and techniques that will overcome similar problems. This is the key to understanding the concept. Design principles work out what works and how it works. They can be spoken of in abstract terms such as space, shape, form, line and movement, but they are essentially real solutions to problems that continually occur in gardens all over the world. Designers then manipulate the elements of design — levels, focal points, views, patterns and surfaces — with living things such as trees, screening and foundation plantings.

WAKING THE SENSES
The principle of surprise

If we can see a garden all at one go, we miss out on much of what makes a garden an exciting place to be. Gardens with nooks and crannies, secret corners or surprises in store are filled with mystery and surprise. It's not difficult to achieve this surprise factor using 'tension'.

Designers use the principles of design to create this tension. 'Garden rooms' are one method. Sections of a garden can be perceived as enclosed or separated from other sections either by real walls or suggestions of dividing walls. In practice it works more like a see-through screen. The separations provided by hedges, garden seats, container groups, a change of level and so on, establish 'tension points'. Each of the above devices can be used to obscure a view, so producing mystery and anticipation. As we walk through, the tension is released and converted to surprise.

SPACE INVADERS
The principle of space

Space is the most overlooked element of design. Space is not merely the gaps between features, buildings or garden beds, it is also how the plants and features themselves are arranged and used. Edna Walling made an acute observation about unassuming plants, those that do not immediately leap out at you for their audacious flowers or foliage. She wrote, '... strip a garden that pleases you of all the quieter things that grow in it, and all its charm will vanish.' What she was saying is that simple shrubs, trees and groundcovers that do not sell themselves with bold flowers also add 'space' to a garden by disappearing into the distance.

Space is there to be manipulated for effect. Plants that are not vying for attention can be easily overlooked. By adding to or forming part of the 'void' (along with lawns, paving or clearings), they increase the sense of space in a garden.

The smaller the garden, the more important even a tiny element of 'space' becomes. Inner city terraces, for instance, may have only one open area, such as paving surrounded by walls and buildings. Larger gardens may have several, including areas of lawn, a swimming pool or even a sweeping driveway. There may be several areas of lawn intersected by flowerbeds or paths that lead to other courtyards or sitting areas.

THE TORTOISE OR THE HARE?
The principle of movement

Space and movement are linked. This is not just a conceptual link but also a practical one. Movement can enlarge or shrink our perception of a space by controlling how fast we move through a garden.

There are many ways to link spaces. Paths link terraces, lawns and patios, and steps do the same on sloping or uneven ground. Sometimes function demands movement between spaces in a garden: hanging the washing, going for a swim or adding carbon to the compost heap. People will always take the most direct route to an urgent destination. The more practical the function, the more direct the route should be — a straight path to the clothesline makes more sense than a meandering one. Generally we will not deviate from a 'desire line', so design should respect this tendency.

If we move through the garden quickly, it will appear smaller. In the case of the washing, the quicker the better, but with less pressing matters, slower movement is desirable. Varying the route achieves this. A serpentine path is one way, but any path requires a reason to deviate. Planting a stand of

OPPOSITE

Mist in this mountain garden enhances the native trees and the sense of mood.

trees or placing a large urn or a seat in the course of the path provides a valid reason for the path to zigzag or bend.

We can modulate speed, too, by the tightness of the curve or the width of the path. You might imagine a narrow path may slow passage down, but in the same way that a narrow neck on a stream creates a rush of water, a confined path quickens our pace. A slight curve is traversed much more quickly than a tight one, making the garden appear smaller.

Wide and winding paths slow movement. So does creating openings and exits into different parts of a garden. Changes of level such as steps and slopes slow us down and also provide valid reasons to regulate movement.

Even such mundane things as paving can make a difference to speed. We move faster on a smooth surface than a rough one, and things like grass and pebble coverings make passage even slower. Brick paving laid in stretcher bond with the pattern running in the same direction as the path can speed up movement. If laid crossways, it tends to slow movement.

BALANCING ACT
The principle of balance

Balance, along with rhythm, unity and accent are principles that come from art but are applicable to garden design. Each is dependent on the other to some extent, but all are essential to a satisfying design. The *Macquarie Dictionary* defines balance as, 'harmonious arrangement or adjustment esp. in the arts of design'. The *Australian Concise Oxford* says 'harmony of design and proportion'. Both imply that a balanced landscape also contains hamony and proportion.

Balance brings an implied stability. One way to comprehend this is to imagine a waiter carrying a tray by the palm of the hand. If the weight of the tray shifts slightly the contents may topple. Our perception of balance in a landscape is similar. We perceive imbalance even though we may not be consciously aware of it. Something may look wrong — that is essentially an imbalance in the visual weight.

Plants and objects in a landscape all carry this visual weight. To look stable they must be strategically placed. Dark-coloured flowers and foliage appear heavier than white and pastels. Fine-textured leaves appear lighter than coarse foliage.

A plant with an open habit and large leaves, such as pomaderris or some of the dwarf lillypillies for instance, may appear lighter than one with small-leafed foliage grown tightly, as in a hedge. Size and form are also variables. A tall tree needs an equal mass to balance it in a landscape. This can be either another erect tree of similar size or it could be a horizontal feature. A mass of shrubs as wide as the tree is tall balances a lone tree if there is insufficient room. It is also a lighter alternative.

Formal and informal gardens rely on symmetry and asymmetry respectively. The formal garden uses an obvious means to achieve balance. A central axis with a mirror image on either side is clear to see. It works best on a level site and often uses a central focal point. On the other hand, balance in an informal garden is less obvious. Asymmetrical plantings need to be well organised and stable. A tall form such as a tree with dark colours and rough textures needs to be balanced by shorter plants with lighter foliage.

LEVEL PLAYING FIELDS
The principle of levels

Sloping gardens offer more natural possibilities for interest than do level ones. The downside is that it is often more expensive to exploit these possibilities. Walls, steps, bridges, boardwalks, cascades and water features can be costly additions. Existing natural features such as rock outcrops and gullies, though, can form the basis of an exciting garden design.

Slopes can be spatially manipulated — even flat sites can be made to appear less level. The general principle is that a downhill slope makes a space appear larger, while one sloping up from the house foreshortens the view and makes space appear smaller.

The latter situation is common on new housing sites in hilly areas. To deal with it, a large level terrace close to the house will balance the upper slope. If the area is steep, retaining walls are the best bet. An artificial slope on a level site is best positioned in the middle distance. It could take the form of a slight rise formed by sleepers or a mound of soil, and can be planted or terraced and paved.

LINES OF SIGHT
The principle of lines

I've heard lines in a garden described as permanent tour guides. Following them leads your eyes and feet from place to place, calling attention to points of interest along the way. These lines are three-dimensional. Paths form curved or straight lines with garden beds and boundaries. All act as threads to tie a garden together.

The line our eye follows is called the line of sight. It often leads to focal points and the location of a line of sight is often determined by the location of a focal point. It is possible to influence mood, appearance and how quickly we move through a garden by altering the width, angle or curve of lines in a garden.

Formal gardens use a central axis to direct views. Focal points create views within a garden, and are usually placed at the end of straight lines or where they intersect. Formal gardens rely heavily on straight lines and so are often found where surfaces are level or where several different level surfaces are created by terracing sloping ground — it is hard to imagine a straight line on undulating ground.

Informal gardens use curving lines. Broad sweeps and curved planting lines are often designed to focus our attention towards the middle of the garden, but usually off-centre. A line directed to dead centre appears too symmetrical and therefore unbalanced.

Lines can be used to introduce complex patterns in a garden design. Parallel lines act as a partial screen and can be used in an informal or formal way. To focus attention on a view or a focal point, we can use lines that converge in the distance. Lines that converge in the distance also create perspective, an important point to consider when designing in a small garden. To open up an area, use diverging lines, which become further apart in the distance. Crossing lines, whether the lines are straight, as in a formal garden or curved, help you create shapes. Shadows from tree branches, buildings and structures can sometimes be used to create a secondary series of lines and hence create a more complex design picture.

SHAPES AND PATTERNS

We look to pattern to give structure to the world we inhabit. Pattern is a repetition of shapes in a set order. Patterns can be repeated and varied with overlays of colour and texture. Combinations of patterns also create effects and determine style. Pattern works by drawing attention. Large-scale patterns catch the eye, and depending on where the pattern is applied, it can serve different purposes.

Living patterns using plants can add interest to a landscape. Espalier techniques, tall wispy plants that cast shadows, topiary, knots and parterres can be used according to the overall theme of the garden.

ABOVE

Architectural features like this timber boardwalk are as important as a garden's plant material for providing 'pattern'. The boardwalk also creates a line of sight by opening up space.

GETTING STARTED

Assess your site for climate, soil, location/surroundings, exposure, views, aspect/orientation — retaining sun and providing shade for winter and summer comfort.

As with all human tasks, there is a logical sequence to designing a garden. To the amateur it can appear daunting, but if we think of it as a series of short steps leading to a unified goal, then it all becomes much less of a challenge and more of an adventure.

Good garden design results from three steps: site analysis, outline plan and concept design. Good design is also timeless. Quirky and quickie gardens don't last and willl date. If anything, err a little on the side of conservative. Later, when the garden has settled in and is growing, add some flourishes, a bit of bold colour here, a feature there, but always keep the main theme going.

To start, simple design works best. The most complicated parterres you find in those inspiring books on renaissance gardens are all very well until you get tied up in knots with planting, weeding, pruning and just keeping the hedges alive and green. If you realise that your garden and your lifestyle are a less than perfect match, you'll have wasted a lot of time, money and effort. A straightforward naturalistic planting using a repeated series of plants will serve most of us well. The way to avoid follies is to keep reminding yourself of your needs. You will be able to itemise these as you read through the site analysis checklist.

If you get stumped, try running with a single idea and developing it as the base plan. Develop a strong, simple skeleton and overlay the idea with detail. Once you have a plan worked out, try to space the work over several seasons. A garden is not an instant thing, so allow it to develop in stages. That way it will still be a joy, not a chore.

SITE ANALYSIS

A site analysis will help you avoid costly mistakes or, as one wit once said, it stops you putting the cart before the horse manure.

It is essentially an inventory of site features with a touch of 'wish list' thrown in. In it you list all the site's advantages and disadvantages, whether you are working on a bare building site or an established garden. The benefit of doing this is that you are less likely to make a move before you have a clear idea of where you want to go with the design. Quite often the existing tree or shrub border that seems to be in the way of the new deck is removed, and this is regretted later when you realise another spot is a better location for the deck.

Where do you start? If you have a house plan, use that. If not, you may have to draw the footprint of the house on a sheet of graph paper. Start by walking around the house at different times of the day and note what you see. There is a point to this and you should use the following list as a guide to what to note.

Site analysis checklist

Note down all the following:
- Features you would like to keep and those you want to get rid of
- Existing vegetation, including trees and shrubs
- Sun and shade. Check at different times of day and also different seasons if possible. Note sunny and shady areas and approximate hours in sun or shade per day
- Soil quality and texture
- Good and bad views
- Drainage patterns such as slopes, moist and dry spots
- Where utilities cross the property — power lines, telephone cables, gas, water and sewerage
- Street privacy, aspect and views
- Neighbours' properties, including impinging factors such as shade or overlooking windows or balconies
- Indicate where north is
- Prevailing winds
- Easements and setbacks.

Once you have done this you have the basic information about the garden as it is and a rough idea of what you want. Now the process of analysing the data begins. Simplify the information. Make a list of what you need well before undertaking any design work. Call the list of things that are essential your 'A' list. This may include space for a pool, a barbecue, somewhere to dry the clothes or park the car or a plot for vegetables.

Your 'B' list could include things you may possibly want to add at a later date. Relaxing can be either active or passive, so consider areas for a basketball hoop, a croquet lawn, a parterre or a hammock.

Building a Garden

ABOVE
Common tussock grass (*Poa labillardieri*), bamboo spear grass (*Stipa ramosissima*) and other grass-like plants such as dianella or mat rush (*Lomandra longifolia*) create a wild effect beside a secluded bend of a river.

The concept of outdoor living is an idea that has more or less taken hold in the minds of Australian gardeners in the last 30 years, with some regional variation mostly according to climate. Gold Coast gardeners, for instance, seem to live for the idea; gardeners in the cooler south are perhaps a little less attuned to it as a design option, but it is Perth and western gardeners who have adopted the notion the most. Perhaps it's the Mediterranean climate and the likelihood of rainless summers and balmy nights. Open courtyards and rooms which open up into the garden are common design elements in Perth gardens.

Certainly climate plays a major role in garden use, and it needs to be a factor in your decisions about what you want from the garden. The other major factor is expectation of use. You need to consider both these factors before you start, and balance the space you have with what you know about your local climate and the uses to which your garden will be put.

The New Native Garden

PLANNING

The site analysis gave you the basic information about the garden as it is; your next step is planning. Instead of looking at the physical aspects of the site, turn the spotlight on yourself. This is where you say to yourself what you really want your garden to be, and outline your expectations.

Think of the plannng process in terms of five broad categories: family, outdoor activities, circulation, and privacy and security.

ABOVE

Chorizema cordatum is a Western Australian plant that has found a niche in just about every native plant garden. Flowers are short-lived in spring but they are spectacular.

FAMILY

The garden has to suit all occupants of the household or members of the family, so pay some attention to defining everyone's needs and routines. Do you have any pets, and will their needs impact on the garden? The future must be addressed too. You may have to include plans for an extension at some time, or other building projects such as a pool or a new garage.

OUTDOOR ACTIVITES

Ask yourself how much time you spend on the following: gardening, entertaining, recreation activities (including hobbies) and utility functions such as washing, cleaning the car and so on.

CIRCULATION

Estimate actual hours spent outside and how often you might entertain. Include likely number of guests and length of functions. Space will determine how many guests you may have in comfort and how easily they will move around the garden. The anticipated guest numbers will determine the size of paths, where they go and the placement of paved terraces, driveways and parking spaces.

PRIVACY AND SECURITY

Privacy can be a big issue, so plan for it. Determine which rooms you use most often and how these may be made more private from the street and from neighbours' houses. Security is another issue. You may need fencing to keep young children or animals within the property or out of a pool. You might prefer not to obscure access points at the front of the house.

Lighting for security, circulation and entertaining can be planned at this stage. The benefit here is that electricity cables can be laid before the hard landscaping goes down, which will be much cheaper than trying to lay it afterwards. A well-lit entry makes guests feel safe and comfortable, and lighting the garden increases its use.

ROUGHING YOUR OUTLINE PLAN

The old axiom 'form follows function' is simply a fancy way of saying why you do something tells you how to do it. After listing the desirable features, a reality diagram is useful. Your 'wish' list will no doubt be in excess of available space, so the whole thing needs to be rationalised. The easiest way to do this is to start with the plan of the property.

Circle areas of the yard according to the following seven categories:
1. Public spaces — what's visible to the public, usually the front garden
2. Entry points — front path and rear courtyards
3. Driveway and parking
4. Entertaining
5. Utility
6. Recreation/hobby
7. Garden.

If there are more categories than space, eliminate categories or rationalise the list. This is where it pays to adopt a lateral way of solving problems. Some functions may be able to be doubled up. You need to think very carefully about what you really want and need.

Be realistic about maintenance. Sometimes a garden will look good for a year or two but as plants grow it will require too much time to keep at a desired standard. Think about how much time you want to spend pruning, mowing, watering, feeding and replanting.

THE DESIGN STAGE

This should be a rewarding and enlightening experience. It can also be frustrating. You need an open mind and patience. Always be prepared to ask for advice, and gather all the information you need before ordering plants.

You will need some tools, which are essentially simple drawing tools:
tracing paper
graph paper
markers
drafting tape
scale
tape measure
straight edge
circle templates.
Use your outline plan as a guideline for tracing. You will need to do several copies of the base plan — about half a dozen large photocopies will do.

PRELIMINARY DESIGNS

You will probably do three to four options.

Step 1

The first plan is the so-called 'bubble diagram' because all you need to do is circle shapes or rough outlines of proposed features. As you do this check the site analysis and outline diagram for aspect. Work out a suitable scale before you begin, and make sure the bubbles are all to the right scale.

The whole process is like a puzzle. Make sure features and elements fit together and relate to each other. An example would be to place the compost bin near to the vegetable garden.

Start with four or five major items such as the drive, patio or utility area.

Step 2

Redefine form

Give features recognisable shapes. Scale the features accurately. Draw circles for trees and indicate the spread at maturity. You must do this, otherwise other plants and features may be swamped. Make several plans with variations and generate a range of solutions. Try one bold plan, and one straightforward and conservative one. Your third will probably be an amalgam of the two.

Step 3

Final design

Put your ideas into final form. If you are using curves, draw them boldly and avoid squiggly lines. The bigger the curve the more aesthetically pleasing the end result; and chores like mowing will be easier too.

Check your features against the site analysis regularly. Seek advice and appraisal from a person you respect. A good garden designer will give you a consultation for a reasonable fee. This could lead to some changes. Think of it as an insurance policy. It could save you money on a costly mistake.

Be realistic about budget. If you can't afford a pool but want one later, include it in the plan, but for the future. Don't plant large trees in the way or build other structures on that location. Get quotes for work. It will give you an idea of what needs to be done and how much it will cost.

SOIL PREPARATION

How you go about establishing a garden of native plants depends on the nature of the land to be cultivated. Your garden may be virgin bush soil or, if you are converting an older garden, it is likely the soil will contain chemicals added for conventional gardening. These may include such problems as high levels of phosphorus and nutrients injurious to some natives. Even the soil in new gardens built on what had been bushland will have been altered by earth-moving equipment, clearing, cement residues and building wastes. Before you start to prepare your soil, you need to find out three things: soil type, drainage patterns and the acidity or alkalinity of the soil.

SOIL TYPES

Soil is made of different minerals and it is the proportions of each that determine whether your soil is described as sandy, clay or loam.

Sand

Sandy soils are made up of small particles of quartz. Some are finely worn by water; others are more coarse and angular. Most soils contain some clay, organic matter and humus. Sandy soil generally drains quickly; this is ideal for plants needing sharp or rapid drainage.

Clay

Clay is a mineral made up of very fine particles of hydrated aluminium silicate and mud that pack together tightly, preventing water penetration. Heavy soils containing clay also contain organic matter and some sand but the higher the clay content the heavier the soil will be. Heavy soils can become waterlogged and sub-surface drainage is often needed.

Loam

The ideal garden soil is called loam. It contains both clay and sand in varying proportions. There is usually a proportion of organic matter to provide additional drainage, nutrients and water retention capability. The proportions of clay and sand, though, determine the nature of the soil. Sandy loam has a higher percentage of sand, while clayey loam is higher in clay than sand. Loam is easy to work as it breaks up when dug and retains moisture while at the same time it drains freely. You can make sandy or clayey soil more like loam by adding the deficient mineral plus organic matter.

DRAINAGE SOLUTIONS

The simplest way to improve surface drainage is to direct runoff to dry areas in need of additional water, or to water-loving plants. Improving the structure of the soil by adding organic matter is another method. A more complex solution is to install underground agricultural drainage.

To work out if your drainage is inadequate, wait for heavy rain. Water collecting in puddles or as marshy ground is a sure indicator that it is not draining away adequately.

Try to follow the natural runoff. Water may run into a natural drainage system such as a stream, or even to an underground spring. This will be obvious if water appears to rise up out of the ground during wet weather. It is a fairly rare occurrence and not something to worry about unduly, but it will indicate a poor position for planting any drought-hardy plants which resent heavy moisture content.

Another solution is to sculpt the ground to direct unwanted water flow away from sensitive areas such as the house or delicate plants. Swales, which are shallow depressions used to direct water flow, can become part of the decorative aspect of the garden if they are covered with gravel and planted with sedges, rushes and other water-tolerant plants. A swale can be disguised as a dry streambed or even a dish-shaped pathway for occasional walking.

Soil porosity may also be a problem. To assess soil's porosity, dig a hole about 60cm deep and fill it with water. When the water drains away, refill the hole with additional water and measure the time it takes to drain away. If it takes less than 24 hours, your soil could be too porous, but if it takes in excess of 48 hours, the soil is too dense.

You can grade density by taking a sample from the top 15cm of soil and placing it in a jar filled with water. Cap the jar and shake it. Then let the mixture settle. It will settle into three distinct layers. The heaviest, sand, will settle on the bottom, while clay, which is the lightest, will float on the top with silt suspended in the middle. Good soil will appear to have roughly equal amounts of each of the three layers. A disproportionate amount of either sand or clay indicates soil that needs improving. Soil density can be improved by adding organic matter and even some clay or sand depending on what is deficient. To improve soil, add mulch about 10–12cm deep. It helps retain moisture in sandy soil and allows clay soil to drain more easily.

Building a Garden

TEST SOIL FOR PH

Pick up a test kit from your local garden centre. At several spots in your garden, rake away 5cm of topsoil to remove the organic matter, which can distort the test results. Take a soil sample 15cm deep at each spot. If your soil is too alkaline, you could add flowers of sulphur. If it is too acidic, add lime or dolomite. Most native plants prefer a neutral to acidic soil, generally about pH 5.5-7.0. In some areas, particularly in South Australia and Perth in Western Australia, soil is naturally alkaline, and the best solution is to grow only lime-tolerant plants native to the local area or to areas with similar soil conditions in other states. Any attempt to alter the pH over a large garden area will result in a heavy maintenance task and an unachievable result.

RAISING BEDS

Another method of setting the soil for a native garden is to build raised beds. This can be done by creating mounds of earth, which, by changing the levels, improve drainage and the physical appearance of a flat site. The cheapest and often the most effective way is to purchase a load of sandstone waste (provided this is the predominant local stone). This is material recovered from excavations, and contains plenty of sharp sand plus rock rubble. The sand provides drainage and the rock creates root protection for new foraging roots. It keeps the roots cool in hot weather and provides moisture in dry spells. Plant directly into the sand/rock mixture and lay a mulch over the top when planting is complete. This is an effective way to provide sharp drainage for many plants which do not need high levels of moisture or nutrients.

ABOVE

Good soil preparation is essential for a spring display like this. Larger shrubs will survive on poor rubble and good drainage is required for heath plants such as *Boronia mollis* 'Lorne Pride' (rear) and *Lysiosepalum involucratum* (foreground). These are surrounded by brachycome with a border of exotic dianthus.

CHOOSING PLANTS

A garden should be a place to create a world of delight and fantasy; a place to lift the imagination and the soul by blending plants with sculpture, stone, timber and other hard materials.

Plants contribute so much to style and garden design; indeed the same plants can be used to give completely different effects, depending on the horticultural techniques employed to grow them. When choosing plants, the style, effect and impact you wish to achieve must be considered in the selection process.

Australian plants can be used in formal styles, but there is no point selecting incompatible plants or plants that fail to respond to training and regular pruning, if this is your objective.

Plants grow at different levels, from the tree canopy to the lowest groundcover, and this is the first thing to consider when arranging a planting plan. Trees provide varying degrees of shade, height and cover for groundcovers, shrubs, climbers and herbaceous plants such as shrubs and perennials. Some plants, like the climbers, reach for the sun with their roots in the shade. Others prefer the coolness of the forest floor where little sun reaches, and others form interesting patterns of shape, form and texture in both shade and sun. Grasses and spear-leafed plants add vertical accents and contrasts to the more common rounded or spreading shrubs. All these shapes and possibilities are there for the gardener to create interesting harmonies and contrasts.

There is a plant for every location and every condition and every plant has a different habit of growth. But many have similarities that enable them to blend and create textural patterns. It is this wonderful variation that allows living material to be used as an art medium. The wisest gardener

will take into account the natural growth tendency of each specimen when choosing plants for a garden. Plants may grow as erect, columnar, rounded, prostrate, open-branched or spreading bushes, shrubs or trees. These shapes can then be moulded to form the style you want, within reason.

There are many other factors that influence our choice of garden plants. Climatic and soil requirements are among the most important. Knowing how a plant grows naturally will assist you in selecting the right plant for a particular location in a garden. Just as in the wider world, a garden is full of microclimates in which plants perform differently. Simple things like the shadow cast by a fence, a house wall or an existing tree create microclimates. The position of a house or structure will influence the climate, moisture level of the nearby soil and prevailing wind patterns. For instance, a garden on the south side of a house is always cooler and more shaded than one on the northern side. On the south, the house casts shade, cooling the ground adjacent to it, and the garden is also exposed to cooler winds from the south, particularly in the southern half of the continent.

Microclimates give us an opportunity to grow a much wider range of plants. You can select plants to match microclimates but it is rarely a good idea to attempt to completely change the nature of the soil and the character of the surroundings. Your site analysis will tell you exactly what your soil is like, where the desirable views are, what needs to be obscured and what the weather patterns are. This will help you in the search for suitable plants.

When it comes to preparing a planting list, an open mind and a close reading of your site analysis will help. Researching plants is one of gardening's most pleasurable activities. Delving into catalogues, magazines and books, and visiting botanical and show gardens will all help you understand what plants suit your conditions and how they will be likely to grow. Drawing up a list from such excursions is the easy part. The editing process can be difficult, and requires discipline. Expect to cull your original list by at least half. Culling favourites is, sadly, an essential part of the design process and the more you do it the more you define what is appropriate in your garden. It limits you to what will grow well in your soil and microclimates and the end result is more satisfying. Only in this way can you be sure you have the blueprint for an exciting garden.

KEY PLANTS

Start with the key plants. These are often trees, because they are the biggest plants in most gardens. They tend to be the most dominating, but they may not be the showiest. Trees provide you with layers that can be filled with shrubs, climbers, annuals and groundcovers. All need to tolerate much the same conditions as your key plants, though with perhaps more shade in the lower levels.

Once you have the key plants in place, it's time to look at filling in the lower levels with shrub banks, groundcovers, camouflage and plants that are needed for specific purposes.

The key to planting choice in these lower levels is to blend plants with similar characteristics, such as small leaf size for dry conditions, or larger leaves if they are rainforest plants. If plants have something in common, it is easier to break the mould with accent plants or groups of contrasting foliage plants in strategic locations.

ACCENT PLANTS

Accent plants are used as punctuations. Many shrubs are strongly horizontal, so the intrusion of a strong vertical plant can lift a design giving it power and dynamic tension. Accents should not compete with other plants, but are added for drama or to relieve or emphasise a flat plane. Repeating accents helps add cohesion. They can be used around the more architectural parts of the garden, close to patios and outdoor living areas, for instance, or as a link to a naturalistic woodland section.

Plants are generally grouped in one of two ways. Either use blocks of the same plant, or group different plants with similar characteristics. Both techniques keep a relaxed atmosphere in the design. Adding too many different shapes, forms and species can lead to a busy character that may become the opposite of restful. Blending several species of *Grevillea* or *Callistemon* with similar leaf shapes and growth habit is a good alternative to the more common planting of several specimens of the one species.

LEFT

Concern for colour should not subsume form. Consider the shape and texture of plants out of bloom. Free-flowering plants like *Eriostemon buxifolius* and *Dampiera purpurea* add structure off-season too while *Grevillea* 'Robin Gordon' flowers all year round.

The New Native Garden

LEFT
Climbers give vertical interest to a garden adding charm to humdrum scenes. *Hibbertia empetrifolia* is a shrub with lax stems that can be trained upwards.

COLUMNAR AND PYRAMIDAL PLANTS

These can be used for screening, for privacy and for variety. They add vertical accents to a garden. Some, such as *Callitris rhomboidea* and *C. columellaris,* adopt this shape more or less naturally, depending on the age of the plant. Others, such as many of the newer cultivars of syzygium, the lillypillies, can be trained into this shape. Both genera also blend well with exotic plants.

BUN-SHAPED PLANTS

These are very useful for creating interesting patterns in the garden, whatever the design — whether it is formal or informal. Correas tend to adopt the bun shape if grown in good conditions, as does the *Baeckea virgata* 'Nana' and *Boronia* 'Lorne Pride'.

SPREADING PLANTS

These can be useful for spilling over walls, softening rock ledges, for camouflage such as hiding old stumps and to conserve moisture and keep soil cool. Some are naturally groundcovers, but others are taller shrubs with a scandent habit that allows them to follow the curves and pattern of the landscape.

Many grevilleas, including *G. hookeriana, G. thelemanniana,* 'Bronze Rambler', 'Ivanhoe' and 'Royal Mantle', together with prostrate forms of banksia such as *B. serrata* 'Australflora Pygmy Possum' and *B. spinulosa* 'Coastal Cushion', can perform this task.

CLIMBING PLANTS

These add height and interesting patterns. They become living boundaries if grown over walls or fences, and screens and dividers if used on trellises near patios or around service areas. They can also be allowed to climb through shrubs and trees. One of the best for the latter role is *Clematis aristata,* a relative of the exotic clematis which is often used in cooler climates in the same way. *Hardenbergia* 'Happy Wanderer', *Kennedia rubicunda* and *K. prostrata* are also suitable. For trellises, one or more of the cultivars of either of the two pandoreas, *P. jasminoides* or *P. pandoreana,* are ideal.

RIGHT
The swamp banksia (*Banksia robur*) is hardy just about anywhere but mixes well with exotics such as this *Helichrysum petiolare*.

LOCALITY PREFERENCES

Seaside plants

Many people agonise over the choice of plants for salt-lashed positions, but in fact there are a multitude of desirable and suitable subjects. Seaside plants create a sense of place more than many other groups of Australian plants. Even in the most exposed position coastal plants have an affinity with the landscape with their twisted shapes and windswept styling. Among the choices are banksias, melaleucas, leptospermums and acacias. These are perfect to form the backbone of a seaside garden and most are fast growing. They provide cover for many smaller plants which can be added once the larger shelter plants are established. Some, like westringia, add structure in the form of hedges or topiary. The effect is easy to enhance with decorative elements such as ceramics, shell shapes and driftwood collages, and landscape features fashioned with bleached timber, sand and fine gravels.

Shade-loving plants

Shade-loving plants are generally divided into two categories — those that like moist conditions and those that thrive in dry shade. Many rainforest and wet sclerophyll plants fall into the former category and are ideal for creating interesting patterns of foliage and texture. Many dry-climate shade-loving plants will also grow in full sun, and it is worth experimenting a little with plants in varying degrees of shade.

Arid garden plants

Arid area landscaping is often a wan attempt at copying a garden more appropriate to a milder climate. However, a little bit of planning and research makes it possible to bring together a range of trees, shrubs and flowering plants that will fulfil all your needs including shade, shelter and privacy. Mulching with gravels, drip irrigation in the early years of growth, and simple earth drains to direct water flow to sensitive plants are essential for the arid garden.

Propagating your own plants from seed or from cuttings is a useful skill to develop. Most arid areas are ill-served by fully equipped and stocked nurseries, so gathering seed from indigenous plants or obtaining it from seed banks or mail order companies becomes more vital to the keen gardener who wants to grow Australian plants. Keep in mind when planning an arid garden that a good garden is like a painter's palette. The beauty of the paints or the colours don't impress us; it's how the colours are merged into a pattern that makes the picture. A garden's worth is not measured by the number of exquisite specimen plants. It's how plants, many considered ordinary, are grouped together, trained or mixed with others that creates the tapestry and the art.

The New Native Garden

Australian plants do not fit into a neat and ordered grouping of colour and texture as easily as exotic plants. The charm of a garden composed primarily of natives is more in the blending of all their separate elements than in creating a flower garden in the European tradition.

It's a cliché to say that a native garden is predominantly a green garden, but it's a muted green, not the green of a box parterre or hedged murrayas. Our greens are subdued, greyed-out and subtle. If anything, it is a 'Mediterranean-ised' green, filled with subtle silvers and greys. But true greens are there in abundance. Mostly they are rainforest or stream plants nurtured by regular water and moisture.

An Australian plant garden can also be as colourful as you wish. Nothing succeeds like excess, and massed displays of native annuals and perennial plants like kangaroo paws, strawflowers, *Brachycome* and *Scaevola* can be used in a cottage style for a garden almost perpetually flowering. When it comes to shrubs, the 'tropical' grevillea cultivars and hybrids are also free flowering, blooming for a full twelve months of the year. Few plants in any country's flora can boast that.

An Australian plant garden is more likely, though, to be a blending of foliage, bark and flowers with shape and texture producing a palette like no other. Form and plant shape from weeping to prostrate, bun shaped, pyramidal and globular are also as much a part of our unique palette as are flowers and colour.

PREVIOUS PAGE

Anigozanthos 'Bush Dawn'.

INSET LEFT

Canberra grass (*Scleranthus biflorus*).

INSET RIGHT

Kangaroo paw *Anigozanthos* 'Bush Ranger'.

MAIN PICTURE

Angophora costata.

The Living Palette

COLOUR

Colour is dynamic. It creates moods — calm, joy, excitement, even unease and distress if used badly. Colour can change the character of a garden simply by blending, adding or taking away colours.

Colours are divided into categories. The first are the primaries (red, blue and yellow). These are 'pure' colours, not made by mixing with other colours. Each has a certain quality: red is powerful and hot; blue is cool, conservative, sometimes detached; and yellow is happy and lively.

The secondaries — green, orange and violet — are blended colours created by mixing pairs of primary colours in equal proportions. Green is a combination of yellow and blue; orange comes from red and yellow, and violet from red with blue.

The tertiaries are a mix of the closest pairs of primary and secondary colours arranged on the colour wheel. Red and violet make purple, blue and violet produce indigo, blue and green beget turquoise, yellow plus green gives chartreuse, yellow and orange turn to gold, and red and orange become scarlet. Different groupings of colours can produce harmonies, contrasts and discords.

HARMONY

Harmonies lie next to each other on the colour wheel and create a placid, calming garden picture because all the colours are related and none clash with any other. They are probably the easiest combinations to use.

CONTRASTS

Contrasts create electricity and impact; colours seem to jump out at you. They occur between opposites on the colour wheel, whether primary and secondary colours, such as yellow and violet, red and green, or blue and orange; or between tertiaries, including indigo and gold, turquoise and scarlet, or purple and chartreuse. Used in moderation, contrast can be exhilarating but in excess, it can be overwhelming.

DISCORDS

Discords have an affinity with each other but are not direct contrasts or harmonies. Use them to create mood and a varied garden without the overwhelming 'riot of colour' effect. Common discord effects include blue with gold and yellow or pink with blue and mauve.

The New Native Garden

REDS AND PINKS

RED

Red is the most commonly seen flower colour of the three primary colours. We see it as vibrant, lively, exuberant, strong, the colour of love and passion. It is essentially a happy colour. But it is also the colour of blood, and Mars, the Roman god of war, is associated with it. Its power can be overwhelming and dominating. It is the colour artists and others use to convey menace and anger.

It is certainly important in the Australian garden, as red flowers are visible to nectar-eating birds and insects whose assistance is needed for reproduction.

Many popular garden plants have red flowers: grevilleas, bottlebrushes and flowering gums, to name a few. Smaller shrubs are less likely to have red flowers, but often red will occur as part of the flower colouring. *Correas*, *Darwinias*, *Epacris* and *Dillwynias* often have red splotches on petals or sepals. White, green, yellow or cream frequently tones down the flamboyance of red in Australian flowers.

Red flowers have sometimes been decried as 'too, bold, too gaudy, so hard to use'. This is not necessarily true. Red is a powerful colour, but its impact can be softened using silver and plum-coloured foliage. While there are plenty of plants with silver foliage, plum and purple shades are not so easy to find. *Ceratopetalum gummiferum* 'Magenta Star', *Dodonaea viscosa* var. *purpurea*, *Agonis flexuosa* 'Jervis Bay Afterdark' are a few cultivars with purple, burgundy or deep bronze leaves.

Because of its dominance, red is best used in the foreground. If used in the distance, it may make a small garden look even smaller.

PINK

Pink is a pastel version of red obtained by adding white, and pinks can be either warm or cool. Adding yellow produces salmon pink, and adding blue results in mauve pinks. Salmon works well with orange and yellow shades, but mauve, candy and pastel pinks are more compatible with flower colours closer to them on the wheel: blue, mauve and violet shades.

Emotionally, pinks are generally warm. Pink can be used as a neutral colour. It is a colour found in many annuals, especially our rhodanthe species and many other spring-flowering plants.

Everlasting daisy
(*Rhodanthe manglesii*).

Mint bush
(*Prostanthera magnifica*).

Swamp fox grass
(*Pennisetum alopecuroides*).

MAIN PICTURE
Gymea lily
(*Doryanthes excelsa*).

The Living Palette

Native hibiscus (*Alyogne huegelii*).

Daisy bush (*Olearia phlogopappa*).

Pink wax flower (*Eriostemon australasius*).

The New Native Garden

38

The Living Palette

BLUES AND MAUVES

Colours in the blue spectrum — blue, lavender, violet and mauve — are the coolest and most sombre colours in the garden palette. A blue/violet garden is calm, peaceful and serene. Purple tends to warm the blue garden, since it is a blend of red and blue.

Blue is used to create perspective. Blues look more distant than they really are, so a blue-flowered garden often appears bigger. Blue gardens, like most monochromatic gardens, look spacious because there are no other colours to distract attention. They can be monotonous, so add lighter and darker shading. Adding white or a complementary colour such as yellow or orange prevents blue becoming gloomy or cheerless, though blues are also the most relaxing colours for a garden.

Contrasting colours, those opposite each other on the colour wheel, enhance the blue effect. Complementary colours (those positioned adjacent on the colour wheel) such as red and crimson tend to make blues and mauves recede. Red makes a blue garden warmer and pink is ideal for brightening the sobriety of violet, a sombre colour at the best of times.

Combinations of pastels tend to be more restful than the two suggestions above. Lilac and lemon would be a subdued blend but deep yellow and purple is a more day-glo combination and much bolder. You could try blending *Orthrosanthus laxus*, one of the native iris-like plants, with *Bracteantha bracteata* 'Cockatoo', a cream-coloured paper daisy. In the same vein but on a bolder note, *B. bracteata* 'Dargan Hill Monarch', a deep yellow, mixed with violet *Patersonia glabrata* would make a good combination. Both have their place depending on the effect required.

Foliage backgrounds make a big difference to how we perceive blue flowers. Blue with silver foliage is the most relaxing combination; bright green foliage is a happy mix because of the yellow component of the leaf colour.

TOP
Left: Blue leschenaultia (*Leschenaultia biloba*).
Right: *Scaevola aemula* 'Purple Fanfare'.

BOTTOM
Left: *Scaevola aemula*.
Right: Cootamundra wattle (*Acacia baileyana* 'Purpurea').

SILVER

Foliage is supremely important in the native garden palette. Combining foliage with a blue–green or silvery sheen adds a cool, relaxing atmosphere on a long-term basis. For instance, *Melaleuca incana*, *Eucalyptus caesia*, *Acacia podalyriifolia* or *Plectranthus argentatus*, combined with architectural plants such as grass trees or grasses like *Poa labillardieri* or kangaroo grass (*Themeda triandra*), can form the basis for an interesting framework.

Many silver-leafed plants have brightly coloured flowers in the warm end of the spectrum. This allows scope for setting and moving the tone of the garden according to the season. Gardens can be cool or hot depending on the flowering season. This is a valuable tool. For instance, silver-leafed acacias flowering in winter give a burst of bright sunshiny yellow in the depths of winter when days can be cold, grey and gloomy. Gold and yellow are happy colours that lift the emotions. Later, when days are hot and dry, the silver and blue–green foliage tones induce a cooler, more restful mood.

Silver is often associated with arid conditions, and can make a garden appear dry and hot if used in excess. Adding a few blue–green tones will keep it cool. For instance, adding blue-flowering groundcovers and patersonias, brachycome daisies and scaevola with blue and violet will give an impression of greater coolness. Blue foliage can deepen a narrow garden. Just as blue flowers recede into the distance, blue–green or silver foliage placed at the rear of a border makes the bed appear wider.

BELOW: *Eucalyptus maculata*.

Eucalyptus caesia.

Coast banksia (*Banksia integrifolia*).

Snowy pimelea (*Pimelea nivea*).

LEFT TO RIGHT: Pinnate grevillea foliage; *Scleranthus biflorus* and *Thryptomene* 'Payne's Hybrid'; Gymea lily (*Doryanthes excelsa*); grass tree (*Xanthorrea australis*); native ginger (*Alpinia coerulea*)

GREEN

Green is the most common colour in the garden. Green is neutral; the perfect companion for all colours. Most of the time we don't even think of it as colour, but the differences in shades of green are what make a garden interesting, especially when flowers are few and far between.

Green is a secondary colour derived from two primary colours, blue and yellow. A garden's green comes mostly from foliage — there are not many flowers that are green, though those that are can be spectacular. *Callistemon pinifolius*, for instance, has the most amazing lime green to emerald flowers on an open bush about two metres high. *Melaleuca diosmifolia* also has small green brushes, again very showy. Many consider the red and green kangaroo paw, *Anigozanthos manglesii*, to be the most beautiful of that family, and one of the best of the green flowers from any continent. Outside of the west it can be hard to grow, or at least short-lived, but *Anigozanthos* 'Bush Emerald' makes a good substitute in more humid regions. Correas are known for their green flowers and many combine green with red or cream shades for greater variety.

There is great variety in foliage colour, with greens ranging from blue–green to lime, dark green and olive. Some are even a limey cream colour or blessed with silvery, rust- or cream-coloured undersides so whenever the wind blows this glint of contrasting colour is always hinted at. This makes for an exciting blend of colours without even a hint of flower colour. New foliage too can be highly coloured, with pink, red, salmon and crimson tips. Occasionally all four shades will appear, as in many rainforest plants, particularly amongst the lillypillies.

Foliage can be invested with emotion and heat too. Green can be cool if the leaf has a touch of blue. It can be warm when yellow predominates. This is not common in natives — it often indicates chlorosis, an iron deficiency — but there are a few melaleuca cultivars with yellow foliage. *Melaleuca bracteata* 'Golden Gem' grows to two metres and 'Revolution Gold' (up to four metres) can both be handy to add variety in the shrub border. They have a tendency to look sickly and chlorotic, but they can serve a useful purpose. Sometimes a dark corner is brightened by yellow–green foliage, but those mentioned above are not the ones to choose for shade. They need full sun to grow well. The green form 'Revolution Green' is often a better choice, especially if you need a dense green foliage shrub.

The modern trend is for a stronger emphasis to be placed on foliage and texture. By blending different shades of green, ranging from blue–green to yellow–green, and then tying these in with other foliage shades such as plum, bronze and variegated leaves, the end result veers towards the monochromatic but is rarely monotonous. Textured plants, such as the moss-like Canberra grass, *Scleranthus biflorus*, can be used in exciting ways. It is a beautiful billowing groundcover that hugs any soils, logs and rocks it comes into contact with. It needs full sun and a supply of constant moisture, but not boggy conditions. It tends to die back if allowed to dry out or if grown in excess shade.

CREAMS AND WHITES

White, along with black and grey, is often called a non-colour. The latter two are the result of pigments blending. White and cream, on the other hand derive their tonal qualities from their ability to reflect light. Silver too has this quality.

As a result they tend to glow at the times of day when light is weakest — dawn, dusk and at night. Garden designers have used the glowing qualities of white and cream flowers to light up the night-time garden. Vita Sackville-West can claim the most credit for popularising the concept of the all-white garden. She had a practical reason for doing so. Her white garden was used for soirées and garden parties in the long English twilight. White flowers were visible. Other colours were not. White and cream show up at night, as our eyes require little adjustment to perceive them even in dim light conditions. The value of white and cream to garden design stems from their ability to blend with all colours. This ability is again related to their light-reflecting qualities. Both cream and white have an ability to bend ultraviolet and infra-red light so that it becomes visible to us.

Light contains all colours, and so does white. As a result, white has an affinity with all colours. You can add white flowers to any combination of colours and it adds brightness and removes the weightiness of dark colours and the dullness of pastels. It doesn't matter whether the colour is considered warm or cool — white will leaven it. This also applies to silver and grey foliage and variegations including white or cream. All can be used where foliage tones are very dark.

Large expanses of white can act as blank space in the landscape. White is a void or a separator. White is particularly useful in the lawnless garden. Lawn serves as space, void and separator in most exotic gardens. A bed of white flowers, such as a field of white everlastings, flannel flowers or a carpet of white brachycomes, duplicates the function of lawn, providing spatial separation. It lightens the composition by providing breathing spaces and resting spots.

White and cream expanses add a restful element in a crowded or complex planting. White is often used as a foil for other colours as it adds energy when used in moderation. Small white flowers such as the white scattered flowers of *Pratia*, allowed to weave through a garden bed, will give all other colours a lift.

MAIN PICTURE
Flannel flower (*Actinotus helianthi*).

INSETS
Top: White waratah *Telopea speciosissima* 'Wirrimbirra White'.
Second from top: *Grevillea biternata*.
Second from bottom: *Melaleuca linariifolia* 'Seafoam'.
Bottom: *Phebalium lamprophyllum*.

The Living Palette

COPPER TONES

Brown is one of the most dominant colours in Australian plants. New growth is often bronze, coppery or rust-coloured, developing more familiar greenish hues as the leaves mature. These colours form a significant element in the palette, particularly in rainforest plants, eucalypts, callistemons, banksias, hakeas and smaller shrubs. Unfortunately, the tendency for vibrant colour of new foliage is frequently overlooked when planning a garden. In some plants, notably the lillypillies and many rainforest plants, the flush of colour on the new spring growth is more spectacular than either the flowering or fruiting stages of the plant's seasonal cycle. We are blessed with little in the way of the frenzied autumn colour of the northern hemisphere's deciduous trees, but our spring is almost a match in some species.

The rust-coloured tones of casuarina flowers can transform a tree in spring, but it is not just flowers that have the power to add such coppery hues. The varying colours of barks are a significant element in providing seasonal colour variation, particularly in members of the eucalypt family. Many regularly shed bark. Their new bark can range from greenish to salmon and through many different shades of brown.

Even ferns demonstrate a propensity for rust-coloured adornments. Staghorns are regularly covered in blankets of coppery or rust-like spores, and when released, the spores of tree ferns carpet the ground and surrounding foliage with a dusting of copper. In the garden this can be quite an attractive feature — closer to the house or near open windows, however, it is not such an endearing quality.

Rust as a colour is often found in bark and new foliage and exerts a subtle influence. Restio or creeping rush often has rust-coloured tips in season. It is a plant that is prolific near water. The tips offer a strong contrast to the bright green of the lower foliage and to other waterside plants such as ferns and bog-loving plants such as *Bauera rubioides* or *Epacris longifolia*. Many ferns, such as blechnum species and rasp ferns, also produce bronzed or coppery new fronds that provide colour where flowers are rare because of low light levels. These can be used in the same way as a seasonal flowering plant, and a mass planting of such ferns can provide colour that is even more more brilliant than the colour provided by many flowers.

Use these foliage tones for contrast too. Bronze and copper leaves contrast well with many plants whose leaves have a silvery reverse. Banksias, grevilleas and other plants display this tendency, often only revealed as a breeze rustles the branches. Further variation occurs after rain as sun shining through water droplets creates interesting interactions with light. There is tremendous scope for subtle colour variations like this in Australian plants, and appreciating it entails almost complete re-education, accustomed as we are to the all-out colour displays of the annuals or spring shrubs of the exotic garden.

LEFT TO RIGHT

Top: Melaleuca bark; native grass; heath banksia (*Banksia ericifolia*)

Centre: Restio (*Restio tetraphyllus*); eucalyptus bark; swamp banksia (*Banksia robur*)

Bottom: Casuarina flowers; *Acacia glaucoptera*; *Eucalyptus haemastoma*

YELLOW AND ORANGE

For some, the sunset colours — orange, gold, yellow and rust tones — are the true colours of the Australian bush but they are rarely used extensively. Unlike the blues and violets, these are colours that are hot, flaring and aflame. In outback areas the very earth is red, but closer to the coast the summer sky at dusk is the closest thing we see to the sunset colours in the garden.

There is no doubt that colours can affect the emotions, and these are colours which, when used in moderation, convey excitement, verve and vivacity. But like red, they can be overwhelming if used to excess. They can be distracting and evince a reaction ranging from edginess to irritability.

An orange garden should not be allowed to dominate, but a small bed dedicated to sunset colours can give a pleasant respite. Like reds, oranges, golds and rusts are best placed in the foreground, close to the house, lining paths, near steps or where people congregate. They stimulate conversation, so courtyards or alongside outdoor living areas are good locations. These dominant colours also tend to make a space appear smaller. They are useful tools if you want to create intimacy or cosiness in a corner of the garden such as a patio or courtyard area. Courtyards are meant to be areas for togetherness, so a limited number of orange flowers over one or two seasons is desirable.

Surprisingly, there are few flowers that fall into the sunset category in the Australian garden. The standout would have to be *Chorizema cordatum*. It passes on every count, with bright orange standards (the upper petals) and a candy pink keel or lower petal. Many of the new kangaroo paw hybrids also come close.

Other low scandent shrubs for the border include *Gompholobium* and *Dillwynia*. Taller plants are harder to come by, though *Banksia ericifolia* and *B.* 'Giant Candles'

The Living Palette

are two that come to mind for eastern gardens. *Banksia menziesii* and *B. prionotes* are two from the west that qualify. Hybrid grevilleas are often found in the sunset colour range.

Orange and related colours are get-up-and-go colours. They are certainly eye-popping, but can make you edgy if overdone, and can produce a garden which is neither restful nor charming.

The colours closest to orange on the colour wheel are red and yellow, yellow–orange and red–orange. When we blend these complementary colours we perceive their 'temperature' to be much the same, so they work in opposite ways from our expectations. They can be soothing. All are warm and therefore cosy and comforting. Yellow adds a bright note to the orange garden, while red heats it up.

Varying the amount of other colours can change the character considerably. Foliage colours can be used to tone orange down: dark foliage, whether dark green or even bronze, is a good foil for orange; silver lightens it by several notches.

Orange also works well with contrasting colours from the blue/violet spectrum. This can be a bold blend, or it can be subtle, when pastels such as pale mauve and apricot or peach shades are used.

ABOVE

Left to right: Strawflower (*Bracteantha bracteata*) 'Cockatoo'; *Banksia* 'Giant candles'; *Chorizema cordatum* (close up); *Chorizema cordatum*; *Restio tetraphyllus*; Showy everlasting daisy (*Schoenia filifolia*); kangaroo paw 'Bush Dawn'; Illyarie (*Eucalyptus erythrocorys*).

The New Native Garden

TEXTURE AND TOUCH

The palette is enhanced by the senses of smell and touch as well as sight. A good many native plants possess aromatic oils which give off fresh fragrances when crushed . These fragrances are apparent too on hot, burning days and after rain.

The smell of aromatic leaves is one of the greatest sensual delights of Australian plants, only matched by the herbs of the Mediterranean: sage, basil, rosemary and the like.

The sense of touch is clearly part of the Australian plant garden too. A cynic would say yes, they have sharp and prickly leaves and dry, twiggy sticks. But there is much more. The rough bark of the old man banksia, the whip-like strands of the grass tree, the furry surface of *Plectranthus argentatus*, or the soft fresh tips of *Melaleuca incana* all invite touching in one way or another.

Flowers too are worthy of touch. The Proteaceae produce many buds and flowers which have a strong tactile quality. The unopened corona has a strokable quality. And banksias have the same wiry coronas that can be pressed and will bounce back just like the teeth of a comb.

Boronias, like other members of the family Rutaceae, possess oils which are highly aromatic. They are some of the most scented leaves in the Australian garden.

INSETS

Left to right: Waratah 'Shady Lady'; kangaroo grass (*Themeda triandra*); *Restio tetraphyllus*.

48

The Living Palette

49

garden STYLES

The New Native Garden

LEFT
The familiar look of the rural landscape dominated by eucalyptus. Select eucalypts carefully as most are too large for suburban gardens.

THE AUSTRALIAN LANDSCAPE

NATURE AS DESIGNER

Nature is a gardener. Not only is she a gardener, but she invented the notion of garden styles. For confirmation, all you need do is look around you. Nearly every garden style popular today has its roots in something already devised by natural forces. Even the geometry of the formal garden owes something to nature: where humans tread a straight line, nature loves to fill in, with avenues of trees or dense hedges along paths or the banks of streams or canals.

When it comes to Australian plants, the dominant style is the one found all around us. The so-called 'bush garden' is the most popular style of garden employing Australian plants. It is a style that stems from our deep love for the look and the ambience of the Australian bush. For many years the notion of the 'dry sclerophyll' bush garden was rigidly defended by some as the *only* style of native garden. The dry bush garden can be an unfriendly style. Most of us imagine sharp twigs, prickly leaves and a tough, uncompromising look that is hard to warm to. But nature is much less prescriptive and far more generous than that. She has given us many alternatives and ideas to develop.

Just about any recognised garden style can be adapted to use native plants. Even formal and parterre styles can lend themselves to native plants. The many new small-leafed cultivars of the syzygium are a case in point.

But what is a garden style? Style in garden terms is the convergence of art and nature. Climate, more than any other factor, determines what grows where and how it grows, which, when you get down to basics, is what most garden styles are about. Most are nature-based, with climate, topography and plant material playing a commanding role. Because climate is so distinctive in different regions around the world, we also come to the notion of 'sense of place'.

A garden style is a celebration of place. It ought to possess a defining sense of its locality. Indeed, styles defined by location — Mediterranean, Santa Fe, Japanese and English — all have this sense of place. If we turn to garden styles using Australian plants, nature has given us many opportunities to create distinctive looks and types of ambience.

There are dozens of 'natural' styles: low heathland, symbolic, dry bush, wet bush and rainforest. There are desert styles and coastal plains, coastal wetlands and sand dune styles. Any imaginable landscape can have a garden style designed around it. Australia's landform and climates are so varied that there is plenty of scope for regional differences to

Garden Styles

be celebrated in garden styles. Nature itself should be one source of inspiration. But it need not be the sole stimulus.

The human condition embraces many experiences, and learning is one of them. The influence of science, mathematics and geometry is as integral to the way we live as the concept of the natural environment. There is nothing unnatural about humankind's domination of nature. If you doubt that, then look around. The formal garden is, like the naturalistic garden, a celebration of learning and knowledge built up over the ages. There is nothing intrinsically wrong in attempting to control plant material, whether it is indigenous or introduced. It has taken us two hundred years to realise that we can use Australian native plants in the place of traditional plants for topiary, hedges and formally structured gardens.

Style should never subsume function, and the styles illustrated in the following pages cover a range of possibilities, from small city courtyards to large country gardens, from medium suburban blocks to tiny alcoves. Look at them and consider the possibilities with new eyes.

ABOVE

Desert landscapes show remarkable variation. The Pinnacles in Western Australia is a landscape of rocks rather than plants, but we can learn valuable lessons about placement of rocks from nature.

The New Native Garden

'SEAMLESS TRANSITION' AND THE WILD GARDEN

Gardening next to natural bushland carries a number of responsibilities. One is the responsibility to ensure a visual continuity between the bush and the lived-in landscape.

The sudden change from bushland to settled suburbia with its incongruous garden exotica is one of the most visually jarring experiences in suburbia. The transition can be a shock to the senses; visually unsettling and unnerving. The challenge for the garden-maker is to prevent this sudden shock, to create a seamless transition from settled garden to natural bush and vice versa.

The history of suburban development has seen many areas of bushland degraded by inappropriate planting in adjoining encroachments. The contrast is strong between badly colour-matched azaleas, flowering prunus and other massed plantings of bright green-leafed exotics with the rhythm of repetition and subtle toning found in the natural vegetation. However good the garden of exotic plants, special considerations need to apply when gardening in this transition zone. It is not enough to simply turn your back on the bush. Indifference will destroy the tranquillity of both zones.

The gardener faces the challenging task of designing a garden that does not appear to be designed, yet still includes features such as paths, patios, service areas and attractive entrances that contribute towards our enjoyment of a garden. A wild garden can still have the comforts of modern outdoor living.

So where do you start? Wherever possible, retain rocks, trees and existing plants. Look for views that can be enhanced or retained. The next step it to remove any weeds or exotic plants that have drifted into the composition. Save the seed of any desirable native plants. When the renovation work is complete, re-sow the disturbed areas with this seed to keep a visual link with the existing plantings. Repetition of a few plants is the rule in nature.

Use nature as the starting point and teacher. The special features of the landscape need to be incorporated into the design, and the plant palette could be restricted more or less to continuing the local theme. For a seaside garden, this may mean including coastal plants such as banksia, leptospermum and others endemic to the area. Here you will occasionally find open spaces and clearings, most often where rock outcrops or gravel seams intersect the landform.

Creating a sense of place is especially important in a garden adjacent to bushland. The design restraints are severe but the end result is a garden that suits its location with a relaxed simplicity and one that also meets the needs of the owners.

The gardens in this chapter are for the most part enhanced bushland, or in one case, recreated bushland. Many are located in a naturally bushed environment and pay homage to their sense of place. They borrow from the surroundings so that the effect is harmonious and peaceful.

The front garden is the ideal place to start your 'seamless transition'. It is mostly for show in Australian gardens, and visible to the passer-by. On the other hand, the back garden is rarely seen from the street and offers scope for a more colourful life. Here we can be more exuberant and use vivid plants such as mintbush to brighten the spaces where you spend the most time.

OTHER CONSIDERATIONS

Gardening next to bushland carries responsibilities not borne by gardeners unburdened by such proximity. First and foremost is the need to prevent any escape of potential weeds into the natural environment. Garden escapees have destroyed much littoral bushland and have cost local government and the environment dearly.

There is a responsibility too, not to hinder the lives of animals that rely on finding food, nest sites and shelter in the bush. In many ways a garden in a transitional zone becomes a wildlife corridor and food store.

The continued healthy existence of wildlife is dependent on not introducing hazardous domestic animals. Cats, in particular, have wreaked havoc on bird, lizard and small mammal populations wherever they have been introduced. Dogs too pose a danger with their tendency to hunt in packs at night, the very time most native animals are moving and seeking food.

Garden Styles

RIGHT
Use mat rush (*Lomandra longifolia*) in place of grass. It has perfumed flowers and attracts birds and insects.

BELOW LEFT
A mix of different textures with *Asplenium bulbiferum* and grass trees.

BOTTOM LEFT
Eriostemon australasius in a bush setting.

BELOW RIGHT
Grass trees (*Xanthorrea australis*) and kangaroo paw 'Bush Dawn' with Billy buttons (*Helichrysum ramosissimum*) as groundcover. The latter is now known (for the time being) as *Chrysocephalum apiculatum*, but you will still see the old name used in nurseries. Don Burke designed both this and the scene above.

Garden Styles

NATURALISTIC GARDENS: BUSH AND RAINFOREST

NATURE ENHANCED: EXPERIMENTS WITH NATURALISTIC STYLES

The naturalistic 'bush' garden has always been the most popular style for gardens using Australian plants. The very informal structure of many Australian plants and the style itself affords many chances for inspiration from nature. But natural gardens are asymmetrical, and are often much harder to compose than formal gardens. On the other hand, the naturalistic garden has greater energy than more static formal plans. Movement is never predictable and the element of surprise is easier to add.

The very impetus for growing native plants, after all, stems from a deep love of the native bushland. The ambience, the scents and the look are all part of this affection. The popularity of the style also arose as a reaction to the destruction of bushland around cities for ever-encroaching housing estates, particularly in the 1960s and 1970s.

The style usually translates to a singular look, based on the dry sclerophyll forest. With such a wealth of ideas for imitation or inspiration, it is perhaps surprising that there is not more variation in interpretation. The flora of the rainforest has only recently been used to create an alternative to this dominant style, but there are plenty of other options.

Imagine a seaside garden using many of the low groundcover plants including succulents and prostrate varieties of common species. Nature sculpts shrubs such as acacias, leptospermum and melaleuca with a windswept look, and there is something magical about walking through a tunnel of coast banksias or honey bracelet myrtles. This effect is ideal for developing as a garden theme. The gentle shade and cool soil creates a wonderful ambience and a great growing environment for native violets and other tender perennials. Best of all, it does away with the hostile, touch-me-scratch-you look of old-fashioned native gardens.

In arid regions, *Eremophila*, Sturt's desert pea and *Senna* could be used in mass for brilliant colour and texture, with copses of mallee eucalypts for shade and height, to produce

LEFT
This naturalistic garden replicates the feel of the rainforest but uses exotics blended with natives. Even the jacaranda works well with the largely native planting in a superb setting.

a gentler version of the desert garden. There are plenty of other examples too, from the coastal heath to the glorious simplicity of wet sclerophyll forests. In southern New South Wales you could find inspiration in the massed plantings of *Macrozamia*, a dramatic architectural cycad with feathery fronds often seen nestling under tall white-trunked eucalypts. It is the perfect recipe for an easy-care landscape with impact that lasts and lasts.

CHARACTERISTICS OF THE NATURALISTIC STYLE

This style is always characterised by its reverence for nature. Followers often talk of their stewardship of the earth and this ethic is a strong motivating factor. It is also a style that reveres simplicity, in keeping with modern ideas of informality. Unlike the formal garden, the naturalistic garden is not established to dazzle, impress or overwhelm visitors with the owners' wealth, power or control over nature. Instead it pays homage to nature. The plan and the planting are always informally arranged, keeping often the original lay of the land intact, or slightly modified to incorporate a stream in a natural fold of the land. This is usually done in a way that embellishes nature and avoids any sense of contrivance.

The plants are the primary features of a naturalistic garden. Herbaceous plantings are arranged in drifts; trees in groves or shady glades. Formalised beds and borders are out — there is no need to keep plants within a rigid structure — and architectural elements are forsaken in favour of natural adornments like rock outcrops or old logs. Interest is added by creating contrasts with texture, form and foliage colour.

Order is not apparent, but as in any garden, the gardener exercises control; here it is subtle, almost subliminal. Above all there is compatibility between plant and place. We shall look further at how to achieve this sense of place in the suburban garden, as it is one of the most important elements governing the creation of a naturalistic garden.

CREATING A NATURALISTIC STYLE

Like the wild bush garden, the seamless transition theory is given a thorough workout in this style. One of the key 'rules' is this: aim to intensify the original natural elements, not eliminate them. This is much easier if you are starting a garden on land which is relatively untouched or had previously been cleared bush. In this case, work within the limits of the site and elaborate on the existing features of the site. The reality is more often that the block will have harboured an exotic garden or non-garden of grass and weedy shrubs. Here you will need to make a choice — purist or blended. Do you aim to plant only Australian plants and eliminate exotics or do you want to blend your garden with the local environment and preserve some of the better exotic plants too?

Designing a naturalistic garden is not about selecting a style and imposing it on the land. In all cases it involves analysing what is there and creating a new, more artful landscape, but one which is sensitive to its surroundings, and relatively self-sufficient. Plants should be adapted to the local conditions. For the most part, this means a reliance on natural rainfall, maintaining the integrity of the soil type and avoiding fertiliser runoff.

The naturalistic garden is perceived as part of the landscape. Consequently it is almost always designed with some impression of a natural scene in mind. Historically it borrows equally from the 'Picturesque' and English garden styles. The naturalistic garden can become a collector's paradise if the gardener's self-control lapses and the tendency to treat the garden as a secure haven for tender plants takes over.

Realistically, there is little room for mollycoddling poor performers. Plants that do not grow well should be replaced. The style demands that the plants perform as structure, not just as specimens to be individually admired; you cannot rely on architecture or built structures to cover up weak or spindly plants.

Self-seeders and groundcovers that spread by stolons or by rooting at nodes are to be encouraged. Plants that evolve and adapt to the artificial environment of a garden also make a good visual fit. Many ornamental grasses fit into this category and are worth incorporating into your plan.

FITTING INTO SUBURBIA

The bush garden is often plonked down amongst unsympathetic gardens where, far from appearing natural, it is the proverbial sore thumb in the suburban landscape. It becomes an oddity — out of place and out of step with the surroundings. This is a major reason why native gardens have acquired such low esteem with the general public.

If it lacks the defining sense of place, a garden of Australian plants fails on the 'naturalistic front' by definition, as it fails to blend with the local environment. If this is overwhelmingly exotic in tone, there are ways to overcome the problem. The challenge is to blend a native garden with existing gardens yet still make sure the garden says 'Australian'.

Garden Styles

HARMONY AND A SENSE OF PLACE

Look around the surrounding gardens and pick out planting features that may have a native equivalent. This will largely involve consideration of the tree plantings, as they are the most dominant part of the landscape visible from your garden.

The first step towards achieving a sense of place is to adopt an 'outreach' strategy. Borrow from the dominant trees and use the character of your neighbourhood to reach a coherent design and planting plan. Borrowed scenery is a term used in Japanese garden design, and is useful as a starting point. Essentially, you need to take inspiration from what exists around and build on it.

Many suburban gardens are planted with exotic conifers, often cypresses and pines, for instance. These can be a sore point with some, but rather than being upset by these alien plants, minimise and disguise their impact by selecting native conifers or conifer-like plants. The native

ABOVE

Harmony is created when a garden feature, like this pool, fits neatly into its surroundings. Designer Paul Thompson works closely with nature to create gardens that are highly naturalistic but also very stylised.

cypress pines (*Callitris* species), for example, are more than a match for the introduced Leyland cypress, both aesthetically and in adaptability. Others include *Casuarina* and *Podocarpus*. The kauri pine (*Agathis robusta*) and the *Araucarias* (bunya and hoop pines) suit very large warm-climate gardens only, but they are handsome trees. The Athrotaxis and Phyllocladus families have members suitable for cooler and temperate areas. Tasmania's pencil pine (*Athrotaxis cupressoides*) and the celery top pine (*Phyllocladus aspleniifolius*) are rare in cultivation, slow growing but attractive either as garden or tub specimens.

The New Native Garden

LEFT
Richly textured leaves like those found on regelias blend best with plants for a Mediterranean-style garden.

OPPOSITE
A rainforest is a moist environment. Joanne Greene's design in this garden includes palms, rhododendrons and cordylines which thrive in similar conditions. 'Prima Donna', the pink-flowered form of the blueberry ash (*Elaeocarpus reticulatus*) is a good match for the pink foliage of the riberry (*Syzygium luehmannii*).

BUILDING BRIDGES AND THE VISUAL LINK

When the selected blending plants are used as the key plants, the addition of other Australian plants will appear much less traumatic. It's much easier then to fill in with plants that have a similar fine-leafed habit. Some of the grevilleas, persoonias, hakeas, melaleucas and other shrubs, such as *Baeckea linifolia* or the cultivar 'Clarence River', can be incorporated into the 'coniferous' planting theme.

If large-leafed deciduous plants such as liquidambar, elm, maples or planes are visible, build a bridge with Australian plants that have similar large leaves. This may be difficult in arid areas as many of our large-leafed plants are denizens of the rainforest, and as such are adapted to fairly high humidity and ground water.

Illawarra flame (*Brachychiton acerifolius*) blends well with exotic trees, as does the silky oak (*Grevillea robusta*). Use kurrajong (*Brachychiton populneus*) in drier areas. Native beeches (*Nothofagus gunnii* and *N. moorei*), though slow growing and rare in cultivation, could also provide a visual link in the right position. Much faster growing and easier to obtain is the deciduous white cedar (*Melia azedarach* var. *australasica*). In high rainfall areas it's worth trying the beautiful timber tree, red cedar (*Toona ciliata* syn. *T. australis*), or the red ash (*Alphitonia excelsa*). Both are deciduous in cooler weather but blend in quite well with a dominant deciduous cover. Other large-leafed trees suitable for blending purposes (and with their own innate beauty) are the tree waratah (*Alloxylon pinnatum* syn. *Oreocallis pinnata*) and the firewheel tree (*Stenocarpus sinuatus*).

In cooler districts where birches are grown, work with Australian plants that have prominent bark. The ubiquitousness of the eucalypts mean we are well accustomed to gums

in exotic gardens, so use them. Some are better than others. *Angophora costata* and similar salmon-coloured gums make the grade by virtue of their trunk colour. In other cases, melaleucas have papery bark reminiscent of birches.

SINUOUS CURVES

Straight lines are rarely found in nature, so the naturalistic garden relies on curved lines. Paths and edges to planting beds follow sinuous lines.

When laying these out it is important to be as generous as possible with the curve. Small, tight curves look unnatural and unnecessarily fussy. The old trick of laying a hose along the proposed edging can work as long as you avoid the short, scalloped effect. More often the curves should follow the natural contours.

Curves also serve another principle of design: to create mystery or surprise. Plant right up to the edge of curved beds so you obscure potential features or focal points. That way, they can be discovered as you turn the corner. In a formal garden, these same things would be placed at the end of a series of straight lines or at intersecting axes. In the formal garden, these same lines help create a sense of balance, but in this type of informal garden it is the asymmetrical planting that serves this purpose. Plants need to be staggered along a path and on either side of the path. Use texture, shape and foliage colour to create a sense of balance. Repetition of the same plants in groups or clusters along the line is one way to achieve the naturalistic effect.

COTTAGE GARDENS

A cottage garden is a blended garden of flowers. Traditionally it was made up of herbs, vegetables and perennials for the most part, but also climbers, a few annuals and occasionally low shrubs too. Of all the recognised garden styles, it is one of the easiest to achieve using native plants. Dozens of popular Australian perennials can be used. Many, including the brachycome cultivars and kangaroo paws, are deservedly popular overseas. So many cultivars have already been introduced to the general nursery market place that there is no difficulty in finding material.

The cottage garden is a nostalgic garden. What we call the modern cottage garden is a gentrified, romanticised pastiche of the original. The name was given to old English village gardens where poor cottagers randomly sprinkled a few flower seeds among the herbs and vegetables they grew for sustenance.

There was an invaluable side benefit too, since the flowers helped attract beneficial insects and reduced the problems of insect pests. Nowadays we'd call it biological diversity, and it points out one of the useful tips cottage gardening can offer to general garden maintenance. A garden of varied plants help create a mini-ecological balance by attracting different pest controllers — bird, insect, reptile and mammal — to the garden. This alone makes it a good style for small suburban gardens.

Because flowers are the principal focus in the cottage garden, the improved forms of native plants are generally preferred for cottage work. Compact growth, small stature and tight flower formation are qualities to look for. You'll find it in the newer forms of kangaroo paw hybrids such as 'Bush Gems', and brachycome daisies.

Gardeners have several criteria that are easily met by these cultivars. The first is colour and regular flowering. The second is ease of cultivation, easy care and low maintenance. The third is interesting texture and good form for garden uses. Last but not least is drought — and heat — resistance.

Other suitable cottage perennials are Sturt's desert pea, the amazingly beautiful leschenaultias, annuals such as the Swan River daisy, strawflowers, paper daisies and Rottnest Island daisy or blue lace flower (*Trachymene caeruleus*).

CHARACTERISTICS OF THE COTTAGE GARDEN

The cottage garden is a contrived garden mixing colours, shapes and textures. It also combines elements of both formal and informal gardens. Often a straight path creates a formal axis through the centre of the front garden to the house entrance. It is this feature that forms the main structural element of the cottage garden and gives it a formal quality. It also borrows some of the informal elements of the naturalistic style with spillover plants used to loosen the structure. Another alternative is for the path to be defined by low hedging, in the manner of the formal garden but softened by loose asymmetrical plantings of flowers behind the defining hedges. Taller hedges are sometimes used along the front fence for privacy from the street or as windbreaks.

This is in contrast to the back garden, which is often laid out more informally. Here meandering pathways edged with overhanging plants tend to be the norm. No doubt it comes from the more informal nature of rear yards and traditional house architecture, which placed service functions there. Nowadays it is more likely to be the living area with glass-walled rooms opening onto broad decks or verandahs.

The main focus of cottage gardens is on plants, their colour, form and composition. The cottage garden relies heavily on long-term colour, and the challenge for the

cottage gardener is to devise a planting scheme that creates floral pictures with flowers for each month. Long performers such as grevilleas and perennial daisies, including the ever-popular *Brachycomes* and *Bracteantha*, are ideal for this purpose. Plants that burst and fade over a few weeks can then be dropped into the scheme for maximum impact. These include spectacular bloomers such as chorizema, olearia, hovea and mint bush as well as annuals. Foliage plants provide some interest in times when fewer flowers are available or in cooler climates.

CREATING COTTAGE FEATURES

The cottage garden is a vernacular garden, for it uses things that are readily at hand. If it's old, rustic and weathered, then it will probably be a good visual fit in the cottage garden.

Seats and benches can be simply slabs of timber set on brick piers or old level stones. They should be chosen to link the garden with the house, because it is this characteristic that gives the cottage garden its old-fashioned look and appeal. Paving, wall materials, fences and garden edges should also be chosen to match closely with the house architecture. Leftover bricks, stone footings, and paths of gravel or brick are often favoured. There is no need to look for exotic materials such as slate or imported stone for the cottage garden — they tend to look out of place.

Though the essence of the planting style is controlled informality, modern interpretations have become quite sophisticated. As noted earlier, a degree of formality is acceptable in the form of straight lines and paths lined with low, clipped hedges, hemming in a lax profusion of flowers overflowing the borders, edges and paths.

Few native gardens have been designed this way, but if you wish to try, there are plenty of hedging plants suitable. For a 'wet' look, the dwarf lillypillies make ideal small hedges. For a 'dryer' look, *Baeckea virgata* 'Nana' is a good alternative, as it naturally grows as a dense, rounded bun of a bush. It may reach one metre in height and spread twice as far. If used in this way it may need plenty of training and a bit of room.

Cottage gardens generally do not have lawns; ground space is devoted to plantings, with paths and paved clearings providing the element of space.

Some of the best plants for cottage gardens are the wildflowers of Western Australia. These blend with a Mediterranean garden and other natives could be used with well-known Mediterranean plants for a garden in that style.

ABOVE

Exotic candytuft is a good contrast to scaevola and *Brachycome multifida alba* in this mixed cottage bed.

OPPOSITE

The rosy everlasting (*Rhodanthe chlorocephala* ssp. *rosea*) can be used with other Mediterranean plants such as lavender in a dry-climate cottage garden.

When designing a planting plan, consider carefully the mature height and shape of each plant, particularly any shrubs used. You may need to grade them to achieve some variety in height. Taller, rounded and prostrate forms should be carefully balanced against each other. Use climbers on trellises to screen intrusive structures such as sheds, garages and other constructions.

The odd architectural feature is frequently used to set off the predominantly low-rise plantings of perennials and groundcovers. It may be a gazebo, an arch, an urn on a plinth or maybe a low stone wall where levels change.

The native cottage garden is an ideal style to attract wildlife. Many of the flowering plants provide nectar for butterflies, insects and birds. If thickly planted and dense they may also provide nesting sites for birds and cover for lizards and mammals.

Like its exotic counterpart, a native cottage garden needs regular maintenance, and tired plants need replacing. Many are perennials with a short lifespan. Many, too, are grown outside the climatic zones for which they have developed special adaptations. For example, kangaroo paws and tea-trees both have difficulty adjusting to humid climates.

OPPOSITE

This well-constructed native cottage garden includes *Grevillea* 'Bronze Rambler', *Prostanthera magnifica*, *Dampiera linearis*, *Kennedia prostrata* and the yellow *Leschenaultia formosa*.

BELOW LEFT

A mixed cottage planting of Western Australian natives includes *Leschenaultia biloba*, hibbertia and showy everlasting daisies (*Schoenia filifolia* ssp. *subulifolia*).

BELOW

A collection of dwarf kangaroo paws *Anigozanthos* 'Bush Gold', 'Bush Illusion' and 'Bush Twilight'.

BOTTOM

Bracteantha bracteata 'Diamond Head'.

ABOVE

An espalier is an easy way to give a garden pattern and structure at very low cost. It adds an architectural element without going to the expense of masonry or building. This is *Pandorea pandoreana*. The hedging plant at the base is *Murraya paniculata*. Design by Michael Bates.

OPPOSITE LEFT

Westringia fruticosa can be trimmed and trained as a hedge or as topiary, as demonstrated by this container plant.

OPPOSITE RIGHT

Traditional teak benches look good in any formal garden. This one has a mixed planting. Mondo grass is used as infill between the pavers. Behind is *Eriostemon myoporoides*.

FORMAL GARDENS

Using native plants in a formal garden is nothing new. The trend goes back to ancient Greece and Rome. In the ancient world the formal gardens of Italy were the pioneers of the notion of using plants native to the region. *Cupressus* and *Buxus* species come quickly to mind, but the long-neglected idea of a formal garden using Australian plants is still one that raises some scepticism.

There are several reasons for this. One is conservatism. The movement for popularising Australian plants grew partly out of a need for bushland conservation. While conservation and conservatism are often poles apart, the conservation movement has embraced a strong preservationist strand. In

Garden Styles

terms of Australian plants this has translated to a conservative philosophy and a conformist ethic. It discouraged the development of new and varied styles.

The second reason is the nature of much of our plant material. Mostly it is from dry sclerophyll forests. In general the growth habit is lax, informal and not suited to major cultivation. Take the eucalypt for instance. It is impossible for any gum to adopt the regular symmetry of the introduced Northern Hemisphere trees so suited to the formal landscape. Gums are, by their very nature, suited to an informal landscape style. There are a few notable exceptions of eucalypts used in a formal way. The famous avenue of lemon-scented gums used to line the grand entrance at Cruden Farm in Victoria, originally designed by Edna Walling, is one. However, the informality of the tree's structure is still unmistakable.

Things could have been different. Gertrude Jekyll and William Robinson were both strong influences on the style of Edna Walling. They were indirectly responsible for the development of the English garden, now popularised by the likes of Penelope Hobhouse and Rosemary Verey. This employs strong structure through the use of walls and hedges. An informal planting style is overlayed onto this structure. Perennials, shrubs and annuals from all over the world contribute to the English garden style. Late in her career, Walling introduced many native plants into her designs and some have suggested that a true Australian style was emerging. Unfortunately, such developments never really got going.

CHARACTERISTICS OF THE FORMAL STYLE

The true formal garden has a perfectly symmetrical form with the design of the garden mirrored on either side of a central axis. Symmetry and repetition create the balance needed for a harmonious pattern.

Geometry is paramount. Straight lines, a strong central axis and intersecting secondary axes are found in almost all formal designs. Circles and curves are laid out with

The New Native Garden

geometric precision and paths are often of gravel or formally laid stone. The style is most suitable when used to complement houses with strong formal features. These include houses with a central door with matching windows on either side or constructions where wings of the building are positioned as mirror images.

In the garden, hedges and shrubs trimmed to form topiary or living 'architecture', such as niches and 'garden seats', are popular. Ornamentation is normally borrowed from the Classical idiom. Urns, copies of Greek or Roman statues, or busts in the Renaissance style are popular. Order, and control over nature, are important concerns reflecting the ferment of the exploration of human existence, endeavour and achievement that occurred in those periods when the style reached its greatest heights. Most modern formal gardens tend to borrow some of the elements of the highly structured originals, but without appearing too rigid or purist.

GETTING THE LOOK WITH NATIVES

Although formal gardens look complex, they can be simple to design. The best advice is to keep the geometry simple and avoid the complex knot patterns and grand designs that characterised the style in Renaissance Italy, Tudor England or Louis XIV's France.

The best place for a formal garden using Australian plants is the little-used front garden. It is here that the architecture of your house is most likely to be symmetrical. The front is the driveway, entrance and formal part of the house, the part that is open to public view. This suits the formal garden's role as a visual feast rather than an active garden. Living activities are centred on the back yard. Alternatively, a small courtyard off the side of a house could be turned over to a formal style.

Start by laying a straight central walkway as a primary axis. If space permits, intersect this with paths at right

angles to and parallel to the main axis. These are your secondary axes.

Focal points can be inserted at the ends of paths and where the straight lines intersect. Enclose a formal garden with a hedge, fence or wall to separate it from the surrounding landscape.

Semi-circular beds or connecting paths trimmed with low hedges can be added to connect primary and secondary axes, provided you can maintain an unfussy appearance and a sense of space. For a formal layout to work, allow space between the elements.

Accessorise with urns or pots placed on either side of the path. Plants are used to adorn not dominate. Try flanking paths or drives with a symmetrical planting of shrubs, flowerbeds or clipped hedges.

ABOVE

Eriostemon myoporoides can be trained, and respond to regular pruning. This makes them ideal for use as hedges, garden topiary and rounded shapes.

OPPOSITE

Westringia fruticosa makes an excellent hedge and looks better trained formally than left to grow. Ferns, even though rarely thought of as formal, have been planted to form a solid mass as if they, too, were a hedge. Behind is *Darwinia citridora*.

CONTEMPORARY AND URBAN INTERPRETATIONS

The contemporary garden has always been good fodder for satire. In the 1960s French film director Jacques Tati savaged the contemporary garden. In his Monsieur Hulot films, he poked fun at minimalist landscapes and horticultural technology. In the 1990s, 'Absolutely Fabulous' ridiculed modernist architecture by raising the mantra of 'clean surfaces'. Minimalist was in and clutter was out. It was always more of a joke than a reality.

The contemporary garden, in the meantime, has moved on from fashion victim to trendsetter. Simpler designs and more intense and varied uses for gardens meant design had to follow function.

CHARACTERISTICS OF THE CONTEMPORARY GARDEN

The contemporary native garden is more responsive to the new urban realities than the older style of naturalistic native garden ever could be. It is more functional, stronger on structure and easier to maintain. The trend is for the contemporary garden to be designed, multi-purpose, mutable and capable of reinterpretation when mood and fashion change.

There's one thing that most agree on, and that is simplicity. The landscape structure of the contemporary garden is reduced to the bare essentials. Shapes and space are simple, with often fluid forms, using flowing lines and geometry, circles rather than straight lines. The classic formal garden, with its perpendicular geometry, is in marked contrast to this trend, though the contemporary garden contains many formal ideas. Axes and paving patterns are often common to both.

In the formal garden, plants tend to be subordinate to architecture. In the contemporary garden, plants are used as architecture and as an adjunct to building and hard landscaping, but acting more as a 'soft' structural element than the strongly geometric topiary in the formal garden. The forms are softer, more billowing and less rigid.

Colour is used in different ways too. It is not uncommon to see walls and hard landscaping coloured with limewash

OPPOSITE
Modern architecture is often spare and stylised. Plants too need these qualities. The designer, Michael Cooke, has used grass trees (*Xanthorrea* spp) in this city courtyard space.

or vivid paints. These are stylistic devices borrowed from international garden styles. The earthy and sunset tones of Mediterranean, the bright colours of Santa Fe and the cobalt colour (known as Majovelle blue) found in Morroccan gardens are some examples. Such architectural flourishes may take the place of flower colour. Furniture too is frequently boldly painted. Contemporary gardens are greener than their predecessors. Plants are used to enhance the form of built objects. This is partly a response to changing uses and dimensions of the modern garden. Many, as will be expanded on later in this chapter, are courtyard-sized and dedicated to extending living space rather than straight plant display areas.

In the style of Roberto Burle Marx, the innovative Brazilian landscape architect, blocks of coloured foliage plants give a bold abstract quality to plantings. Form and texture have as great a role to play as flowers. Characteristically, colour is bold, with foliage used for long-term effects. Many Australian plants have small, even dainty blooms, but foliage can be more distinct. For instance, banks of silver-leafed plants such as *Plectranthus argentatus* posited next to banks of purple-leafed *Agonis flexuosa* 'Jervis Bay Afterdark' or *Leptospermum* 'Rudolph' and other cultivars could replicate the variation of leaf colour found in the Brazilian's use of bromeliaeds and tropical foliage plants.

AUSTRALIAN TRENDS

In the Australian context, a contemporary garden is turning to plants from our rainforest and employing them in ways not purely naturalistic in style. The contemporary Australasian garden operates as an amalgam in the same way that culinary styles have fused into a pan-Pacific style. Ingredients and techniques from Asia to the US West Coast and Australia and New Zealand have been blended. In gardens this fusion manifests itself as a blend of formal and informal styles, using plants in a structural way.

In each location, indigenous plants are being used, but in ways that are similar. New Zealand garden design has its 'Pacific Rim' style, using native plants from moist forests blended with sub-tropical plants from other regions. Australian gardening has been slowly developing a blend of Asian and European influences with Australian plants, especially those from our too-long-neglected rainforests. This alone is the single most important step towards the evolution of an 'Australian style'.

There are two threads running together in current

garden design in Australia. Smaller spaces and greater attention to outdoor living have increased the importance of the small or courtyard garden, and at the same time American gardening has exerted a strong but subtle influence. In some quarters it has been largely ignored or unobserved. Let's look at the latter first.

Australians long ago embraced the essential heart and soul of the Californian garden, the concept of outdoor living. Every summer we see it emblazoned across magazine covers and extolled on television lifestyle programs. Yet few Australians know anything of Thomas Church, the Californian landscape architect who popularised the notion of 'outdoor living'.

Historically, Australian gardens have looked to England for inspiration. The irony is that there is possibly no less likely place to use as a model for the Australian garden. Cool, moist and mild, the English climate is the opposite of our own conditions. Ours is a land at the opposite end of the climatic spectrum.

The Californian garden, however, has much to offer in climate and in outlook. Much pioneering work has been done on the use of dry climate plants as well. The California style borrows from the Spanish garden as well as the northern European styles. The Spanish influence contains elements of the Islamic garden, with its cooling fountains, covered verandahs, enclosed gardens and open patios. Interestingly, our early colonial gardens were influenced by some of these same ideas via India and the British Raj. Unfortunately, architecture and gardens retreated into an insular Britishness in the Victorian and early Edwardian periods. By a stroke of good fortune, these Spanish/Indian influences have been revisited and are now accepted.

Style choice is almost inexhaustible. Many styles which may at first appear alien — Spanish, Moroccan, Japanese or Balinese, for instance — can be adapted using Australian plants. Because of our geographic position and cultural heritage, borrowing and blending is perfectly acceptable, and will in time lead to a distinctly Australian style. Our gardens need creative flourishes, and if a light hand is employed, decorative elements from these styles can serve as inspiration.

OPPOSITE

Ornamental features turn ordinary into extraordinary. Designer Michael Bates used green river stones, found in nurseries and landscape suppliers to soften the impact of the purple wall.

ABOVE

A dramatic use of colour is combined with espalier techniques in this modern courtyard.

BELOW

Epiphytic native ferns and exotic container plants blend to create a strikingly modern garden composition.

URBAN AND COURTYARD GARDENS

Let's turn to the physical appearance of the urban garden. Many tend to be small and enclosed on all sides, a description that sums up the courtyard garden. The courtyard is not a style in its own right, but a vessel for interpretation. The courtyard turns its back on the outside world and focuses interest internally, to create a private 'paradise', a word derived from ancient Persian. It describes a garden, an enclosed and private sanctuary, sequestered from the hustle and bustle of civilisation.

Although the courtyard garden has been around for a long time, it is also a modern concept. The courtyard operates as an extension of the house, an outdoor room, close to our modern ideas of outdoor living mentioned above. A courtyard is a place for entertaining, recreation and relaxation. It also affords an opportunity for highly personal artistic expression. No other type of garden fulfils these functions.

CHARACTERISTICS OF THE COURTYARD GARDEN

The use of space is crucial, especially in the inner city, where gardens can be minuscule. Space needs to be carefully allocated, a measure that calls for extreme discipline. For a start, too many pots can clutter courtyards. One or two large well-selected pots can obviate the need for masses of smaller ones. Raised beds can often be used to take the place of pots. Because the courtyard is enclosed, taking plants to the walls as espaliers or in wall pots can maximise the sense of space.

Colour can also be used to manipulate space. Colours can foreshorten or enlarge our perception of space. Red in the foreground of a short, narrow block adds a sense of depth or distance to the rear. Conversely, for a garden that is deep and narrow, adding red into the middle ground can bring the distant view closer so the garden seems less elongated. Use flower colours, wall colours or painted furniture to achieve this.

Hard surfacing plays a vital role, and so does the internal/external transition. Coordinating colour schemes between interior and exterior spaces is another means of changing perceptions of space in a positive way. Large pots inside, if repeated outside, will strengthen the links.

Courtyards are intimate spaces, and each one (if there are several in the same property) may be given a distinct character by using features and colours. One may boast a pond and fountain, while another may be used primarily as a breakfast nook, with table and chairs. Sunny courtyards will need shade; small trees or climbing plants, supported by pergolas and beams, can act as a ceiling to further the outdoor room notion.

In all courtyards, attention to detail is especially important. Both modern and older urban buildings often include odd shapes, which can foster creative solutions to design. The long narrow space outside older terraces can harbour a wall fountain or mosaic, for instance, which can be viewed from the kitchen. Adding lighting gives the space yet another dimension.

ABOVE

Raise grass trees (*Xanthorrea* sp.) as seedlings from nurseries rather than buying plants dug from the bush. The latter are often slow to regenerate and generally die young.

OPPOSITE

Outdoor living is the key to courtyard gardening. Shade, raised beds and seating contribute to the ambience.

Because courtyards are enclosed by walls, a degree of protection is afforded even in cooler areas, and many rainforest plants adapt better to close cultivation than 'bush' plants. A degree of formality is often desirable. Courtyards designed on an informal or naturalistic model tend to fail, though there are many exceptions, as seen above. Sometimes the scale is wrong, and the idea of an urban bush garden may be incompatible with the reality of the city garden as a formal, intensively used space. The small size of most courtyards means 'preening' and tinkering are likely, and more formal styles can accommodate this care much better.

A courtyard is intensively used, so plants should 'perform' for long periods of time, both in flower and out. Foliage, form and texture are just as important as flowers. Many short-term spring flowers offer little other than this short burst of bloom, but some are acceptable. Mint bush, particularly dramatic species such as *Prostanthera ovalifolia*, for instance, can be planted as a mass and can be lightly trimmed after flowering to maintain a dense semi-formal shape. *Thryptomene* 'Payne's Hybrid' can also be shaped into an informal round shape, and several planted together make an ideal border hedge. The fresh new foliage with its soft pinkish tinge is most attractive. Many of the taller baeckeas can also be treated this way, becoming attractive weeping shrubs less than two metres tall.

Because courtyards are small, intimate spaces, plants with sharp leaves, or those prone to stickiness, are best avoided. There is nothing more irritating than swatting away a sharp plant when trying to relax with friends. If you wish to use such plants, place them away from main congregating points or place them in raised beds.

It is wise to raise the canopy, a pruning technique that bares the trunk by removing most of the lower branches. Many dry-looking natives look excellent treated this way. Trim the tops too, to achieve a tighter-than-natural look that does away with the dead, twiggy appearance of many species. Plants need to look good for long periods of time, and unless they are regularly maintained and pruned with discrimination, even the most suitable plants can become rangy and unattractive. Highly naturalistic plantings are prone to degenerate without this kind of regular attention.

Garden Styles

ABOVE
There is little need for massed flowering plants when colour is used so effectively in architecture. Here elements of the Santa Fe and Mexican styles are borrowed using Australian plants. Designer: Michael Bates.

LEFT
In a small terrace garden, space is at a premium, and the area in front of an old outdoor toilet has been turned into a sunny court with outdoor decorations, palms and native plantings. Designer: Michael Bates.

OPPOSITE
Rainforest plants fit into a small city courtyard far better than the traditional plants used in native gardens. Designer: Gordon Rowland.

STYLE AND CLIMATE

TROPICAL GARDENS

Australian plants that can be used in tropical and subtropical gardens have never been in short supply. There are plenty to choose from. Not all require rainforest conditions to thrive; many suit the arid tropical inland.

The design of tropical gardens has come a long way in the past twenty years. Borrowing from the Hawaiian resort style and sometimes using a twisted view of Brazil's Burle Marx, who popularised the use of geometric foliage patterns, exotic gardens have frequently gone overboard with colour. It is possible to blend the best of the imports with massed plantings of native trees, shrubs or perennials. Rainforest trees have one advantage over dry forms of plants: they are more easily blended with exotic tropical plants, many of which have coloured or variegated leaves.

Palms and ferns are the archetypal tropical plant form, and Australia possesses many excellent varieties of each. Staghorns and birds' nest fern, for instance, are popular throughout the world. Perennials such as cat's whiskers (*Orthosiphon aristatus*) with its white or mauve flowers, work well as bedding plants and even in cottage style gardens.

Rainforest plants have only recently been touched by the hand of horticulture, and most are unavailable except from specialist nurseries. Those that have made the crossover include golden penda (*Xanthostemon chrysanthus*), the midyim (*Austromyrtus dulcis*), Leichhardt bean (*Cassia brewsteri*), *Rhododendron lochiae* and the ivory curl tree (*Buckinghamia celsissima*).

A design for a tropical garden will include shade, covered walkways, moss-resistant walking surfaces and foliage plants. While it is possible to go overboard with colour using exotic plants, particularly red-leafed plants, this is less likely with Australian plants. Green splashed with a hint of colour from ginger, native tibouchinas and tropical grevilleas is a more balanced expectation. The tropical garden compares with the wings of a parrot in flight. You will most likely see occasional flashes of brilliance within an overwhelmingly green framework. It is this quality that makes a tropical garden one of the most relaxing and inspiring to walk through.

In the absence of well-designed tropical gardens using native plants, inspiration can come from picture books of tropical gardens.

ABOVE

In a tight space, use walls to provide room for more plants. Coloured walls highlight the form and texture of non-flowering plants such as staghorns, elkhorns or epiphytic orchids with small, delicate flowers.

RIGHT

Cordyline rubra has red fruit.

Garden Styles

ABOVE

The coin pod tree fern (*Cyathea cooperi*) grows in temperate areas and sub-tropical gardens. Here exotic tropicals such as flamingo flowers make a colourful groundcover.

ABOVE

Many rainforest plants give temperate gardens the fashionable look of the tropics. The light-coloured clay pavers also give this garden a modern, fresh look.

LEFT

With a touch of the 'Australiana homestead' school, this courtyard is given added sophistication with rainforest plants. A partially shaded terracotta limewash wall adds warmth and colour.

THE ARID GARDEN

Gardeners in arid zones have special needs, and the conventional green lawn and flower-filled beds are not feasible. Choosing Australian plants with low water needs is essential but planting with a sense of style needs inspiration. As mentioned earlier, garden styles such as Californian, Santa Fe or Mediterranean provide that inspiration. In Phoenix, Arizona, an Australian nurseryman, Paul Chambers, has been influential in introducing many Australian desert plants into Santa Fe style gardens. It just goes to prove that Australian plants can be used anywhere in any style of garden, provided the climate is appropriate.

The location of plants will have a bearing on comfort levels within the house as well as outdoor enjoyment of the garden. Trees located around the house itself act as natural air conditioners, and the denser the foliage cover the deeper the shade is likely to be. To increase the amount of shade cast, look to the use of groves or several copses of the same or compatible species. Wherever possible, retain the existing mature vegetation. Plants can grow slowly in arid areas, and any large trees and shrubs provide instant shade and a cooling environment for new plantings. They help stabilise soil and maintain microclimates and shade around buildings.

Features such as seating and fountains can be located within these encompassing circles of trees. Pergolas and loggias can also be built to provide shade. Choose a densely foliaged climber for maximum shade — several may need to be planted to achieve a dense cover. The *Sollya*, *Pandorea* and *Kennedia* genera have many suitable species for arid areas.

For purely practical reasons, lawns should be kept small. A circle or rectangle of well-kept lawn acts as a mental restorative in contrast to the brownness of the summer landscape. Make sure, however, that the water supply is adequate. The alternative is to plant green-leafed shrubs in large groups to achieve the same oasis effect. Gravels make ideal mulch and can be softened with groundcovers such as Sturt's desert pea.

Borrowing from the gardens of Santa Fe, we could find sheltered and shaded courtyards enlivened by walls daubed with blue, green or turquoise, rich colours indeed but at the same time cooling and refreshing. Wall tones can take the place of flowers, which often only appear in winter or spring. Foliage texture and plant forms can then be allowed to provide year-long interest.

Water is a significant feature of arid gardens the world over. Water cools the air and is restful. A water feature could be a formal pool in a courtyard surrounded by buildings or a natural billabong-style. Try to make any pool in arid areas as deep as possible. Evaporation is fierce, and a cover of floating aquatics and lilies will help stem water loss.

Garden Styles

OPPOSITE FAR LEFT

An avenue of ghost gums (*Eucalyptus papuana*) and heavily trained senna bushes with the blue desert sky as a backdrop. Designer: Paul Chambers.

OPPOSITE LEFT

A stream in an arid garden should not be a raging torrent; more a gentle passage of shallow water through rocks in a garden as here. Designer: Gregg Chapman.

ABOVE

Weeping acacias and fiery Sturt's desert pea. Designer: Paul Chambers.

The New Native Garden

ABOVE

This water feature draws inspiration from several sources. The terracotta comes from the Mediterranean tradition, the sago palm from the Japanese, and the grass tree is pure Australiana. Designed by Andrew O'Sullivan and Henri Lekeu.

OPPOSITE

Australian plants predominate but this contemporary garden, designed by Barry Jarrott, blends plants from Japan, New Zealand and Europe, yet still retains an Australian feel.

BLENDED OR TAPESTRY GARDENS

There has been next to nothing written in the literature on Australian plants on how to blend exotics with the indigenous flora. Yet even the most cursory glance at the average Australian garden will show that most gardeners like to use a combination of Australian and exotic plants. The argument that we should choose one or the other has drawn battle lines, with purists decrying any use of exotic plants on one side and are those who refuse to even consider any Australian plant on the other. Most of us are more even-handed. We have a strong heritage of exotic horticulture, and it is hard to get away from the plants of other lands. Besides which, it is actually difficult for an Australian garden to avoid native plants. Think of all the bottlebrushes, grevilleas, lillypillies, strawflowers and kangaroo paws that are bought at nurseries every year. If we need good plants for screening, colourful flowers, foliage effects or shade, we tend not to worry about where they come from. What is important is whether they will do the job. On that score, many of our most popular plants rate very highly, in aesthetic terms and also in adaptation to climatic and soil conditions.

Yet we still are faced with a challenge — how to create a coherent garden that treats native and exotic plants as equal partners in an artistic partnership.

A blended garden is not so much a style. Rather it takes a style or a concept and uses plants to create a mosaic of living material. There are no defined rules in this other than to use plants whose growth habits and foliage types blend together. It is somehow easier if we start with a garden that has a clearly defined look or style. Mostly it involves close observation of form, texture and growth.

The New Native Garden

ABOVE
Within an exotic planting this Australian tree may sometimes go unnoticed. The white cedar (*Melia azedarach* var. *australasica*) does not fall within the accepted look, but native it is and it works well in suburbia.

BLENDING NATIVES INTO EXISTING GARDEN

The first step is to decide on the look you want from your garden. Most Australian gardens could be described as 'tapestry' gardens: using plants without regard to country of origin. It is the appearance and how foliage and habit fit together that is important. Nowhere is this more so than in the cottage garden. Let's look at that as an example, because it presents us with a relatively easy choice. But there are some pitfalls.

We tend to think of cottage gardens as having a single style, but there are several variations. These are roughly divided by climate. There is a dry, warm cottage look which blends plants from the Mediterranean, southern Africa, California and Mexico. There is also a cool-climate version with plants from the forests of Europe, Asia and North America. The former, naturally, is the one with the greatest potential for using Australian plants.

The most popular Australian cottage plant, the brachycome daisy, has fine, feathery foliage, prolific flowering and a neat bun shape that looks good both in and out of flower. It blends extremely well with a wide range of exotic perennials, among them: dianthus, gazania, snow-in-summer, kalanchoë and sedum. These are all ideal perennials for the Mediterranean-style cottage garden, familiar to us from the gardens of Provence. Added to cooler-looking polemonium, epimedium and other soft cottage plants, the brachycome daisies can look very harsh.

The other great Australian cottage plants, kangaroo paws and members of the *Bracteanthus* genus, the strawflowers, both annual and perennial, often look even more harsh against the softer European perennials. Each of these will work successfully with statice, lavender and rosemary and the Mediterranean feel is a good one to work with, given the overwhelmingly warm (and dry) climate we enjoy.

The key is to look for similarities in leaf shape, colour and texture. The higher the number of similarities, the easier it will be to blend plants from different lands. Popular native shrubs such as callistemon, grevilleas and melaleucas also have a dry look, for the most part, and can be difficult to blend with a garden of deciduous 'woodland' plants like purple-leafed plums (*Prunus cerasifera* 'Pissardii') or plants from cooler climates, such as dogwoods or maples. Our plants do, however, merge quite well with plants from other hot or dry climates. Southern Africa, Mexico, Turkey, the Middle East or parts of India and China, for instance, offer plant groups that can work well with our native species. Many are already popular garden plants. They just need to be rediscovered as partners. The South African proteas, including the *Leucodendron* and *Leucospermum* genera; salvias and some succulents from Mexico and drier parts of South America are a good match for many Australian plants.

Plants with similarly shaped leaves generally have similar growing needs. For instance, grey hairy foliage often indicates a plant from a dry or seaside climate where exposure to the elements requires special adaptations. Large and soft leaves can be an indicator of a need for good rainfall. So look carefully at the plants in a well-stocked nursery and then check their growing needs if you are not already familiar with them. Also consult a good general plant reference before buying. If you have ever watched a florist add branches and flowers, you will have an idea of how to display and mix plants.

Sometimes going for a strong contrast is appropriate. Even blending strong-leafed local plants like Gymea lily (*Doryanthes excelsa*) can be hard. But in their native habitat, the forests south of Sydney, they stand like beacons, even when not in bloom. The leaves offer a strong contrast to the mass of tiny-foliaged plants surrounding them. Take a cue from this and use such plants as accents. Group a few in a corner, not evenly distributed around the garden, but positioned where they stand out and lift themselves above the other parts of the garden.

If you are blending native with exotic, even-handedness does not seem to work. Gardens that are most successful tend to be composed mainly of natives with a few exotics carefully chosen for their compatibility, or vice versa. And always the similarities need to be considered above all other considerations. Mixing camellias with waratahs or grevilleas is likely to be uncomfortable, but add lillypillies, native rhododendron (*R. lochiae*), *Cordyline stricta,* birds' nest fern and other rainforest plants with similar leaves, and it could prove beneficial.

BELOW

A non-traditional use of a native Lomandra in this Mediterranean-inspired design; it works well because it simply pays it dues. Designer: Peter Nixon.

garden DESIGNS and Plans

A MEADOW GARDEN

Native annuals may be small in number but they make up for it with impact and their ease of cultivation. The wildflowers of Western Australia are justly praised for their beauty and spectacle. For a few brief weeks in early spring they carpet the ground for mile upon mile. With the wealth of exotic annuals available to us, it is perhaps understandable, if not entirely excusable, that we have overlooked the largely Western Australian natives.

Through all the neglect, there are glimmers of hope for native annuals. Perth's King's Park Gardens and Mt Annan Botanical Garden in Western Sydney are two large public institutions to have absorbed their importance. Each spring their lawns become home to fields of native everlastings in a display every bit as breathtaking as the tulips of Keukenhof in the Netherlands, the azaleas of Winterthur, or the massed bedding of begonias around the palace of Versailles.

Made up of members of the families *Rhodanthe* and *Bracteantha*, they are perhaps better known by their former botanical names, *Helipterum* and *Helichrysum*, by which names they are still sold by seed merchants and garden centres. Paper daisy and strawflowers are even more familiar. The gardeners of Victorian England knew them as 'immortelles', a romantic (and ironic) moniker for flowers whose life in the wild is fleeting and temporary.

Essentially, the design plan illustrated on this page is a meadow garden planting, a popular trend in parts of the Netherlands, Germany and the north-eastern United States. The very notion of a 'meadow' planting and all it entails, however, does not sit well with Australian conditions. The reason is climate. Meadows are a European construct, as alien to Australians as hedgerows and copses, dales and downs. Maintaining one is not nearly as easy as the European writers tell us. We need to adapt our gardening methods to our own conditions.

There are some difficulties in translating a phenomenon of hot parched plains to small domestic gardens. The flower fields are in effect growing in a sandy desert. These wildflowers are adapted to growing when rain is plentiful, flowering quickly before heat evaporates precious soil moisture and setting seed as the summer haze takes over. The show is brief and spectacular. Their outpouring of colourful glory can be sporadic too, dependent on good autumn and winter rains. Without these conditions, the show can fail. In a garden, we control the supply of water but we demand a stronger, longer show.

How can we overcome that? The answer is simply to fudge a little. Mix annuals with perennials, mostly from the same few families but others also, so the show is extended over a much longer period. Some of the best colour comes from paper daisies, particularly *Bracteantha bracteata* and native buttercups (*Rhodanthe appaceus*), the latter new to

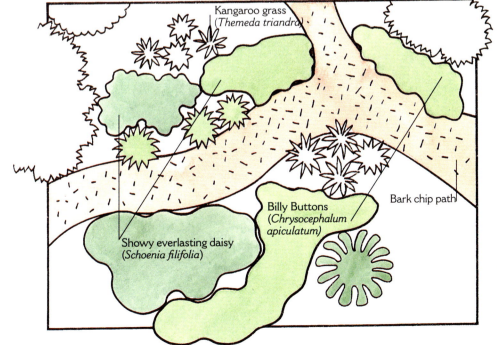

OPPOSITE

A meadow planting of mixed daisies has been kept to two colours. Grasses and other loosely structured plants help to support their thin stems.
Mt Annan Botanical Garden, NSW.

PREVIOUS PAGES

Pages 86–87: Planning is the key to designing a beautiful garden. Designer: Roger Stone. For more information on this garden see 'A Stroll Garden,' pages 100–103.

cultivation and hard to find. You can extend the display by planting perennials too. Strawflowers, mostly bracteantha and helichrysum are the most prolific but brachycome daisies, both hybrids of *B. multifida* and the annual Swan River daisy are also worth using.

For late season colour, drifts of hybrid kangaroo paws keep colour going through summer and into autumn.

Paper daisy seed can be purchased in bulk packs for mass sowing. Mail order firms, which specialise in seed sales, are the best source. See plants by mail order in the resource list on page 216.

Ground preparation is important for the paper daisies. The best soil is sandy and well drained. Too much fertiliser will result in weak and sappy growth. A reasonable amount of organic matter such as well-rotted compost will enable rapid growth with strong stems, but plants should be watered less frequently than exotic annuals. In areas with mild winters, plant in autumn to harden off the young plants gradually before winter frosts. They will develop a strong root system over the winter months. Sowing is often delayed until early spring in regions with hard frosts.

Dig the soil, rake it and remove clods of earth. This will create a friable seedbed. A layer of mulch will preserve soil moisture without the need for daily watering.

Native annual varieties:

Rhodanthe chlorocephala ssp. *rosea* (Rosy Everlasting). Papery flowers in a range of shades of pink with narrow leaves. Excellent in the garden or for cut or dried flowers.

Rhodanthe manglesii (Mangle's Everlasting, Silver Bells). Flowers in both pink and white with broader leaves. Smaller growing than *R. chlorocephala* spp. *rosea*.

Schoenia filifolia ssp. *subulifolia* (Showy Everlasting Daisy). Yellow papery flowers with very narrow leaves.

Brachycome iberidifolia (Swan River daisy). These flower in white, pale blue, dark blue and mauve. Good foreground plants.

Native daisies will grow in most areas of Australia except severe frost zones. They are frost resistant down to 0°C. Sow seeds directly where they are to grow in autumn in mild climates. They will flower in spring. To improve drainage, plant in raised beds of sandy soil. Feed with liquid fertiliser during warmer weather to encourage strong growth before winter. They also grow well in pots.

ABOVE LEFT

The most common of the pink everlastings is Mangle's Everlasting (*Rhodanthe manglesii*). Flowers vary from pink to white and some have dark centres.

LEFT

Showy everlasting daisy (*Schoenia filifolia* ssp. *subulifolia*).

Garden Designs and Plans

ABOVE
Smaller growing is another *Rhodanthe*, *R. chlorocephala* ssp. *rosea*. Members of the *Rhodanthe* genus are frequently sold as *Helipterum roseum*, the former name for these pretty paper daisies.

Garden Designs and Plans

A COTTAGE BORDER

The cottage look has been one of the most popular trends in recent years, and it's one of the easiest looks to achieve using native plants.

A true cottage garden uses perennials, annuals, vegetables and herbs in a mix that's contrived to look haphazard. It can all become quite labour-intensive, as many gardeners have found out. If you still want the look but with a fraction of the workload, use small flowering shrubs and fewer annuals and perennials. They make a longer-lasting and easier-to-care for alternative to the high-maintenance perennials of the traditional exotic border. There is an enormous range of native plants suitable for this purpose.

A mixed border allows you to create a framework planting of trees and shrubs. The transient (or at best semi-permanent) nature of most flowering plants used alone — annuals or perennials — often requires some form of structure to bring them together. Linking with shrubs can prove a much cheaper alternative to hard landscaping in the form of stone paving or masonry walls.

There is the added advantage of planning for year-round colour. Many of the popular native plants flower in spring, which can leave the bushes looking rather dull through the other three seasons. But there are some that flower at all times of the year. Prominent among these are the grevilleas. Many are used in our featured garden, which also contains several native perennials to keep interest going through all seasons.

The garden below and on page 95, designed by Professor Ron Laura, fits into the typical quarter-acre block — it is relatively small but it looks much larger. There are plants of varying heights, some only miniatures, others tall shrubs and trees used as background plantings. Some of the larger grevilleas can be trained and pruned to scale, others should be allowed to grow to a more natural height but regularly pruned to keep them youthful.

Any mixed garden, whether native or exotic, needs a blend of textures. This can come from foliage but also from height, habit and shape. Variety is introduced by using different shapes side by side — a low-growing squat shrub can be planted next to a spreading taller shrub and other pyramidal or tightly foliaged plants can blend in behind and to the sides. The achievement of balance can often be a hit- and-miss affair, but pruning and training play a significant part.

Some plants are short-term and others grow for many years. The longer-term plants should be arranged so that they form the backbone of the garden. Position them so that whenever some of the short-termers such as the mint

OPPOSITE
A mixed planting of natives includes several grevillea cultivars, the delightful silver-leafed and mauve-flowered *Eremophila nivea* and Geraldton wax (*Chamelaucium uncinatum*).

RIGHT
Blend foliage and flowers together. Geraldton wax, *Leptospermum* 'Cardwell' and a red-flowered grevillea form a good colour composition.

The New Native Garden

A COTTAGE BORDER

Garden Designs and Plans

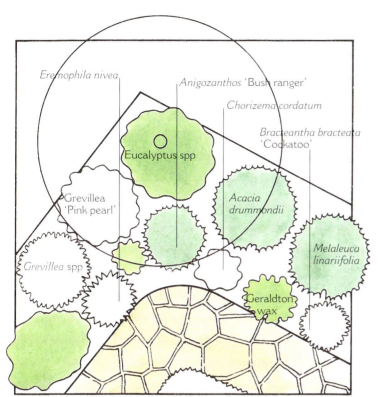

bush, croweas or correas are being culled, the garden does not look like a bombsite. Plant craters caused by the inevitable need to replace and change the arrangement can destroy a garden and give it a never-finished look. With a permanent framework the gaps are far less obvious, and can be filled with temporary annuals and perennials such as brachycome and kangaroo paw, which will add seasonal colour and variety. This is important because a shrub border can become static. Adding a mixture of perennials, annuals and groundcovers allows for a changing look from season to season and from year to year. But at the same time there is some permanence and structure.

BELOW

Left to right: The garden is colourful not only in spring but also for many other months of the year. Among the varied planting are groups of grevilleas including *Grevillea* 'Pink Pearl', with white and pink forms of Geraldton wax (*Chamelaucium uncinatum*), *Anigozanthos* 'Bush Ranger', *Acacia drummondii* and *Chorizema cordatum*. Designer: Professor Ron Laura.

The New Native Garden

A ROCK LILY GARDEN

Mention orchids and the mind conjures up images of exotic hothouse plants covered with sumptuous blooms of unimaginable opulence. Mention natives and we think small, insignificant, and dry. But what happens when you put the two together?

Native orchids do indeed have small flowers in comparison with their gaudy South American cousins (but remember these are often the products of hybridising and human interference). Individually the flowers do not match the flamboyance of a cattleya or a cymbidium but mass them and the effect can be stunning.

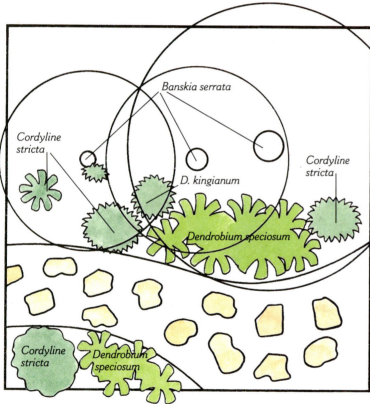

RIGHT

The rock lily (*Dendrobium speciosum*) is the easiest to grow and certainly the most spectacular in a garden setting. The smaller orchid is the king orchid (*D. kingianum*). The garden was designed by author and illustrator, Betty Maloney.

Garden Designs and Plans

The New Native Garden

Garden Designs and Plans

Simplicity is one of the keys to good design. A well-designed garden can be made spectacular by the simple device of massing or repeating the same or similar plants. If you seek a display with impact, this is an ideal method.

The garden of botanical illustrator and native plants enthusiast, Betty Moloney (pages 96–98 and 132–135), uses a single planting of rock lily (*Dendrobium speciosum*). It's a native plant, widely spread through the eastern states and commonly grown all over the Australian continent. In spring it sends up large sprays of white, cream or yellow flowers. The true beauty of this species is its simplicity — it's simple to cultivate and its form is simple and uncomplicated.

The forms of this orchid are quite varied. Some are a pale cream, some have flowers which appear to be still opening. There are also several hybrids of a number of different native orchids. The small pink orchid seen tucked into the middle of the bed is the king orchid (*Dendrobium kingianum*). When crossed with *D. speciosum* the resultant cross, *D. X delicatum,* has a long, elegant pseudobulb and sprays of white blooms as large as, but more erect than, those of the rock lily.

Like most of the Australian dendrobiums, this one is an epiphyte. It attaches itself to tree trunks, often in rainforests or wet sclerophyll forests. In the wild it can also be seen clinging to rock ledges, frequently in the most exposed, west-facing positions where it is hit by the full force of the afternoon sun. Scorching, bleaching heat seems not to affect its flowering potential though obviously a blend of partial sun with dappled shade would be more favourable. These are growing in a rough mixture of coarse materials including large boulders, rubble and bark. Rock lilies need good drainage, so a rasied bed may be necessary if you are planning to grow them as a bedding plant. In the centre of the raised bed throw large rocks and a large grade of gravel and mix in a layer of coarse compost. Don't worry about leaves and twigs falling into the mass of bulbs. These will break down in time and feed the orchids.

An occasional deep watering is preferable to short splashes with the hose. Orchids should be moved or transplanted only in the spring. This gives the roots time to establish and develop over summer until autumn. They will anchor themselves onto the rocks and other hard material before winter. Reduce water as colder weather sets in. In frosty areas some overhead protection will be needed, either from a dense canopy of shrubs or trees or with shade cloth.

OPPOSITE
A winding bush path through banksias and eriostemon leads to this large bed of rock lilies.

Garden Designs and Plans

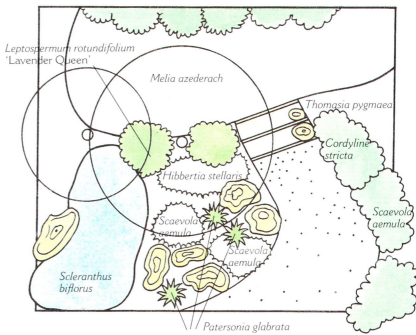

A STROLL GARDEN

Imagine a large garden with winding paths and views cut by trees or shrubs. Beyond, there is the expectation of some enchanting surprise: a secret garden or some special view, a statue or specimen tree perhaps.

Creating the illusion of space in a small area is one of the classic skills of garden design. It reaches its apogee in Japanese gardens, where available land is always at a premium.

But the garden here (also on pages 102–103) is not a particularly large garden. It just looks as though it is.

Creating this illusion is a skill. It's one that has fallen into disuse under the onslaught of the 'garden rooms' fad, where large garden space is broken into small 'garden rooms'. Now this is all very well, and the division of a larger space into smaller components is not in itself a bad thing, but the divsion is more successful when it is seamless. Too often the notion of the 'garden room' is called upon to justify separating a French parterre from woodland, from a formal rose garden and so on. Feature after feature vying for attention. In a native garden this technique can safely be avoided.

LEFT

Wide steps and a planting almost entirely composed of groundcovers lends a feeling of space to this garden. *Scaevola*, *Scleranthus* and *Hibbertia* are among the flowering and non-flowering plants giving a cushioning effect. This mixed planting displays interesting colour contrast.

The New Native Garden

CREATING SPACE

The techniques used by the early Japanese garden designers to create the illusion of space are worth revisiting. The tradition depends upon a close observation of nature. Gardeners looked at how rocks were placed, trees grew, water flowed and eddied, and how wind and the elements shaped plants. Their perceptions were then translated into garden designs in an artistic or abstract way. It wasn't merely copying nature; it was more interpreting it.

They saw that nature favours asymmetry over symmetry. This became the basis for creating harmonious gardens free of discord. The Europeans, on the other hand, used symmetry to create harmony, with altogether different results. Their gardens displayed geometric precision, strong axial lines and mirror imaging along the axis.

The Japanese struggled with the problem of balance and harmony in the absence of symmetry. The solution was found in grouping plants, particularly in arrays of odd numbers. Groups of three, five and seven, for instance, appear balanced when arrayed.

Perspective and scale were also problems. They discovered that when something appears out of scale, adding another element (itself possibly out of scale), can reinstate the balance. They used height, weight and mass to create a sense of perspective and depth. In other words, if a large rock is placed in a small space, it will look over-scaled. The addition

Garden Designs and Plans

LEFT

Scleranthus biflorus is a cushion groundcover that needs full sun and moist soil.

OPPOSITE

A pond and gravel landing extend the open feeling adjacent to the path. Plants are maintained by careful pruning and ongoing care.

of another large rock, perhaps differently shaped or placed on its side, brings them both into a more acceptable perspective.

Space, the area between the elements, is just as important. Designers sometimes refer to spaces such as lawns, paths, paving and gravel courts as voids. Essentially they are the flat areas between the high points, and are essential to create balance.

Setting rough and smooth against each other can also create a sense of balance. For instance, setting the ruggedness of stone, gravel and coarse plant textures adjacent to or in view of a still body of water is one way to create balance.

In this stroll garden, designed by Roger Stone, the void in the foreground is the gravel steps. In the middle ground a level of lawn does the same job and in the background you can just see another level of gravel.

The masses are provided by the plantings at the side of the path. To the right is a barely visible building hidden by mass of low-growing shrubs and strong vertical accents from the cordyline. The placement of rocks within the garden and also along the path creates balance and harmony, a feeling enhanced by the curve of the path and the way the view is obstructed in the distance.

In this garden even the placement of the trees adds to the sense of harmony. The by-product of balance is the creation of mood. Contrasting textures also creates differences in feeling, an important feature of a good design. You can see it here in the way the design flows through the scene.

Garden Designs and Plans

A GRAVEL 'BEACH'

The beach exercises a powerful pull on the Australian psyche. Anyone who has gardened near a beach knows that the ocean is an unforgiving neighbour. Salt spray and leached-out sandy soil make gardening a difficult task.

But a beach is not the sole preserve of oceans. Freshwater rivers and creeks, too, possess pretty sandy beaches and coves. And the possibility of gardening in such an environment is an altogether more appealing and more thankful task than that faced by coast dwellers.

A garden without spaces or voids can be very dull. This gravel beach acts as a substitute for lawn, providing open space. The crunch of gravel has an evocative feel and gives the design a sense of place.

A rainforest stream with a small expanse of fine gravel is the inspiration for the garden pictured here and on page 107, and even though it uses several exotics it is still clearly defined as an Australian garden.

The use of lawns is much overrated in Australian gardens, though the benefit of a lawn as a foil for the surrounding plantings is well established. Here is one way the lawn can make way for more naturalistic settings.

Lawns are environmentally unsound. To look good, lawns need grading, levelling, weeding and feeding. They are voracious feeders and invasive as well. They also need attention and manicuring. If you neglect these tasks, the lawn will invariably look shabby. And no more so than in a native plant garden, where even the well-kept lawn will often look out of place.

In the garden design here, the garden owner, Bev Hanson, solved the problem by adding two of the essential elements, water and stone. Groundcovers planted around the space help soften it and allow it to still retain the green look provided by lawns.

The pool that the beach fronts is set close to the house, with a path running between the two.

For a design like this to work, you would need an expanse in front to open up the scene and shubbery behind to close the scene.

LEFT

The area surrounding this pool has been turned into a feature with a beach of fine gravel. Native and exotic plants, such as *Banksia ericifolia* and the Judas tree (*Cercis siliquastrum*), work surprisingly well when used in close proximity.

The New Native Garden

A GRAVEL 'BEACH'

Garden Designs and Plans

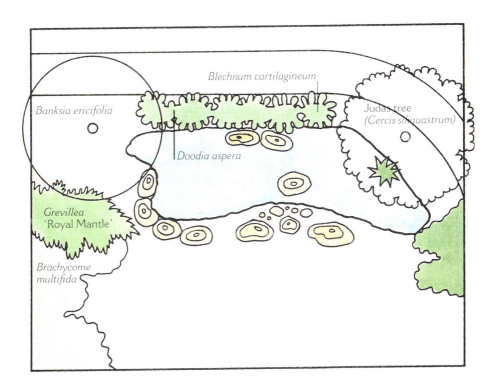

LEFT
Plant species such as ferns and rushes, that would normally be found beside lakes or streams, are ideal plants for a gravel beach design.

A RAISED GARDEN

Raised beds offer plenty of opportunity for garden making. In some cases they are a major design element, defining or articulating a particular garden style. More often they are used for practical reasons, but, offer valuable aesthetic side benefits as well. They provide the opportunity for increasing the depth of the soil. They make gardening easier by reducing the need for excessive bending, especially for elderly or infirm gardeners. And on slopes, they can define changes of levels, providing design advantages and practical solutions to real problems, such as drainage, soil stability and access.

What part do walls play in garden style? The walled garden has become a defining element in the English garden, and it's hard to imagine a Santa Fe garden without its trademark adobe walls. More often than not, though, they define a place. The raised bed in the garden here, designed by Gregg Chapman, forms part of an entrance planting. A wall at the rear defines the boundary of the garden and retains soil behind the gentle slope. Walls therefore serve a dual purpose in this garden. The perimeter wall limits the garden and encloses it. All attention is directed to what lies within it. The retaining wall at the front limits the focus too, but it also serves a practical purpose.

Soil retention is the primary use of low walls. Where a planned wall exceeds one metre in height, you may need to obtain approval from the local council, so seek the advice of a qualified builder or landscape contractor before proceeding. Points to consider include drainage and the provision of weep holes for water runoff, soil weight and the depth of soil to be retained.

These walls are a finishing touch rather than a defining one. The grey colour used in both walls provides a good foil for the predominantly grey or glaucous foliage tones and the flower colour scheme. Pinks in spring are followed by a mass of blue from the *Scaevola* planted to hang over the edge.

RIGHT

A raised bed offers plenty of opportunity to grow a wider range of plants requiring sharper drainage. *Boronia denticulata*, pink *Prostanthera rotundifolia* and *P. lasianthos* have been chosen to blend with the wall colour. The *Cordyline australis*, a New Zealand native, adds height and architectural form. Designer: Gregg Chappman.

Garden Designs and Plans

The New Native Garden

A RAISED GARDEN

Garden Designs and Plans

ABOVE

The colour of *Prostanthera rotundifolia* and *P. lasianthos* are a softer pinkish mauve than the common purple mint bush *P. ovalifolia*.

ABOVE

The exotic groundcover *Convolvulus sabatius*, a Mediterranean plant, works well with natives such as *Westringia fruticosa* 'Wynyabbie Gem' and *Orthrosanthus multiforus*.

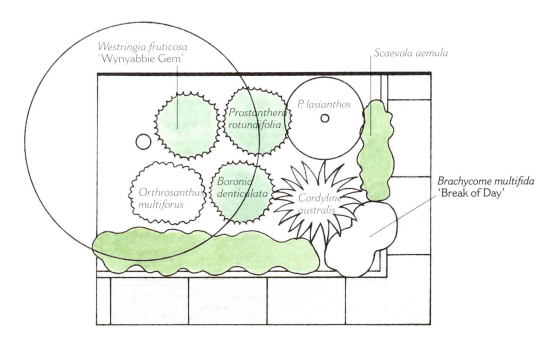

A BOG GARDEN

The most calming places in a forest are those near creeks and streams. The gentle rush of water, the abundance of soft green foliage, the enveloping canopy of leaves and flowers and the fresh, clean smell of damp leaves underfoot are the things we think of.

Few of us are lucky enough to be able to set our home beside such an idyllic scene. This is probably a blessing. Nature is seldom as romantic and giving as to provide a chaos-free existence — there is always the probability of flood or some other catastrophe.

But we can control nature in a garden. An artificial stream or wetland garden is devoid of the risk of natural calamity but still full of the charm and peace of a natural watercourse.

Start by identifying the wettest point in your yard. There are usually two ways to treat a wet patch in the garden. The first is to lay in agricultural drainage or engage a drainage engineer to draft a plan to remove the excess water.

The second is to go with the flow and make the disadvantages work for you. A bog garden or even a shallow pond is a useful place for water to accumulate and gradually seep away after wet spells.

MAKING A BOG GARDEN

Mark out the area to be used for planting, then dig out to a depth of 45cm. The sides should be sloping — a gradient of about $60°$ is sufficient for most bogs. If you wish to have an area of water dig it a little deeper in the centre. Smooth sides and remove any sharp sticks, stones or roots.

Cover the surface with impermeable sheeting such as heavy-duty polythene. Unlike a pond, where butyl liners are preferable, the idea is to retain soil moisture but not permanent water. Pierce some weep holes into the surface so the water does not become sour or stagnant. Cover the holes with gravel to prevent them becoming blocked.

Lay a length of irrigation tubing, the type used for garden watering, on a bed of gravel so water will have a free run. Connect this permanently to your home irrigation system. Refill the bed with good garden soil. Plant, allowing plenty of room for plants to grow, and mulch the soil heavily.

PLANTS FOR THE BOG GARDEN

A bog garden is the natural alternative to a real spring. A variety of plants are suitable for growing in damp conditions and range in size from trees such as *Melaleuca armillaris*, *M. bracteata*, *M. quinquenervia* and *M. styphelioides* to low growing groundcovers such as *Phyla nodiflora*, various ferns and creeping rush (*Restio tetraphyllus*).

Shrubs suitable for planting on the edge of a water garden where moisture is permanent but not stagnant or constantly wet include the river rose (*Bauera rubioides*), *Baeckea gunniana*, *Goodenia humilis* and *G. lanata*, *Epacris lanuginosa* and *E. reclinata*, *Kunzea capitata*, *Leptospermum lanigerum* and *L. scoparium*. Some will also grow where roots are permanently wet. Look for *Juncus pauciflorus* and many of the bottlebrushes, including *Callistemon citrinus*, *C. sieberi* and *C. subulatus*.

Ferns are ideal for bog gardens. The availability of ferns varies from region to region, so choose from among the available native species rather than any named here. Some outstanding ones are tree ferns (*Dicksonia antarctica*), the king fern (*Todea barbara*), the rasp fern (*Doodia aspera*) and members of the Blechnum family, *B. fluviatile*, *B. nudum* and *B. wattsii* among them. Good groundcovers include Canberra grass (*Scleranthus biflorus*), *Pratia concolor*, New South Wales Christmas bell (*Blandfordia nobilis*) and *Ranunculus rivularis*, none of which like to be inundated but prefer a moist root run. The very best groundcover for this situation is the native violet (*Viola hederacea*), a stoloniferous or creeping groundcover, or its clumping relative *V. betonicifolia*.

OPPOSITE

In this garden, owned by WIRES volunteers Lorelle and Rhonda Mercer, swamp banksia (*Banksia robur*), dianella, cunjevoi (*Alocasia brisbanensis* syn. *A. macrorrhizos*) and ferns abound. Cunjevoi grows particularly well in bog gardens, as it needs constantly moist soil and part shade to produce its perfumed flowers.

The New Native Garden

A BOG GARDEN

Garden Designs and Plans

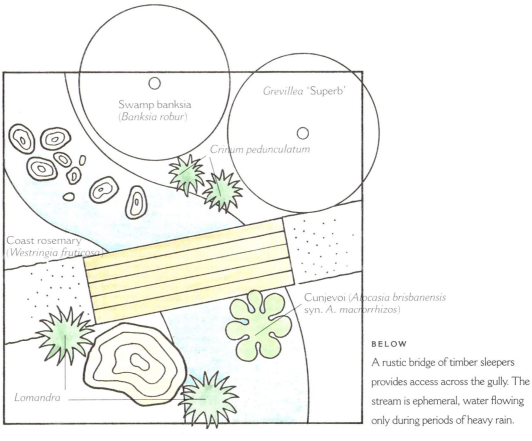

BELOW A rustic bridge of timber sleepers provides access across the gully. The stream is ephemeral, water flowing only during periods of heavy rain.

The New Native Garden

A GREEN WOODLAND

There's something about a green garden. Perhaps it's the absence of flowers competing for attention, the patterns of a single colour blending into a tightly knit tapestry, or maybe it's just the gentle sway of foliage textures in the breeze.

This garden, pictured on pages 117–118, designed by Don Burke, replicates natural bush, but it's an idealised version. It has its highlights, in spite of the monochrome colour scheme. There are bright greens against dull greens, dark and olive greens with paler, and through it all, texture is paramount. Most of the plant material has an architectural quality. There are some grasses, but mostly it relies on a few shrubs and grass-like plants. The effect is billowing and poetic as the tall slender blades move in the slightest zephyr.

One of my fondest memories is walking through the local Sydney bushland as a young child after rain. The trunks of the angophoras were the richest shades of salmon pink overlayed by rust and terracotta as the moisture was soaked up by flaking bark and became enriched with colour in the process. Native grasses, lilies, swordgrass, *Lomatia* and *Dianella* all looked their best at these moments. They were a little clammy to touch, of course, but the smell of eucalypt leaf mould with its wonderful oily scent still thrills, to this day.

That is the inspiration behind this garden. It looks like bush but it is well tamed, with paths of bark chips and ordered routes. It is a garden that could easily fill a small backyard. The woodland style has a cool and tranquil feel. The planting is unostentatious and informal. The blending of tree fern and groundcover plants allows space between ground planting and the canopy, giving a relaxed and enclosing feel.

The tree ferns add height and provide shelter for ferns, as this garden gets a fair and generous share of natural rainfall. Where moisture levels are constant, ferns thrive, and here they grow in shady pockets.

Grasses too are adaptable plants and thrive in many ecosystems and habitats. They have become very popular landscaping plants in the northern hemisphere in the past two decades. Designers such as the Dutch Piet Oudolf and the Americans, Wolfgang Oehme and James van Sweden, have used mass plantings of grasses as large-scale perennial plants where their seasonal display adds variety

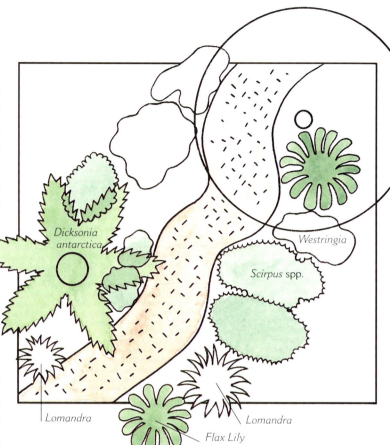

and character to gardens, even in winter under a carpet of snow or frost.

Australians are less enthusiastic, and there are very practical reasons for this. Grasses grow and die quickly in our climate. Their active growing season is shorter, with rapid growth in spring followed by a quick brown-off in summer, when scorching heat dries them out. In a hot, dry climate, grasses are a fire risk, an ever-present problem in outlying urban and rural areas. This garden attempts to counter this by offering the look of grass with greater fire-retardation. Using alternative strap-leafed plants such as *Lomatia* and *Dianella*, and rushes such as *Restio*, which have a higher leaf moisture content than grasses, makes a lot of sense.

Start with key plants such as tall trees and accents like tree ferns, perhaps *Cyathea cooperi* or *Dicksonia antarctica*. Both have well-defined trunks, though the former has softer, more airy foliage and a lighter, more slender trunk, to give a gentler feel to the woodland garden. Tree ferns have a cathedral-like quality. Their fronds make a canopy or an umbrella over other plants and direct the eye downwards and along. They are excellent in a garden on a steep slope. Looking down on the symmetrical pattern of fronds makes a view more enticing.

Garden Designs and Plans

ABOVE

In Don Burke's native garden, groundcovers mixed with tree ferns, low shrubs and native lilies create a lush green landscape. The overall effect is softer than the traditional naturalistic garden.

Straight-trunked eucalypts are good in this type of garden. They make a strong visual statement without casting heavy shade. Light and sun is still permitted to permeate the canopy, and this allows you to grow a wide range of plants, including some flowering ones. In a shady location, white-flowering shrubs or low, ground-hugging perennials are possibly the best choice. White lightens what can sometimes be a dark or shaded spot.

The New Native Garden

Garden Designs and Plans

ABOVE

Flax lilies are easy to grow in a shaded, moist garden. Two species are commonly grown — *Dianella caerulea* and *D. tasmanica*. Both have blue flowers and berries.

ABOVE

The drooping leaves of the grass and the flax lilies have a flowing, wave-like quality, attractive even when covered in berries or blooms.

OPPOSITE

The path wends its way through a combination of plant forms, some pruned and tended, like the westringias; others flowing naturally for continuous movement.

The New Native Garden

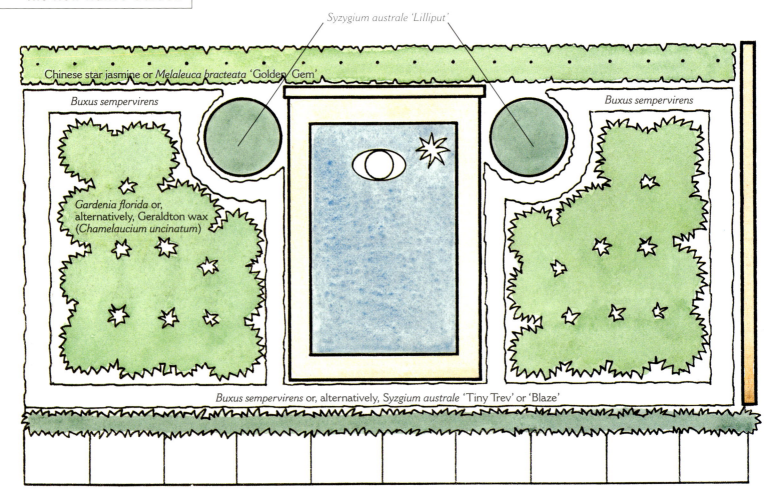

OPPOSITE
This formal garden is primarily exotic but uses topiarised lillypillies as a strong accent plant. The same style could be transformed using native plants like *Austromyrtus dulcis* and *Syzgium australe* 'Blaze' as the infill and outer hedge respectively. The garden designer is Peter Fudge.

FORMAL GARDEN IDEAS

Formal gardens have returned in a big way in the last decade. It's hard to say why this has happened, because formal gardens are nothing if not labour intensive, especially in warmer areas. The full explanation is most likely a combination of many factors. Perhaps it is a reaction to the softness and lack of definition of the cottage garden, or the laxity and unkempt nature of the bush gardens of the 1970s or perhaps it is just because they photograph well in glossy magazines.

Strictly speaking, a formal garden uses symmetrical plantings and axial lines to complement the strict symmetry of architecture. Most modern houses tend to be assymetrical, but repro-Georgian and neo-Mediterranean houses are built with a strong and visible symmetry. Formal gardens blend well with these styles. Informal gardens, on the other hand, tend to look artificial and out of place. While it has not been common to use them, there are many native plants that can be used to further this look. Most, though not all, tend to be rainforest plants. The

Garden Designs and Plans

principal quality to look for is a plant's ability to respond to vigorous pruning, an essential horticultural act to achieve the formal geometric lines.

This design, pictured above, uses two large topiarised lillypillies as the main focus. It demonstrates the benefits of keeping an open mind when it comes to choosing plant material. This is a blended garden. The hedges are buxus and the infill is mostly gardenia. The supporting green structure could just as easily have been native.

Some of the potential substitute plants would give a very different feel to the garden, probably less green and lush. Some would give it a more Mediterranean feel, drier and more drought hardy, but the native substitutions could also give the formal design greater affinity with our surroundings than the plants originally used.

First let's consider alternatives to the box hedge (*Buxus sempervirens*). Box is used because it is green and easy to grow. It can be kept low and responds to pruning. The same is true of lonicera, another small-leafed hedging plant.

The many new cultivars of *Syzygium* are the best source of new hedging material in the same vein as box. *Syzygium australe* 'Tiny Trev', 'Bush Christmas', 'Lilliput' and 'Blaze' are just some of the outstanding new introductions that can take the place of box or lonicera for formal gardens. They also have the advantage of being more or less adapted to the environment, at least in terms of temperature range, soil fertility and rainfall of most areas. Their only disadvantage is that they are not frost hardy. In cooler inland areas box may still be needed to produce an evergreen hardy hedge.

The New Native Garden

ABOVE
An alternative treatment of the topiarised lillypilly, designed by Jonathan Allin, places two pyramid shapes framing a gateway. Other native plants include *Syzygium paniculatum* and *Podocarpus elatus*.

OPPOSITE
Another view of Peter Fudge's design shows how the formal pond is positioned to be viewed from the terrace.

Try *Syzygium australe* 'Bush Christmas', a promising plant with the smallest leaves of the lillypillies. It has naturally compact growth, which reduces the need for continual summer pruning.

'Blaze', only 150cm tall, has fine foliage and compact bushy growth. It can be pruned to shape, is ideal for hedges, topiary and borders, is disease resistant and responds to regular pruning.

'Lilliput' grows to 1.5–2m in full sun or light shade, making it extremely versatile under tree cover, something that box is not renowned for. It has naturally dense growth with white flowers followed by edible pink berries. It can also be used as a magnificent garden specimen, tub plant and hedge. It grows vigorously and is easily pruned for the formal garden. Its performance has been proven from Cairns to Perth.

Other small hedges to use instead of box include *Westringia* 'Wynyabbie Gem' and *Baeckea virgata*. Both are commonly available, though, they may need searching out — and both respond to pruning. Some of the westringias have had in the past a tendency to die off in the middle of the row for no apparent reason but it is still a worthy family to consider for hedging plants.

Melaleuca armillaris 'Green Globe' will remain dense if given plenty of water and fertilised. It grows well in light soil if there is little or no competition from large trees or greedy shrubs.

For a slightly varied look using coloured foliage, *Melalauca bracteata* 'Golden Gem' is hardy if given summer water. Leaves are slightly golden and it shoots from hard wood after pruning. *Leptospermum rubrum* 'Nana' needs a dry environment to thrive. Like many of the tea-trees it often fails to perform well in humid zones. There it is likely to be short-lived, but there are many dwarf forms with interesting bronze or purple foliage. It could be used to replace *Berberis thunbergii* 'Atropurpurea Nana' in the exotic garden. It also has the advantage of having masses of white, pink or red flowers.

The spaces between the box hedges do not need to be as tightly controlled. *Austromyrtus dulcis* or many of the correas would make good substitutes to fill in the spaces between the hedges. Another, and one that requires some searching out from specialist nurseries, particularly rainforest plant nurseries, is *Graptophyllum excelsum*. It is soft-stemmed and easy to strike from cuttings.

For more colour in the infill zone, consider Geraldton wax (*Chamelaucium uncinatum*). Borrow some pruning techniques from commercial floriculture to train it for this purpose. The cutflower growers of Western Australia coppice Geraldton wax, so the plants form strong straight new stems which are an ideal length for cutting, and develop plenty of flowers.

While they will never attain the strict precision of box, they can be contained within an outer hedge. Chamelaucium can be grown as a balled specimen too. Start when very young. Regularly trim all new shoots to keep the plant tight for the first couple of years. When the trunk has developed to a thickness of about 3–4cm, cut back to about 10cm from the base of the plant. It will look devastated for a few weeks, and should not be heavily

watered in this time. But new growth will start to form at the base and these will grow to the same height very quickly.

When cut back hard into old wood, chamelaucium will normally sprout again and again, hence its value as a cut flower filler. It needs sandy soil to grow well. Raised beds may be needed in wetter areas. This is an advantage for the formal style. In our garden, this planting is contained with a masonry wall.

For a 'dry' look, *Leucophyta brownii* can be used as a lightly clipped hedge in much the way the exotic santolina or lavender cotton is used. Just clip to keep a general shape without the sharp creases and right-angled geometry. Because this is a dry-land plant, if trimmed into too dense a bun, there is the risk that warm humid conditions may encourage fungal attack. It is worth experimenting with this one if there is plenty of air circulation.

For informal hedges in dry conditions, try *Rhagodia spinescens*, *R. crassifolia* and *R. nutans*. They prefer very free-draining dry sand. They will grow to a one metre hedge and can be pruned hard. They will shoot from old wood low on the plant.

The New Native Garden

A CONTEMPORARY FORMAL GARDEN

Garden Designs and Plans

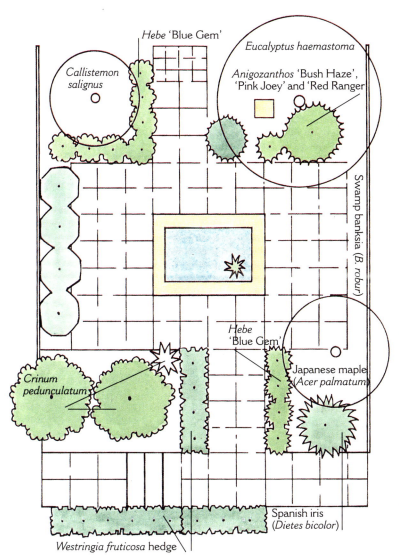

A CONTEMPORARY FORMAL GARDEN

One of the ironies of modern gardening is the concurrent popularity of two garden styles that are at opposite ends of the design spectrum. Most probably the popularity of one is a reaction to the other. Frequently, the advocates of one vociferously reject the design philosophy of the rival camp. I speak, of course, of the cottage garden and the formal garden. Cottage gardens are exuberant, filled with plants of every variety and bursting with flowers. A formal garden is spare in its choice of plants and highly structured; symmetry is prized and geometric precision is paramount; colour is a secondary element in the design. Formality is the ultimate display of man's mastery of nature.

But it is possible to have the best of both worlds. This courtyard garden, pictured on page 127, blends formality and informality. The hard landscaping provides a formal framework with strong geometry and a dominant structure. The planting itself borrows from several traditions. It is a mix of naturalistic plantings with formal hedging. These soften hard features such as paving.

There is symmetry here but it is balanced by asymmetry. For instance the pathway near the main access point is positioned off centre, but it is balanced by the positioning of the path at the far end as a mirror image. The whole effect is balanced, and a sense of harmony is achieved between natural and formal, between native and exotic.

Water is part of the formal structure. The shape of the pool is rectangular, with a sandstone coping flush with the surrounding paving. Its position in the centre of the main court gives it a dominant emphasis as a focal point. It also serves as the point of departure for the strict symmetry often demanded of the formal garden.

In the formal tradition, this is a garden to be viewed. It can be walked through, of course, but its main purpose is to be seen, and seen from several different angles. The steps will give you an idea of the elevation of the garden and location of the front door of the house. So it is viewed from two main perspectives; an eye level and a bird's eye view. The patterning of paving thus assumes far more importance than it would otherwise.

The planting also becomes more important than it would in a strictly formal planting. Formal plantings can become static gardens, lacking any surprise or expectation.

The New Native Garden

A single glance is often sufficient to take it all in. Here, though, by mixing the informal with the formal, we are tempted to linger. The informality of the eucalypt and kangaroo paws adds interest at eye level that simply would not exist if a purist formality had been adhered to. There are other little touches that invite inspection. A sculpture in the corner, abstract and also naturalistic, captures the eye.

That leads us naturally to the planting structure. The most arresting point is that natives are used both in a naturalistic tradition but also as hedges, clipped and trained in a formal mode. There are plenty of exotics, too, but they serve to emphasise the 'Australianness' of the garden.

This blending of exotics with native plants signals the true evolution of an Australian style. There is no mistaking the 'sense of place' here. It could only be an Australian garden, but there is not a purist ethic dictating that only Australian plants should be used. Just as English gardeners discovered it was possible to intermingle British plants with those from China, the Americas, the Mediterranean and every other part of the world, we too are realising how to use our plants in concert with those from other lands.

Some work better than others. Many from similar southern hemisphere lands: southern Africa, New Zealand and South America, seem to work particularly well. Here a New Zealand native, *Hebe* 'Blue Gem' blends with dietes, bird of paradise (both of African descent) and gardenia (China) just as easily as it does with kangaroo paw, kennedia vines and grass trees.

Texture is used to emphasise the structure. The grass tree to the left of the entrance path sets the scene and is an amazing architectural element by itself. Another is located at the far end for balance. The westringia hedge, kept low and clipped, is used as a foil for the more rambunctious kangaroo paws at the end of the path.

If you prefer a native grass between the cracks in the paving, *Scirpus* 'Fairy Lights' could be substituted. Kangaroo grass, if trimmed to prevent flowering, can be kept to a low border of blue–green hued grass. Similarly, any of the correas would be a suitable replacement for the hebes.

Garden Designs and Plans

ABOVE
The garden is designed to be viewed from the step and elevated verandah. Visitors pass the garden on their way to the front door, so the symmetry can be enjoyed from both positions.

OPPOSITE LEFT
Anigozanthos 'Bush Haze' in front of a sandstone sculpture of a kookaburra.

OPPOSITE RIGHT
A hedge of westringia frames the informal planting of dark red kangaroo paws behind.

A NATURALISTIC COURTYARD

A courtyard is an intimate space. It is also a social space. It is where we tend to gravitate for peace and solitude and to meet with friends for lunch, coffee or a quiet drink on the weekend. This duality leads to several design problems requiring different approaches.

First there is the division of space. A courtyard fulfils its role as a meeting place when there is a proper balance between the plantings and the hard landscape.

Second, there are the practical problems. Anywhere people gather you will find the need for a firm, level surface. That's where paving and other hard surfaces come into their own. The main seating areas of this courtyard are located on the paved surface.

Last, there is the plant selection. A courtyard is a reasonably structured area of a garden. It needs some degree of formality, but it also needs warmth and a human scale. Plantings that are too prim or ceremonious can be alienating. They run counter to the notion of casual outdoor living. They can also defeat the purpose of the courtyard as a forum. Rarely do we find formal courtyards used as meeting places. By their very nature, they cannot induce the mood needed for conversation and geniality. A formal courtyard is often merely a viewing garden for this very reason.

In this courtyard, pictured here and on page 131, owned by Australian plants enthusiast Jeff Howes, an informal native planting using natural objects for decorative purposes serves as a backdrop to conversation. A brick wall provides privacy, and in winter the area is also a sunny refuge. In this corner, the strap-like leaves of *Lomandra* and Gymea lily provide the architectural interest while groundcovers like blue and white brachycome daisies, patersonia and poa grass are the linking plants. They provide seasonal colour and, in the case of the daisies, almost permanent colour.

Living plants are essential in any design, whether it is a large or small space. Repeating one colour, here blue and white, unifies the various areas of the garden. It is not necessary to use the same plant. In shadier spots scaevola or native violets may be better choices. But all have the same low spreading habit and similar coloured flowers. Using the same colours and growth habits throughout ties together the disparate sections of the garden. Even foliage plays a part in this linking. *Poa*, which has bluish foliage, serves the same purpose. The thin grass-like leaves refer back to the strappy leaves of the Gymea lily and the *Patersonia* and provide a link to them.

ABOVE

The pretty king orchid (*Dendrobium kingianum*) grows well even in this exposed position atop a large sandstone boulder. It can also be grown in containers and placed in a more shaded position than the larger *Dendrobium speciosum*.

OPPOSITE

An old log provides the focal point for the courtyard planting. brachycome daisies, *Lomandras* and Gymea lily blend in with lacy bush-like shrubs.

The New Native Garden

A NATURALISTIC COURTYARD

Garden Designs and Plans

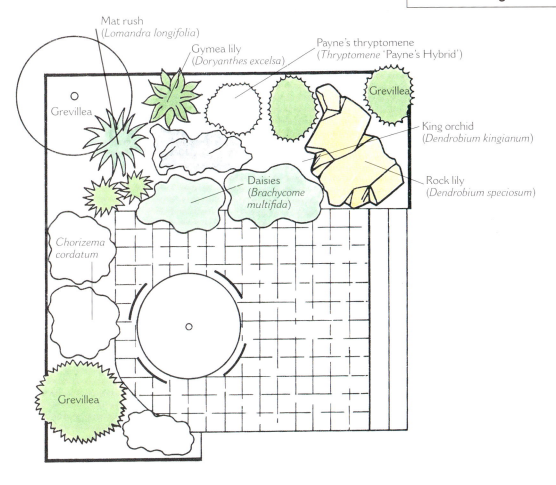

LEFT
Rustic features such as this hollow log are appropriate additions to a naturalistic design. A hollow log is also a good way to attract insect-eating lizards.

The New Native Garden

A RAINFOREST GARDEN

To many, the rainforest is alive with suggestion, like a dream. Lush green canopies and verdant undergrowth are the apogee of nature's gardening skill. It hints at tropical abundance and warmth. It embraces and cocoons everyone who ventures in. It is a garden from which to drink in the atmosphere, a garden capable of intoxicating and inducing a mood of calm and reflection.

It is also slightly threatening, and carries with it a sense of menace and even foreboding. In part this is derived from the majesty of its form and our wonder at its size, but it's also because of the myriad habitats it hides, homes for tiny creatures that some of us may prefer never to encounter. A true natural rainforest is all these things — a living, breathing entity.

A garden is an artifice, and the gardener takes inspiration from the natural world and abstracts it. The rainforest garden, no matter how large or how small, is always an idealised representation of nature, an impression formed from a brief visit.

Betty Maloney's suburban garden, pictured here and on pages 134–135, is a good case in point. The forest has been shrunk to just a tiny portion of a suburban backyard, but still the essence is here. Palms and ferns represent the ever-present greenness of the forest. The profundity of epiphytic orchids which spray from high up in the canopy in nature are here lowered for even the casual viewer to experience and admire. And so it should be. These things would not exist here if it were not for the hand of the gardener. It's only right that she should see what she has created.

Suburban gardens sometimes suffer from being undistinguished from an aesthetic point of view and from under-use and wasted potential. This one, however, is a refuge for birds, lizards and insects. Humans, too, come here to find sanctuary. The combination of wild and tamed landscapes can create peaceful places. It's akin to the concept of hybrid vigour. Cross two different but similar things and the strongest characteristics of each will overcome the weaker elements of the other. This works well for a garden.

RIGHT

A path of gravel and crazy paving is a natural addition to a rainforest style. Tree ferns (*Cyathea cooperi*) and birds' nest ferns (*Asplenium nidus*) planted in generous quantities are enough to create the effect.

Garden Designs and Plans

The New Native Garden

CREATING A SANCTUARY

One of the measures of success of any garden is its ability to attract birds and other wildlife to visit and perhaps even make their homesthere. Birds are naturally drawn to many different habitats. Some prefer open grasslands; others need the cover of low, dense and bushy shrubs. An overhead canopy of trees provides cover and shelter from predators. Smaller birds, such as nesting wrens and finches, need copses and thickets.

Provide insect-attracting plants as well as the more conventionally attractive nectar-bearing flowers for honeyeaters and other nectar feeders. Include native grasses, as they produce seed for finches and seedeaters too. They may even provide the habitat for nesting if the planting is dense enough.

Add a water supply. Birds need to drink and a regular supply of fresh water will have them coming back throughout the day.

BELOW

Tree ferns are ideal for creating a walkway and directing the eye to the ground details.

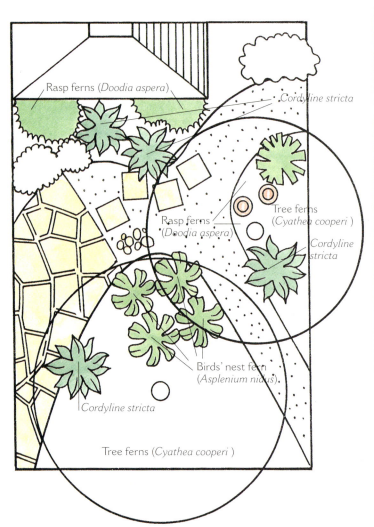

Garden Designs and Plans

RIGHT

Birds are wary and need a good line of sight to be enticed into your garden. Place birdbaths in an open space surrounded by light cover that will reveal potential predators. Strong upright leaves, weeping strap-like foliage, tree-borne orchids and lacy fern fronds in varying hues are all part of the composition.

BELOW

Additional texture comes from *Cordyline stricta*, rasp ferns (*Doodia aspera*) and birds' nest ferns.

BELOW

Birds' nest fern (*Asplenium nidus*).

design DETAILS

The New Native Garden

ACCESS ROUTES

DESIGNING PATHS

Paths do much more than get us from point A to point B. They help us to see. Let's examine the humble path.

Though we rarely acknowledge it, the paths are the most conspicuous element in any garden. They combine the functional with the aesthetic more than any other hard landscaping feature.

On the one hand, they provide a direct passage and a clean walkway. But they also act as an organising element connecting all the different parts of the garden. And they enable us to explore both the garden and the views. This is where the seeing comes in. In many ways they actually create views and vistas, as they lead the eye as well as the feet. How we view the garden is dependent on how we lay out the paths in the first place.

How can we make the most of the potential of paths? We need to go back to some of the design principles discussed earlier. Paths create the lines in a garden. These can be informal or formal. We can use straight lines or wavy lines. The space or plantings next to them further accentuate the lines created by paths.

In the naturalistic garden, paths operate as a series of informal axes. In this style they are arranged so that strict geometric precision gives way to curved patterns and sweeping lines. Natural or loosely formed groves of trees or shrubs create enclosures and open spaces without the need for the hedges or walls of the formal style. The openings between these plant groups are perhaps not as structured, but paths will always remain the means of access. These paths could be hard or soft landscaping, depending on the distance from the house. The further they are from the dwelling, the less traffic they take, making grass and soft mulch paths more practical.

Winding paths link back to the 18th-century 'Picturesque' garden school at the heart of much of our naturalistic native gardens. Larger gardens adopt some of the characteristics of landscape paintings — the garden is

138

Design Details

ABOVE
Sleepers are not common as a path but their rusticity gives them a charm and simplicity that suits this garden, which is sited next to national park. Designer: Graeme Greenhalgh.

RIGHT
Bark chips are a good choice for a level garden. On sloping ground, add crossbeams at regular intervals to contain the bark chips during rain. In heavier rain, loose materials, even gravel, tend to drift.

OPPOSITE LEFT
A formed concrete path has a formal quality that matches the structured planting of the garden. More than just an access route, it wends its way in and out, inviting exploration. Designer: Paul Thompson.

OPPOSITE RIGHT
Light shining through the trees falls on this path through a wild garden. The fall of light and shadow can add to the drama. Designer: Graeme Greenhalgh.

PREVIOUS PAGES
Pages 136–37: A large expanse of water adds a restful quality. Designer: Paul Thompson.

The New Native Garden

seen as a series of foreground, middle and background scenes. Distant views are led into by features in the foreground and focal points in the middle distance. Of course, meandering paths play a vital role in connecting these elements and ensuring that we really do look at them.

Paths also have an important part to play in relation to another design principle — movement and the creation of mystery. If a path disappears around a bend or is obscured when it bends, it arouses our curiosity, and creates a sense of mystery and surprise when the bend is finally passed.

In a formal garden, walls and hedges hide views, and the passage from one space can be more dramatic and intentional. In the informal garden, passage from one space to another can be slower. This has an impact on the width of paths. As we saw earlier, the narrower the path, the quicker we traverse it. This has implications for the paths of both formal and informal gardens. Because the surprise element is quicker in the formal garden we can get away with narrower paths. The informal generally needs wider paths so that we come upon surprises more gradually.

BELOW

As this path disappears around the bend, it veers out of sight, creating a sense of anticipation and mystery.

STEPS

Steps and sloping sites are undetachable. It takes us back to the principle of levels. Steps can be seen as purely functional, but it is more satisfying to use them as features in the landscape.

On a slight slope, large slabs of stone, timber sleepers or similar material can provide easier access. All that may be required is to dig out soil from the sloping site and place the rocks into the depression created. To ensure that the steps are secure, cement or peg the material.

Steps have 'treads' (the flat surface) and 'risers' (the vertical height). There are a few guidelines worth following to make steps safe and comfortable:

- The tread should be consistent and of equal size.
- When the depth of the tread and twice the height of the riser are added it should come to 600mm.
- A standard dimension step is a riser of 150mm and a tread of 300mm.
- The proportions of these can be varied according to the location but the 600mm should always be used as a guide.
- Allow for a 'landing' area (at the top of the flight) that is twice the tread.
- On steep slopes, landings between each set of eight steps are recommended.
- Making the tread wider slows down movement. A shallow tread is best for fast passage.

OPPOSITE

Top left: Large timber beams or railway sleepers make effective steps. They look natural and placement can be curved to interesting effect. Gardens top left and top right designed by Roger Stone.

Top right: Composite steps using natural materials suit naturalistic gardens as well as more traditionally designed gardens. This one uses timber sleepers for the risers and crazy paving for the tread.

Bottom left: These steps pass through a very informal planting and were chosen so as not to appear too contrived. Timber and packed earth are about the simplest way to construct a reliable and sturdy outdoor staircase. Designer: Paul Thompson.

Bottom right: A gentle curve gives steps an architectural feel and also helps to add to the mystery of the garden. Mt Tomah Botanical Gardens.

Design Details

141

ON THE EDGE

ENTRANCES, BOUNDARIES AND DIVISIONS

Entrances and boundaries can ultimately set the style of a garden. We usually think of them in utilitarian terms. They divide up space within a garden, provide security, define entry points and control traffic.

Gates and fences can be attractive as well as practical. They should be tied in with the style of the house and can be used as a backdrop to the garden. They also help to set off certain plants and features. One of the most common uses of a fence is to provide axes in a garden and a planting line along which to stretch a row of shrubs or trees. Plantings are often used as little more than a means of privacy or to hide an ugly fence or wall, but as these examples show, plants and boundaries can go together as an exciting design element.

ABOVE

For a more formal entrance to a block of units, ficus on sticks provide a strong architectural statement. The surrounding garden is exotic, but swamp lily (*Crinum pedunculatum*) and spear or Gymea lily (*Doryanthus species*) could just as easily be subsituted to give a similar look.

ABOVE

The picket fence and cottage garden are a good combination for a Federation house. The traditional front hedge would probably have been privet, a monstrous choice given the extent to which it has become an environmental weed. Instead, the purple leafed form of Cootamundra wattle is an inspired choice. It is trimmed to allow 30–45cm of growth showing above the fenceline. Viewed from inside the fence, exotic lavenders cover the bare stems, but, from the front the effect is colourful and exciting, far more interesting than the ubiquitous box hedge.

OPPOSITE

Bottom left: A more naturalistic impression is gained using blue gums and grass trees, but there are many formal elements, proving that a bit of structure can go a long way to advance the style of a 'bush' garden. A front perimeter hedge of *Syzygium* defines the front and accompanies the fence. This is an entrance garden strong on texture. It doesn't rely on colour or aggressive bush statements to define itself as an Australian garden.

Bottom right: Lattice backs a large bush of *Eriostemon myoporoides*. The turquoise treatment was popularised by the French impressionist Claude Monet, and it is a colour which lightens dark colours and subdues overly bright tones. Here it blends very well with the more subdued foliage colours of grevilleas and bottlebrushes behind.

Design Details

ABOVE

A more formal hedging treatment encourages the tea-tree *Leptospermum scoparium* 'Red Damask'. This cultivar is derived from the New Zealand strains of the species both countries share, but we can consider it an 'honorary native'.

ABOVE

Naturalistic plantings can be as private and as restful as you want. Careful pruning and good plant selection ensures that this small front garden shields the front rooms of the house immediately behind. Queensland bottle tree, *Banskia* 'Giant Candles' and *Baeckea virgata* 'Nana' are the three main feature plants.

143

The New Native Garden

ABOVE
Pools require careful landscaping to appear part of the landscape. Here sandstone boulders add a natural feel. This garden and the garden at the top of this page designed by Robert Boyle.

POOL PLANTING

For something different, splash out with native plants around your pool. A pool adds value to a home so it makes sense to complement its monetary value with a garden that's as inviting as a cool dip on a hot day.

Landscaping around a pool calls for sensible planting and forethought. A good poolside planting provides shelter, shade and privacy, all of which will enhance your initial investment.

Gardening around a pool is often one of the most difficult planting exercises of all. Surrounds are usually narrow and needed for paths and access. There is little room left for plants, as a rule. This, like most gardening, is a problem-solving exercise. Australian plants have not always been popular for pools. If twigginess were measured like sunscreen lotions, natives would have a scratch factor way up in the 30+ range. But there are many that do not meet this negative expectation.

Pools call for a sensible choice of plants that meet clearly defined needs. There may not be ten commandments related to plants near pools but there are certainly eight. These are:

1. There should not be too much litter. Anything that requires more time spent on maintenance and less on leisure is a no-no, so avoid any plants which drop too many leaves, flowers, twigs or branches.

2. They should not be too spreading. Because of the confined space, spreading plants intrude into walkways, and ever since the demise of neck-to-knee swimwear, most of us understand that sticks and swimmers are a bad match. We are all averse to bare skin rubbing against foliage.

3. They should not be prickly. As above. The all-over crown of thorns effect is much less fashionable than an all-over tan, and is likely to remain so.

4. They should not have invasive roots. This is a special problem for above-ground pools though in-ground pools are susceptible to damage from very large trees. Avoid siting a pool near a mature tree with a known propensity for cracking foundations.

5. They should not shade the pool. Generally we demand sun over the entire pool surface, on the pool surrounds and in the entertaining area. Swimming in cold water and sunbaking in the shade are about as popular as moonbaking. That rules out large shade trees.

6. They should not require too much maintenance. Pruning, watering and feeding needs have to be considered before planting. Many containers need constant watering and the runoff can be a problem — it depends on the pool coping you have chosen.

7. They should give privacy. This is essential if you are given to wearing less than the dress regulations prevailing at most beaches.

8. They should be chemical-tolerant. Pool chemicals can cause chlorosis if plants are constantly drenched. Select only the hardiest native plants if this is likely.

Design Details

PLANNING AND CARING FOR POOL PLANTINGS

Pool gardens require an element of basic logic. Water implies lushness, so dry land plants are inappropriate choices. Tropical-looking plants or those with at least a rainforest feel are the ideal choices. They fit into the waterhole ambience and the very notion of water so well that it's hard to imagine any other choice. Of course you could go with the 'Australiana' garden, the outback waterhole look with grasses, embankments, bush sheds and hitching posts.

The problem with most pool landscaping is that it is seen as an afterthought. But often a pool is the very hub of family life, a place for entertaining, recreation and relaxation. It deserves attention. Easy care and room to move are a boon to busy city swimmers. Go for a dominant plant like lush tree ferns or palms interspersed with a few tropical-looking shrubs to create the impression of space, especially if the surrounds occupy only a small space. Pittosporum, golden pendas and many other rainforest plants have lush and soft leaves.

CARE

Pruning and maintenance are important not only for the look of the plants but to keep the foliage lush, soft and green. Bare skin and sharp sticks don't mix. Brushing against a large leafy bush is not likely to leave welts, scratches or red marks.

Pool finishes may help make your pool more at home in a natural Australian garden. Painting a pool with a dark colour removes that stark swimming pool blue allowing it to fit into the surroundings much more placidly.

Most states in Australia require special pool fencing and some insist on safety instructions being prominently displayed. Check with your local council before starting any work. Plan carefully to incorporate regulations into your design.

TOP

Dry bush plants are located well back from the access to the pool, making it comfortable for swimmers.

CENTRE

Design and plants should blend in the formal garden. Topiary, mostly native plants westringia and lillypilly, gives an elegant look, especially against the dark tiles, a change from the bright blue–green of many pools. Designer: Gregg Chapman.

BOTTOM

This planting uses *phebalium*, *Eriostemon myoporoides* and *Grevillea* 'Robyn Gordon'. The latter may cause irritation to some susceptible to skin rashes. Other more suitable plants include mint bushes, boronias, pomaderris, pittosporum and dwarf lillypillies. Ferns such as tree ferns, birds' nest and king ferns are suitable for areas where shade is a factor. As a rule, soft-leafed plants are more suitable than plants with spiky or sharp leaves. Designer: Paul Thompson.

The New Native Garden

ABOVE
Repetition and massed planting help to unify this sloping bed. Tight pruning gives the grevilleas a dense and manicured look in keeping with the style of the house and the lawn. Designer: Andrew Davies.

DESIGN PRINCIPLES IN ACTION

Repetition creates balance and stabilises the visual weight formed by groups of plants. It can occur by repeating the same plant species either in blocks or distributed around the whole garden, so the one plant creates a visual link. Flower colour can do the same thing. Using many shades of one colour, say blue or white flowers from several different species, can tie together disparate elements, features or even clashing styles in the one garden.

Repetition can also be achieved using hard landscaping. Paths in the same material from one end of the garden to the other provide a chance for all sectors to be tied together.

Your point of view will determine whether a scene is balanced. If you choose to view the garden from a verandah and the family room, the first step is to establish a priority. Which is the more important viewing point? This primary viewpoint is the point which balances the composition. It will change over time as a garden matures, and minor adjustments can be made by selective pruning or moving garden furniture.

Determining balance is largely intuitive. We step back and take several looks. Photographs of the garden can help you assess balance. When you turn a picture upside down, if it looks as if some part will tip over, it is probably unbalanced. In a garden, if things seem in imbalance, try a few experiments. Lay tracing paper over the image and draw some rough shapes until you are satisfied. Sometimes all that is needed is a new focal point, which can be as simple as a pot of flowers.

CORRECTING IMBALANCES

The chances are good that this sense of imbalance is caused by a lack of repetition. Collectors' gardens often fall into this trap. The desire to have one of everything can spell trouble for the design of a native garden. This is, surprisingly, most important in the naturalistic garden where the collector trait is most apparent. In nature, all species occur in repetition. The overall effect is of a handful of dominant species. A garden, especially an informal one, needs this restraining effect too. It provides structure within which other less commanding species can find refuge, and can even provide the sense of surprise and discovery so necessary for a strolling garden.

Often a genus of plant will have similar characteristics, and this will provide the element of repetition. Collectors tend to specialise in families, and this is one way to design a collection. Sometimes adding several plants of a different species will highlight the similarities in the collected group. An excellent plant for this purpose is the sago bush *Ozothamnus diosmifolius*. Its dense heads of white (or pink) flowers in spring, followed by a rounded mass of dark green foliage, make it the ideal 'filler' plant. It is not a standout plant on its own, but just dotting a few, singly and in groups, throughout a garden of disparate plants, helps tie it together.

Across different genera there are often plants with similar foliage or flower shapes and this tendency can be used to provide variety and cohesion. Often weeping plants such as many baeckeas can be visually linked with weeping plants from other genera. Some to consider are *Acacia iteaphylla*, *Agonis flexuosa*, *Eucalyptus caesia* and some of the callistemons and leptospermums. Adding colour variation such as the purple form of *Agonis flexuosa* 'Jervis Bay Afterdark' or the lime green cultivar of the bower wattle, *Acacia cognata* 'Lime Magik', can highlight the impact of weeping foliage.

Repeating colour from foliage and flowers is another useful device. If flowers only are used, the effect may be hard to achieve out of season, but it can also call for subtlety. Many of the wonderful naturalistic native gardens based on Victorian, and particularly alpine flora, can be a tapestry of colour in spring, when the impact of repeated blues and pinks works well. Elsewhere, more long-term colour schemes may be called for. Plants such as grevilleas and bottlebrushes flower often, but have an overwhelmingly warm colour palette which needs to be leavened by grey foliage contrasts and softer flower colours to prevent an over-busy appearance. Groundcovers such as brachycome daisies, *Scaevola* and *Dampiera* come to mind, but also foliage plants such as *Restio*, *Scleranthus* and grasses are suitable.

OTHER REPETITIONS

Hedges and borders of single species to line paths or garden beds are a more traditional way to introduce repetition. Many gardeners in the naturalistic style tend to dismiss this as too contrived, but it can work well. Add slight changes to the alignment of rows and drop extra groundcovers or annuals into the spaces thus created. An occasionally incongruous addition can also break the 'monotony' for bush garden fans.

ABOVE

A low hedge of *Acacia howittii*, the sticky wattle, defines the edge of a modern garden. This otherwise nondescript wattle is never grown for its flowers, but it responds to pruning, sending up masses of weeping stems with small, bright green leaves. It is also useful for tall hedges.

GROVES

Trees are the key plants in most garden schemes. They give structure and impact to the landscape. These are the plants to be placed first as the 'cornerstones' on which the rest of the planting will turn.

Trees provide punctuation points and vertical relief to the horizontal plane of a flat site. They can be used singly or in groups. A grove of trees is a common design techniques well suited to naturalistic garden styles. Achieving the right effect is dependent on close observation of the way nature distributes its plant material, enabling us to shape and define our planting plan.

Groves give life to the principle of space. By surrounding an open area with a collection of trees, areas for relaxation and fantasy evolve. Children in particular love the idea of an enclosed wood, and that is essentially the value of the grove of trees. The element of fantasy for children converts the space to a fairy bower or a magic kingdom, an interplanetary stage or whatever location the imagination can summon, depending on the age, sex and interests of the child.

Adults have similar notions of fantasy, but we tend to see areas like this in terms of romance or sensuality, as secret places, private refuges or havens from the world. To adults it's somewhere to read the Sunday papers, curl up in a hammock for a snooze, or read a good book on a warm autumn day. Because a grove is an element of space, it lends itself to furnishing in interesting ways. Groves can be functional as well as aesthetic or ethereal. They can be special areas for sitting or congregation.

Best of all, designing a grove of trees is simple. You do not have to be a design expert, or have a degree in botany and horticulture. Nor do you need to be a walking plant dictionary.

A grove uses a few species often. It is the principle of repetition at work.

Groves serve another higher purpose as well. Tree canopy is natural shade, and groves are also 'green architecture', providing a garden with natural features and a strong artistic statement. The talented English garden designer Dan Pearson talks of these shade trees as 'filling the garden with shifting silhouettes' from the patterns of shade and shadow they create throughout the day.

Using trees as structures in the garden or in place of built structures is a feature of the naturalistic style, and it is certainly less expensive than art. What's more, it's more secure too. An old gnarled tree rooted to the spot is a lot harder to make off with than a heavy sandstone sculpture, even if it is concreted to the spot.

Often, architectural plants are used to create particular effects. Eucalypts and banksias are ideal. For instance on a windswept seaside site, a grove of coastal banksias, (*Banksia integrifolia*) or the honey bracelet myrtle (*Melaleuca armillaris*) could be planted to create a tunnel of trees or provide an umbrella of shade and shelter. Groves work most effectively when they are of the same species — not mixed.

Groves can divide spaces without resorting to the tired cliché of the garden room. In a large garden, looking out on an expanse of lawn, or even bushy growth, without visual relief can be tiresome. The small room concept is more appropriate to the formal garden, a self-contained courtyard or terrace garden (the latter two by virtue of their small size). A grove can create a sense of mystery without resorting to high-maintenance hedges or expensive walls.

ABOVE LEFT

The pattern of shadow is one advantage gained by grouping trees. It is one way to introduce pattern into a lawn or other area. Both gardens on this page designed by Paul Thompson.

ABOVE RIGHT

Groups of trees provide direction and act as signposts. Here the pathway they provide leads to the only access across the creek.

OPPOSITE

Left: A grove of eucalypts planted in lawn is given sculptural form by adding two large boulders in a Japanese style. Designer: Richard Stutchbury.

OPPOSITE

Right: Native trees edged by lawn are grouped as a natural grove. Trees indigenous to the site are used extensively. The scribbly gum (*Eucalyptus haemastoma*) is the dominant tree, but the grey gum (*E. punctata*) is also growing. Designer: Don Burke.

The New Native Garden

Groves can be achieved in a small garden just as easily as in a large garden. The scale needs to be reduced, however, and shrubs could be substituted for trees.

Many of the small mallees are worthwhile in this situation or, in a sunny warm location, grevillea cultivars also. Again, simplicity is essential. For a small entrance garden, one of my favourite plants for compact spaces is the New South Wales Christmas bush. A group of seven or so of this plant used as a grove works well with perhaps a single feature tree such as *Angophora costata*. This will provide shelter for tree ferns and groundcover plants. The planting can be arranged around a path and occupy the entire front garden. This solution satisfies because it is so simple and it unifies the all-important front entrance. The Christmas bushes look good from the time they flower in spring until bracts begin to drop around January. Pruning at this time encourages masses of warm coppery buds. These in turn make a good contrast to the tree ferns. They come into their own when summer heat starts to bite and the soft green has a cooling effect.

Design Details

ABOVE

A grove doesn't have to be a manicured parkland. Grasses and other free-growing plants enhance the play of light and sun throughout the day. Designer: Robert Boyle.

OPPOSITE

Use groves of trees in conjunction with other garden features such as this dry stream which channels excess water in time of high rainfall. Designer: Paul Thompson.

The New Native Garden

ABOVE

A sandpit always appeals to young children and can be replaced as they grow out of it. Here the planting of soft-leafed ferns and mixed perennials has a sub-tropical feel. It's like having your own deserted island to play in.

OPPOSITE

Built on a sloping site, the topography allows scope for differences in levels. This makes it a wonderful garden for childhood fantasy. The bridges and raised pathways offer room for amazingly varied games and exercise. Designer: Andrew O'Sullivan.

KIDS' GARDENS

'Home, home on the range' is not a song known to the modern child, and the vast prairie garden of grass, stretching from fence to fence, is a relic from the long-gone 1950s. Gardens for kids in the new millennium should contain creative elements to develop healthy attitudes. Gardens need to have a sense of adventure, with activity, creativity, fantasy and enough depth to stimulate an inquiring mind and an understanding of nature.

The paddock of parched grass — hot, open and empty — is not the place to bring out creativity and imagination. It's more a place to foster aggression, boredom and children who are unable to create their own play and games. While there may be no empirical evidence to link graffiti, vandalism and destructiveness to dull backyards, we all want to see children with a respect for the world around them. A child who creates his or her own fantasy play in a backyard which is filled with promise of things to do and see is less likely to succumb to the 'I'm bored' line in later years.

Kids need room for games and scope to practise them, to fulfil their need for pretend reality. Games help children make new friendships and cement old ones. They teach them how to behave in groups and how to work in teams. Play stimulates imagination, self-reliance and creativity. It reinforces social relationships and bonding with other children, brothers, sisters and family, and lays the foundation for social success in later life. It is essential for producing well-adjusted, healthy adults.

So how does that translate to garden design? Kids love to find places they can call their own and make fantasy worlds within their everyday surroundings. Plantings that create tunnels and runs, and areas that can be converted into do-it-yourself cubbies, are the best of all. A dense border of shrubs could be hollowed out to provide a small clearing with room for a meeting place, a tea table or a pirate's lair. Plant shrubs about one metre from the fence so a narrow space is created for a pretend enchanted forest or a lean-to cubby. A long avenue of shrubs planted on either side of a path or as a double row is great for fantasy play. It can become anything from a tunnel under the earth to a hidden passage to some very secret rendezvous. With plantings like this, kids do not need expensive timber huts. Often, these constructions costing thousands of dollars are the least used items in any kid's garden. They would rather make their own huts and cubbies.

Design Details

Mulch any conventional playground area of swings and roundabouts with fine pine bark or wood shavings to give a soft, safe landing for the inevitable falls. Paths around shrubs can be covered with the same materials to prevent soil compacting and allow worms to improve soil condition.

Paved areas close to the house are ideal for young children. They can ride bikes and scooters and practise rollerblading or skateboarding when they get a little older. Young toddlers love a sandpit and this is the best place for one — in view of the house and easily accessible.

The built structures should be easily moveable when kids outgrow them. This includes things like swing sets and trampolines. If you design a garden with all the nooks and crannies, secret boltholes and secluded corners that you would like yourself, they can be converted to general garden use in years to come when the children are tooling around in cars or hanging out at the local coffee shop.

Design Details

OPPOSITE

Top left: Garden art can take many forms and plants should be used to enhance. These metal birds are perched atop old gum logs with a planting of low shrubs and annuals.

Top right: Sandstone is a good sculptural medium and if you can find pieces of the quality of this gecko by Chris Bennetts, place it in a prominent place in a garden.

Bottom left: This mosaic fountain has been placed under ferns with a gravel bed. It adds a touch of bright colour without being gaudy.

Bottom right: This frill-necked lizard by Carol Brennan has been used as a Japanese shishi-odoshi, the bamboo deer scarer. Water drips into the lizard's mouth and is recycled. The design is subtle and unmistakably Australian.

GARDEN ART

THE ARTFUL VIEW

Focal points, views and the use of art are all part of the same equation in the design of a garden. Art and decorative pieces allow you to create focal points and views, even in a small space. It doesn't really matter much what you choose. Whether it's an urn, ceramic sculpture or a modern stainless steel sculpture, art adds year-round interest even when flowers are few, and helps create mood, atmosphere and a sense of place.

Artworks should form an integral part of the landscape. If you are consciously aware of a piece of sculpture, if it stands out like a sore thumb, then it's probably in the wrong place. One option is to disguise its incongruity with plants.

Art is often used as a focal point — an object at the end of a long view to which the eye is drawn by the plantings along a path, for instance. Focal points add drama and structure to the whole composition. Used discreetly or in splendid isolation they can engender excitement. When they simply breed, we lose this potential as well as the opportunity to manipulate movement and emotion.

By definition, a focal point is something for the eye to focus on. If the intention is to draw the eye, then several items in the one space tend to create confusion. When there are too many, all compete for attention.

A focal point can be just about anything. Your imagination can transform everyday objects, 'olde' objects, plants themselves. Topiary, bonsai, a large container of annuals in flower or simply a bush or tree planted in a prominent place, can become a focal point.

VIEWS AND FOCAL POINTS

Not everyone is lucky enough to have a great outlook, but garden vignettes and vistas can be created in the even average garden.

Garden art is one way to create views within a garden. Presentation is all-important. More often than not it's the placement of garden art and the setting created around it that makes the difference. Art and other decorative features often look best when viewed against a backdrop of foliage or even within a garden bed. Experimenting with placement, including the use of plinths or stands, will lead you to settle on the right location.

INTERNAL/ EXTERNAL TRANSITIONS

The internal/external transition becomes important as the purpose and function of a garden changes. You see the garden just as often from inside the house as you do from outside, so being able to view art or decoration from inside is as vital as looking at it from outside.

There's not a lot of point placing important or much-loved pieces of art or decoration where you will not see them, so the most-used places around your house and garden should be the points you use to decide placement. These are your vantage points. Concentrate on creating views out to the garden from the most frequently used rooms. These will most often be the family or living rooms, kitchen and possibly the main bedroom. Concentrate your attention where the interior gives way to exterior too — verandahs, back steps, decks, patios and paths. Sitting down, as you would if you were using the space, gives you a better idea of what you will see and helps you find the exact spot.

Art can help determine the style of your garden, so the choice needs to be made carefully. It can also draw attention either to itself or away from negative features, so strategic positioning is a must.

CREATING THE SETTING

Statues, urns, pots — any form of artwork needs a specially constructed stage; it's a rare piece that will fit into a garden without some adjustment. You may need to add a plinth, create a special base or just rearrange the plantings.

Plants can improve or detract from the look of the garden depending on how you use them. Set off the foreground with low groundcovers or keep it unadorned. Keep backgrounds plain to avoid conflict with the view. Use dark-foliaged evergreens, for instance.

FRAMING

Look at views as you would the frame of a picture. Study what you see. Look for potential to create internal views even if there are no external views. The view can be framed from both inside and outside the house. Do this by using windows, doors, verandah posts and trees as frames.

Frame the view in two ways. Use plants (in borders or edges) to direct the eye along the main axis and create a view. Alternatively, use built structures such as arches, pergolas, walls or gates to focus attention.

POSITIONING

Tie the statue into the garden and the paths. Try different locations to see how you need to modify sections. Sometimes extra paving or a low groundcover is all you need. Never just plonk it down somewhere.

SETTING UP

If you use pots, urns or stone vases you may need plinths or bases. Make sure scale and size are in proportion.

WALLS

Use walls as if they are a backdrop on a stage set. Paint or leave bare to suit the piece. A bold terracotta limewashed wall makes a great curtain for a pale-coloured sculpture while a terracotta statue or urn may need a strong contrasting colour, such as electric blue. Choose a more neutral-toned background for brightly coloured ceramics.

CHOOSING MATERIALS

Paving and ground surrounds should be compatible with the 'architecture' of the piece. Pay attention to texture and colour.

Design Details

CREATING MOODS

Once the basic structure of the setting has been established (particularly the foreground and background space), create different moods using a small vase of flowers or dry twigs or perhaps a float bowl with flowers. Change these with the season for an added dimension.

LIGHTING

Night lighting spotlights special features, but it needs purpose. If you do not use entertaining areas on warm evenings, don't waste your money on lighting installation.

PICKING PIECES

Everyone's personal taste and budget vary, so choose what you can afford and design around it. There are many inexpensive items available in garden stores and nurseries. Even mass-produced items can be effective in the right place. Try customising concrete sculptures with milk paint or Porter's Lime Wash. You can locate pieces for garden use in nurseries, craft shops, ceramic stores, wrought iron shops, glass stores and antique shops. Even broken pieces can be given an antiquated look with artful finishes.

ABOVE LEFT

Bird with nest by Tasmanian artists Folko Kooper and Maureen Craig.

ABOVE RIGHT

Old implements find a new role as art in the Australiana style. Artifacts can be found in old wares stores and have a rustic, olde world feel about them. The colour of rusty metal blends beautifully in this mainly green garden.

OPPOSITE

Rudi Jass designed this dolphin sculpture. It is a fine example of how to set modern pieces within a contemporary garden. Essentially a mobile piece, it is surrounded by a mixed native and exotic planting, but an exclusively native garden of bold leafed plants would be just as suitable.

The New Native Garden

BELOW LEFT
Make a gentle cascade by running a stream over a rock shelf. If necessary carve some light channels to direct water to fall across the face like a natural waterfall.

BELOW RIGHT
Water bowls carved from sandstone add a drinking supply for birds but rinse them daily to prevent mosquitoes breeding in stagnant water.

WATER

Water is life. Whether it's the lively splash of a fountain or cascade or the pensiveness of the still garden pond, water makes a garden more interesting, more appealing and more inviting.

Style plays its part. The type of pond, container or lake should have a close connection with the garden as a whole. For a formal garden, a regular pond with geometric proportions is a better addition than a free form and informal one. Similarly, for a naturalistic garden, a formal pool with strictly geometric proportions and classic ornamentation usually looks out of place. Of course there are always exceptions to the rules, and as we grow more confident with our design skills, design outside the boundaries is easier and more successful.

There are technical limitations as well. The size of the pump and how much water you will need to shift will

Design Details

determine what your pond, cascade or fountain will look like. The size of the property and correct proportioning will determine how big your pond ought to be, but construction costs have to be borne in mind, and safety and security also need careful consideration.

Aesthetics will dictate success, and it is often hard to design a pool to fit comfortably into a naturalistic garden. Try, where possible, to follow the natural contours. A body of water always gravitates to the lowest point. Many streams start from a spring hidden by plants — this is a good point to remember when designing your own pond. On level sites, a pond offers an opportunity to give the illusion of a rise and fall in the topography by mounding the earth to create a cascade.

Incorporating cascades increases the expense of installing a water feature. You will need to consider the volume of water that a pump can move and the additional landscaping costs and materials.

BELOW LEFT
An old industrial pot makes an unusual but interesting water garden. The metal needs priming to prevent rust and decay.

BELOW RIGHT
Not all gardens are big enough to include a pond or fountain. A small bowl may be all you need to add water to your garden.

PLANNING YOUR POND

Getting started

A pond needs sunlight for at least half a day. Too much sun can cause excess algal growth — this can be corrected by using water plants and fish to create the right ecological balance.

Avoid siting water features beneath overhanging trees. Roots can puncture liners or lift frames out of the ground and leaves and flowers create a biological imbalance.

A pond should be located where you can see it. Look for a position in view of the house either from inside or out.

Pond design

Pond styling comes down to formal, informal or natural. Your choice will depend largely on surroundings, topography, space and siting limitations. Consider your surroundings and visualise how a pond will fit in before buying any materials. A small rock pool in the middle of a flat expanse of lawn will look out of place, but a large formal or natural pond may suit perfectly.

The life of your pond depends on the life in your pond. For a healthy pond ecology, size is important. It should cover at least 3sq/m. This means a pond 2.4m long by 1.8m wide and at least 45cm deep. This creates a good biological balance for plants and fish. (In very cold areas where water may ice over in winter, make it 75cm deep.) Sides should not slope any more than 45-60°.

LEFT
Terracotta paving tiles create regular rectangles around this contemporary design. Thryptomene and brachycome soften the angular geometry of the plan. Designer: Gregg Chapman.

OPPOSITE
A terrazzo reflection pond is designed to be viewed from an upper terrace. It can also be drained and used as outdoor space. Designer: Diana Pringle.

BELOW
A small stream trickling through rocks.

Design Details

The New Native Garden

SEATING AND OUTDOOR LIVING

A garden without seats is not a garden at all. There are two ways of looking at what a garden is. One is a slightly archaic use of the term but still valid. In the old sense, a garden was a place for growing plants or, as Thomas Church put it, a garden was:

a place to walk through, to sit in briefly while you contemplated the wonders of nature before you returned to the civilized safety of the indoors. It was generally designed to provide a long vista from some dramatic spot within the house, such as an entry hall, the front steps, or a bay window. It was a place to be looked at rather than a place to be lived in. [6]

ABOVE

The natural ochre colouring of mud brick walls require only simple seating. Wrought iron gives a modern twist to a slightly Mediterranean style. It's as much at home in the standard bush garden as it is in a city courtyard. Designer: Gordon Ford, Fülling Garden.

CENTRE

A curved masonry seat constructed as a permanent feature of the garden only needs cushions and a few guests to make a party. The central barbecue pit can be used to heat the space on cool evenings. Designer: Michael Bates.

OPPOSITE

Top right: A rustic timber bench fits nicely into the larger naturalistic garden but would be less successful in a sophisticated urban courtyard. Designer: Don Burke.

Design Details

This idea of 'living in' the garden is what makes our gardens so different from the European ideal. We have a climate that can be enjoyed more or less throughout the year. Most of us treat part of the garden as an extension of the house itself: patios, verandahs, terraces and courtyards are entertainment areas. We can sit outside in winter, and seating is essential for enjoying an Australian garden. Again, Thomas Church put it succinctly when he wrote:

> *The new kind of garden is still supposed to be looked at. But that is no longer its only function. It is designed primarily for living, as an adjunct to the functions of the house. How well it provides for the many types of living that can be carried on outdoors is the new standard by which we judge a garden.*[7]

From a design perspective, this translates into provision of rest areas. These can still be areas intended to be looked at from inside, but are more likely places to sit and enjoy in the garden. While the selection of the actual seat is often given plenty of thought, the location for the seat is less well considered; yet it is more important. If the purpose of a seat is to provide a restful haven, the surroundings too need to be restful. It should be visually quiet. If a large variety of plants and special features are added, it will be busy and 'uncomfortable'. Where possible, the position should be sheltered, with some open space to provide visual relief.

A seat does not have to be expensive or the latest in designer teak. It can simply be a stone wall, a log or a rock ledge, none of which need cost the earth.

CONTAINERS

From a design perspective, plants growing in containers act as features, as an architectural element and as decoration. They can be placed on a deck, patio, balcony or other outdoor living area, or they can be placed as focal points at the end of a long view or open space.

There is a practical point to containers as well. They enable us to grow plants outside their normal range by allowing us to regulate position, growing medium and exposure to the elements. A plant grown in a pot tends to have far more attention lavished on it than one growing in the open garden. Containers are for special plants. We grow them close to the house where we see them frequently because the plants themselves may have a special significance, and a group add a special decorative ambience to an outdoor space.

Containers vary enormously, but clay and terracotta are possibly the most attractive for growing a range of different plants. Some newer plastic pots are aesthetically pleasing as well as being practical, and are less likely to break than clay. In windy or high-traffic areas, this is an important consideration.

DRAINAGE

All pots must have drainage holes — in most cases the bigger the better. Native plants especially need sharp drainage, so it may even pay to drill extra holes in most pots to ensure water is not prevented from passing though quickly and efficiently.

POTTING MIX

Standard potting mixes are suitable for most Australian plants, especially rainforest species or their cultivars. For plants with sharp drainage needs, some mixes contain too much water-retentive material. I find it useful to add a few scoops of coarse river sand to each bucketful and to lighten it with the addition of perlite. The amount of perlite needed depends on the texture of sand used — the coarser the sand, the less perlite you need. The water storage gel often found in these mixes can prove damaging to exotics in areas which receive high rainfall, particularly in summer. Typically this is along the east coast and in tropical regions to the north.

Design Details

If you wish to make your own potting mix, try this recipe and vary it according to the drainage requirements of the plants used:
2 parts loam or standard potting mix
1 part well-rotted cow manure
1 part peat moss or coco-peat
1 part leaf mould
1 part coarse river sand.

WATERING

Container plants, especially those grown in small pots, dry out quickly in summer. Most will require watering daily; some twice a day. Adding a mulch of pebbles, leaf mould or peat will reduce moisture loss. When soil does dry out completely, it is often difficult to re-wet. Use a soil wetting agent and gently rake the top layer to break the surface tension. It is a good idea to dunk smaller pots in a bucket of water when conditions are drying to make sure the soil is thoroughly wet.

As plants outgrow smaller containers they will need to be potted up into larger containers. Some resent root disturbance, though; these are best in large tubs from the beginning. Most plants can be grown in containers for long periods. Annuals make a good seasonal show if grown in shallow plastic or terracotta dishes or bowls.

THIS PAGE

Top left: Formal but contemporary, these refreshing geometric pots are an attractive way to display strap-leafed plants in a modern interpretation of the formal garden.

Bottom left: *Restio* is a plant with a strong architectural feel. It works just as well with modern courtyards and paving materials as it does with naturalistic plantings.

OPPOSITE

Top left: Containers need to match plant and location. The design of this blue glazed tub is simple enough to blend with a contemporary design and the architecture of the grass tree.

Bottom left: A combined planting of native perennials is used to add colour, and is a good way to grow more difficult plants. Soil and drainage requirements are more easily attended to like this than in the open ground.

attracting WILDLIFE

The New Native Garden

ABOVE
Eastern water dragons are attracted to gardens on the edge of the city or near nature reserves. Avoid using insecticides when visitors like this are present. They will often clean up many pests for you.

PREVIOUS PAGE
Meadow argus on strawflowers. Strawflowers are a good source of nectar for butterflies, and many varieties can be planted over different seasons.

POSSUMS, LIZARDS AND FROGS

We can all do our bit for wildlife conservation by planting habitats for animals that would otherwise be displaced by housing developments. One way to do it is by the creation of urban wildlife corridors. Householders become part of a community, planting in railway land, nature strips and parks. These corridors provides access and cover for small animals such as lizards, bandicoots and echidnas, which have been driven to near extinction in suburban areas.

LIZARDS

Lizards mainly eat insects and pests such as snails so they more than pay their way if provision is made for them to live in your garden.

They need basking points such as paving, rocky outcrops or walls. If possible, think in terms of a corridor of plants. If a thick covering of plant material can be allowed to reach to the edge of the sunniest spot, it affords them secrecy and a degree of peace of mind. They need cover to crawl into if danger is apparent. For instance, blue-tongued lizards, slow-moving animals, are often attacked by domestic dogs and cats. If not killed outright, they are likely to die from the stress of the molestation, so a large log, some old terracotta drainpipes or other shelter can be added at the back of garden beds or under dense bushes. Logs have the advantage of being rustic, sculptural and quite easy to incorporate into a naturalistic garden.

FROGS

Frogs and amphibians seem to be the wildlife litmus test. Just as canaries were taken into coalmines to test for dangerous gases, frogs respond sensitively to changes in water quality. Urban runoff has been blamed for their demise but you can help by providing ponds for frogs and tadpoles.

All you need is a small pond or even a series of large pots used as water containers. You can introduce tadpoles from a nearby stream or leave it up to the frogs to spawn when they are ready.

If using tap water, allow it to settle for a few days so that contaminants added to purify it at the treatment works can evaporate. Ponds should be planted with a range of water plants. It will take a few weeks for a suitable level of food to accumulate. Tadpoles feed on algae and decaying vegetable matter. When they mature, they switch to a carnivorous diet, with insects as their main food.

Approximately two-thirds of the water surface should be in shade. Water plants growing in submerged pots and water lilies help shade the water. Too much sun encourages the growth of algae which can upset the biological balance.

A WILDLIFE POND

If you own a tract of land on the city outskirts, you can develop a large wildlife pond. A large pond can double as a bird and wildlife haven for birds, tortoises, native fish, frogs and insects. It's a pleasurable biology lesson for young and old. Even a much smaller pond will harbour a host of interesting and beneficial creatures.

Following are some ideas that can be incorporated into a wildlife pond.

- A central island creates a refuge for small birds and animals. It gives a measure of protection from many feral pests.
- Large logs protruding from the water at an angle of about $60°$ make resting points for tortoises and water-going lizards. A gravel beach, as well as being attractive, is another spot for lizards and tortoises to bask in the sun.
- A planting of grasses provides plenty of food for wildlife even if not 'pretty' in the traditional sense. Allow the grass to grow and set seed without mowing.
- Dragonflies are desirable because they eat mosquitoes and their larvae. Insecticide used to remove other pests, however, can be detrimental to the dragonfly. A pond is the ideal place to raise dragonfly nymphs. They hatch and live underwater until ready to emerge as adults. After shucking off their larval case, dragonflies spend several hours resting and unfurling their lacy wings. The insects pump fluid into the soft ribbing of their wings and wait for it to harden. This usually happens in the early evening, so you will need to shine a torch around reeds in your pond to watch the process. After some hours the wings lose their opacity and take on the familiar beautiful glassy look. Body colours vary from brilliant reds, blues and yellows to more sombre shades.

POSSUMS

Possums seem to cause more angst in gardeners than any other native animal, mainly because of their habit of eating new rosebuds.

Possums are protected native animals and two possums are commonly found in urban areas — the brushtail and the ringtail. Ringtails have specialised feeding habits, eating native fruits and leaves, but brushtails are expert scavengers and the cause of most complaints.

All possums have a home territory which they fiercely defend. Beyond this they have a range in which they search for food and a mate. In suburban areas, it may be one hectare, roughly the space covered by 5 to 7 house blocks.

POSSUMS IN THE GARDEN

Brushtails cause some problems to exotic plants because their feeding on natives is less noticeable. It's mostly where natural foods have diminished, due to habitat destruction (usually for housing tracts), that conflicts occur.

The simple solution is to grow some food for them. Leaves, native fruits, buds, grass, insects and nectar from flowers are part of their natural diet. So large trees and shrubs — grevilleas, melaleucas, bottlebrushes, eucalypts and callitris — will help replenish their larder.

It's generally considered unwise to feed possums. It disrupts their normal social behaviour, especially since most animals spend a lot of time foraging for food. Dependence on scraps and handouts is not a good social policy for possums, as they can forget how to forage and have been known to starve if the supply is stopped.

A nest box gives the animal a home away from yours. Simply removing the possum to another location can kill it. Eighty-five per cent of relocated possums are hounded from new areas by existing possums and killed by foxes or domestic pets. Anyway, other possums soon fill vacant territory. A possum resident in your yard, safely housed away from your roof, is the best way to keeps others out.

BELOW
Wildlife experts recommend against artificial feeding of possums but some gardeners have found it a way to deflect damage from fruit trees and vegetable gardens. Use only fruit and natural foods if you must feed them.

BUTTERFLY GARDENS

FOODPLANTS FOR BUTTERFLIES AND ATTRACTING THEM TO YOUR GARDEN

Butterflies are a summer phenomenon except in the tropical north. They need warm weather for breeding and feeding. Like reptiles they need warmth to stimulate their internal engines.

There are two ways to attract butterflies to a garden. The first is to provide the foodplants for the young caterpillars. The other more common approach is to provide plenty of nectar for the adult butterflies. Butterflies in general are attracted to brightly coloured flowers containing nectar. Nectar, rich in sugar, is a carbohydrate which the butterflies need to fuel their flight muscles. The butterfly's wings beat at a fast rate and their demand for nectar is great.

Clearly the most butterfly-friendly garden will find a balance between the two. Providing host plants, though, can often conflict with the needs of a garden setting. Unfortunately many of the plants some butterflies need to raise their young are considered weeds in a garden. The pretty Australian admiral, for instance, feeds on stinging nettles, both a native species and the introduced weed. Mistletoe, camphor laurel and some rough reeds and grasses may be hard to house. Many do not fit the criteria usually laid down for an attractive garden plant. So encouraging butterflies to breed can be a difficult task.

What you choose to plant will depend on what butterflies occur in your area. This information is usually available from local libraries, conservation groups, state departments concerned with wildlife conservation and zoos or animal sanctuaries. Once you know which butterflies are endemic to your region, you can usually obtain a list of foodplants from the same source.

Exotic citrus provides food for many of the swallowtail family of butterflies, including the large orchard butterfly, the dingy swallowtail and some other less widely distributed species. Another exotic providing food for Australian butterflies is the oleander, which is a host plant for the common Australian crow (*Euploea core*) and Eichorn's crow (*E. eichorni*). Several introduced milkweeds (*Asclepias* spp.) are the foodplants for the wanderer or monarch butterfly.

The tailed emperor is one beautiful butterfly that is never particularly common in its range but could benefit from additional foodplants in gardens. To its advantage, many of the acacias on which it feeds make attractive garden plants. They include *A. decurrens* (black wattle), *A. baileyana* (Cootamundra wattle), *A. dealbata*, *A. longifolia* (Sydney golden wattle) and *A. podalyriifolia* (Queensland wattle). They also feed on *Brachychiton populneus* (kurrajong) and *B. acerifolium* (Illawarra flame tree), both of which are common and attractive garden specimens with a widespread range.

Nectar providers can be found among the callistemon, corymbia, eucalyptus, leptospermum, melaleuca, grevillea and pimelea families. These are all freely flowering plants with good nectar production.

Butterflies are attracted to flowers by sight, not scent. It is possible to identify plants which are likely to attract these delightful insects by characteristics of the flowers. Look for flowers forming a dense cluster or spike of small bloom and tubular flowers with flat rims. The flat rims are an adaptation of the plant to the needs of the butterfly for a convenient landing pad and their own insatiable demand for pollination. The flower provides nectar, and in return the butterflies transfer pollen from flower to flower.

They are colour conscious too. Petals that are yellow, orange, blue, violet, purple or white are the best colours to attract butterflies. Interestingly, the sexes of the adult Ulysses butterfly (*Papilio ulysses*), found in the rainforests of tropical Queensland, differ in their attractions to colours. The male is attracted to bright blue colours while the female flies towards red flowers. The variation is said to be associated with courtship since butterflies initially recognise their own species by wing colouration. Blue triangles (*Graphium sarpedon choredon*) are also apparently attracted to red, so include a few red flowers in your planting design.

AUSTRALIAN PLANTS THAT ATTRACT BUTTERFLIES

Acacia spp.	Tailed emperor (*Polyura pyrhus*)
	Common imperial blue (*Jalmenus evago ras evagoras*)
	Fiery jewel (*Hypochrysops ignita ignita*)
Acmena smithii	Common tit (*Hypolycaena phorbas phorbas*)
	Eastern flat (*Netrocoryne repanda repanda*)
Aristolochia spp.	Cairns birdwing (*Ornithoptera priamus poseidon*),
	Richmond birdwing (*Ornithoptera priamus richmondia*)
Dodonaea spp.	Fiery jewel
Elaeocarpus spp.	Eastern flat
Eucalyptus spp.	Fiery jewel
Ficus spp.	Common Australian crow
Gahnia spp.	Swordgrass brown
Scaevola spp.	Meadow argus
Themeda australis	Common brown

RICHMOND BIRDWING

Gardeners from Grafton, New South Wales, to Maryborough, Queensland, can do their bit for conservation by planting the foodplant of the Richmond birdwing (*Ornithoptera priamus richmondia*). Because of habitat destruction and an introduced plant, Dutchman's pipe (*Aristolochia elegans*), which has leaves toxic to the caterpillars, the Richmond birdwing has become rare. It feeds only on two related but beneficial native vines, *Pararistolochia praevenosa* and *P. laheyana*. (These names have recently changed from *Aristolochia*.) Both need a shady position, rich soil and support from a trellis or fence. They are a light vine and can also be grown up trees but, if adopting this method, plant vines a metre from the trunk so that they are not competing for nutrients with the tree. Tie a rope from a branch for support and allow the vine to climb. If Dutchman's pipe is growing in your garden (from Grafton north) it should be removed. It also poisons the larvae of the Cairns birdwing (*Ornithoptera priamus poseidon*).

BELOW
The Richmond birdwing is a rare butterfly that can be protected by gardeners in its natural range by planting the correct foodplant.

CREATING HABITATS FOR BIRDS

Birds bring life to any garden. Many can be beneficial too, by eating insects as well as bringing added colour and the music of birdsong. Australian trees and shrubs are the best way to attract birds. An added advantage is that many of the introduced pest species, such as Indian mynas, actively stay away from bush areas and native plantings.

Gardens need birds as much as birds need gardens. Bushland recedes as suburbs sprawl, but gardens can replace shelter and foodplants lost. You owe it to yourself to help provide some habitat for these unique creatures.

THREE-TIERED LANDSCAPING

Bird habitats occur in three layers.

The tree canopy provides a haunt for larger birds such as magpies, larger parrots and kookaburras. They use them for roosting and surveying prey, and as lookouts for danger and food supplies.

The denser shrubby undergrowth is used by smaller birds. These include honeyeaters and wrens. Lorikeets and smaller parrots often feed in these plants and take to the trees when disturbed, so they occupy several layers.

Seedeaters such as finches forage in grassy clearings and seek refuge in dense shrubs when threatened.

You should understand some of the basic needs of birds and try to replicate natural habitats of the birds in your local area as much as possible. In most cases, taking care of birds' needs will not be inimical to your ideas of a beautiful garden, but it does take some planning. But plan also for pools and grassed areas. For instance, when it comes to grass and seed-eating birds, incorporate several sweeps of ornamental grasses and back them with a low screen of dense shrubs such as *Baeckea virgata* 'Clarence River' mixed with a few prickly leaves or stems to keep invaders out. Even a small clump of mundane yellow millet (the seed fed to caged birds) can add plenty to a finch's diet.

Where possible, try to use plants native to your area, as birds are most adapted to using them as an avian deli. Local councils and bushland groups can assist with seeds and other plant materials.

COPSES AND COVERS

Two of the most important uses of plants by birds are for shelter and nest sites. You can encourage birds to visit and make their home in your garden by planting thickets or copses of low and medium height bushes. Wrens, finches, pardalotes and some of the honeyeaters and robins also take advantage of such sites. They require a thick canopy for nesting and feeding. Wrens feed on insects, so shrubs with insect-attracting flowers — for instance, kunzea and melaleuca species — should be planted. Plants with prickly leaves or branches give protection from predators such as currawongs or cats, and make good nest sites. Finches retreat to thick undergrowth when disturbed and wrens need it for nesting. Prickly plants are not the gardeners' most favoured plants, so try to include a good variety of dense 'sharps' in an out-of-the way part of the garden. Pardalotes nest in burrows and have been known to nest in hanging baskets in gardens.

AVIAN DELICATESSEN

Plants are the birds' supermarket or delicatessen. They provide food for many species. Nectar-bearing shrubs and trees such as grevillea, callistemon, kangaroo paw and banksias are loved by honeyeaters, noisy miners and lorikeets.

Noisy miners are extremely aggressive birds when it comes to feeding territory, and tend to drive other birds away. Some commentators recommend planting the smaller flowered varieties of natives because the branches are lighter and less able to bear the weight of the noisy miner. The argument goes that the spread of the large grevillea hybrids has unduly influenced the occurrence of miners in gardens.

Seedeaters (such as parrots, pigeons and finches) fancy *Callitris* (native cypress), *Casuarina*, grasses and *Acacia*.

Plants are the best long-term solution. But to attract birds immediately, bird feeders are handy. A pot plant saucer is all you need, but make sure it is placed high up, away from local cats. Feed rosellas and parrots sunflower seed; for pigeons and small finches, millet is a good staple. Fresh, chopped soft fruits such as paw paw or ripe pear suit nectar feeders such as lorikeets, honeyeaters or wattlebirds. Beware of dependence, though. Birds could starve if you move or go on holiday.

Birds love honey or sugar mixed with water, but like our own junk food, it's poor nutrition. If birds neglect natural diets, protein deficiency affects feather growth. Young nestlings will be left flightless and defenceless. Commercially available nectar mixes with added vitamins are a reasonable alternative, but the natural food is always the preferred nutrient.

Attracting Wildlife

FOOD PLANTS SELECTION
Species of both plants and birds vary in every corner of the continent, so we have mentioned families rather than specific species where possible.

SEEDS AND BERRIES
Callitris – native cypresses
Casuarina – she oak
Danthonia
Ficus – figs
Goodia lotifolia
Grevillea
Juncus – rushes
Lomandra
Poa species – grasses
Scirpus – club rush
Ornamental grasses

NECTAR
Castanospermum australe – black bean
Correa – native fuchsia
Syzygium species – lillypilly
Alloxylon – tree waratah
Persoonia
Stenocarpus sinuatus – firewheel tree

INSECT ATTRACTORS
Agonis
Ceratopetalum gummiferum – New South Wales Christmas bush
Chamelaucium uncinatum – Geraldton wax
Isopogon
Kunzea
Melaleuca
Verticordia
Xanthorrhoea – blackboy, grass tree

ABOVE
The kookaburra is a familiar visitor to suburban gardens even in Western Australia where it is an introduced species.

NESTING AND SHELTER
Acacia ulicifolia – prickly Moses wattle
A. boormanii – Snowy River wattle
Castanospermum australe black bean
Hakea leucoptera – silver needlewood
Leptospermum flavescens – lemon-scented tea-tree
L. laevigatum – coastal tea-tree
Melaleuca styphelioides – prickly paperbark
M. armillaris – bracelet honey myrtle
Pandanus spiralis – screw palm (for warmer subtropical and tropical areas)
Persoonia levis – broad leaf geebung
P. pinifolia – geebung

ALL-PURPOSE
These will provide food, shelter AND nest sites.
Acacia – wattles
Banksia
Callistemon – bottlebrushes
Eucalyptus
Grevillea
Hakea

plant SELECTION

TREES

COAST BANKSIA (*Banskia integrifolia*)

This east coast banksia occurs often on windswept cliffs from Queensland to Victoria, making it ideal for coastal gardens. The attractive yellow flowers mostly appear in autumn and winter but occasionally earlier.

Size: 15–25m in protected sites.
Care: Well-drained sandy soil suits it best, but it will survive on clay provided water drains away quickly. It is frost hardy.
Uses: Street tree, coastal plantings, flowers, bird attracting. It also has attractive silver foliage on reverse of leaves, a distinctive bark and an architecturally gnarled shape. There are several prostrate forms available, some of which seem to grow better in pots than in the open ground.
Related species: For east coast gardens, old man banksia, (*B. serrata*) is also salt-resistant and has a venerable appearance with gnarled trunks and branches. The closest to a tree shape of the Western Australian species are the acorn banksia (*B. prionotes*) to 8m and *B. menziesii*, which grows to 7m.

NEW SOUTH WALES CHRISTMAS BUSH (*Ceratopetalum gummiferum*)

Though usually classified as a shrub, this plant is ideal as a small tree in small gardens. Several can be grown as a copse. It occurs naturally in moist wooded gullies but needs good drainage and plenty of sun to flower well. The fairly insignificant flowers appear early in spring and are followed by bright coral red calyces around Christmas in its native state. Further south it tends to show colour in January. It is relatively frost hardy to –7°C. Foliage is a soft green with bronze new tips.

Size: Grows to 5m with a spread of 1.5–2m.
Care: Pruning is essential for flower production and well-shaped bushes. Prune by cutting branches for vases at Christmas or immediately after bracts fade. Feed with native plant food or blood and bone in spring and again after flowering. Soil should be kept moist so mulching with leaf mould is advisable.
Uses: Specimen tree, cut flowers, screening, hedging, group plantings.
Cultivars: 'Albery's Red' is the best red strain, a strong and consistent coral red colour. 'White Christmas' has white calyces and is best used to contrast with a red form. 'Christmas Snow' has green and white variegated foliage. This is recommended for tub plantings as it is less vigorous than normal forms. 'Magenta Star' has burgundy or bronze foliage.
Related species:
The coachwood (*C. apetalum*) is a tall tree of wet sclerophyll and rainforests in New South Wales and Queensland. Covered in bronze coloured bracts at Christmas but is less spectacular. Growing to 25m in forests, in drier gullies it is considerably smaller.

GUNGURRU (*Eucalyptus caesia*)

This is one of the very best of the mallee eucalypts. These are all multi-stemmed trees with thin trunks arising from a lignotuber. A single specimen can take the place of several to give a grove effect in the small garden. In this particular species these can spread from the base at angles from 45-60° from perpendicular. It is a Western Australian species and tends to struggle when transported to the humid east. It performs well though in the dry country in Victoria and west of the Great Dividing Range. The gungurru has very attractive red or deep rose flowers with whitish or glaucous buds. These are large and prominent. The large leaves are also silver.
Size: 8-10m with a spread of up to 4–5m.
Care: Well-drained soil is essential. It grows best on light sandy soil out of prevailing winds. Give it room to spread. The plant is subject to scale and chewing insects. It is frost hardy to –7°C.

Uses: Specimen, bird attracting, foliage plant, attractive bark and fruit.
Cultivars: 'Silver Princess' has larger leaves and a more pendant habit than the species. Recommended.

ILLYARRIE OR RED CAP GUM (*Eucalyptus erythrocorys*)

This beautiful gum from Western Australia can grow either as a tree or a mallee. It needs a dry climate to thrive and grows well in such areas outside its native state. The flowers are borne in prominent clusters and are generally bright yellow but with a hint of lime as the buds open. The operculum or flower cap is bright red and just as prominent as the stamens. If you live close to the coast on rocky sandstone cliffs in New South Wales and Queensland, you just might be able to grow this species.
Size: In mallee to 8m, generally smaller.
Care: Good drainage and dry air are essential. It is frost tender. Prune lightly after flowering. If you want to encourage a multi-stemmed feature, it may be possible to coppice or cut the trunk at the base to encourage shooting. Do it only when the lignotuber has developed after several years of growth.
Uses: Specimen tree, attractive foliage, flowers and fruit, street tree.

YELLOW GUM OR WHITE IRONBARK (*Eucalyptus leucoxylon*)

This tree is quite variable and ranges from South Australia to inland New South Wales and Victoria. Flowers can be pink, white or red and appear mainly in the winter months. The coloured forms are particularly attractive against the glaucous foliage. Unlike many inland and dry climate gums, this one seems to thrive in the humid city environments

found along the east coast. Its size is acceptable for most suburban gardens if not crowded by other trees.
Size: Grows to 16m with a spread of about 8m.
Care: Good drainage, hardy in sand and clay soils. Frost hardy.
Uses: Street tree, specimen or feature tree, winter flowers.
Cultivars: *E. leucoxylon* 'Rosea'.

BLUEBERRY ASH (*Elaeocarpus reticulatus*)

An attractive tree for forest-style gardens, the blueberry ash likes a moist environment similar to its wet sclerophyll home on the east coast. It ranges naturally from Queensland to Tasmania and is always found in moist gullies. In gardens it takes a fair amount of shade but can take on a stressed appearance in full sun with little moisture. The leaves become blotchy and leathery with twiggy, knotty stems quite unlike its normal lush look. For this reason it is not recommended as a street or specimen tree but is perfect in the well-wooded border. The pink-flowered form 'Prima Donna' flowers more freely and seems to tolerate more sun. The berries are large and blue but not often noticed until they fall to the ground.
Size: A small tree to 15m, spread 3–5m.
Care: Plant in a well-drained position but with good moisture retention and high humus content in the soil. Prune if a hedge or large shrub effect is desired.
Uses: Rainforest and gully gardens, screening tree. 'Prima Donna' is also useful as a hedging and large container plant.

NATIVE FRANGIPANI (*Hymenosporum flavum*)

Fragrance is always desirable in a garden tree, and the native frangipani has a gentle perfume that is strongest in late afternoon. It is common in cultivation and has sometimes been grown as a street tree. but its narrow columnar shape means it is poor as a shade

tree. Flowers, borne in spring, are cream aging to yellow and most abundant when the tree is grown in full sun. It tolerates some shade and prefers a moist, humus-rich soil. It is found in the rainforests of New South Wales and Queensland.
Size: While it will reach up to 12m in its native rainforest, garden specimens are more likely to reach only 6m. It is a slim and narrow tree, so is never likely to become a nuisance.
Care: Regular watering and mulching with leaf mould.
Uses: Rainforest garden or blended with exotics.

WHITE CEDAR (*Melia azedarach* var. *australasica*)

This is a wonderful tree for the dry garden. The species is widespread from the Middle East to China and northern Australia in mostly arid, warm regions. It has a stack of common names, and whether the familiar horticultural form is an indigenous one is a moot point. It is known as Persian lilac, chinaberry, bead tree and in Perth a common form is called Cape lilac. It has a spreading crown and a deciduous habit. Flowers vary from a greyish mauve to a pale mauve with white in spring. These are followed by attractive yellow fruits in summer. These fruits are considered toxic.
Size: Quite a large tree, certainly as big as a jacaranda in some locations. It can grow to 40m but 10–12m is more likely. The spread is similar so make sure it has room to grow.
Care: Attacked by processional caterpillars, especially when planted in shade. These can completely defoliate the tree. The best remedy is to tie a length of hessian around the trunk about 0.5–1m from the base. The caterpillars retreat to this as their daytime haven and can be slaughtered with impunity and ease in the morning.
Uses: Good shade tree, attractive feature or specimen tree, street tree.

QUEENSLAND FIREWHEEL TREE (*Stenocarpus sinuatus*)

The flowers of this lovely member of the Protea family found in Queensland and New South Wales are shaped like the spokes of a wheel and open in a 'crown roast' shape. These are vermilion to scarlet and profusely produced in early

summer. The blooms are rich in nectar and popular with lorikeets and honeyeaters. The seeds are retained in hard woody capsules in autumn. The seeds germinate readily and volunteer prolifically. The leaves are large, leathery and lobed. They can be up to 30cm long with several 'fingers'.
Size: Like all rainforest trees, the firewheel tree can reach great heights in the forest: in this case 25–30m. In a garden it is likely to reach 10–20m only. It is slow growing and narrow but tends to develop a wider crown after 20 to 30 years.
Care: Normal watering and mulching is all that is required. They are rarely attacked by pests and are as close to a trouble-free tree as can be found. Not frost hardy, but grows as far south as Melbourne.
Uses: Feature tree, street tree, container plant for well-lit indoor positions, bird attracting.

Plant Selection

SHRUBS

SCARLET BANKSIA (*Banksia coccinea*)

One of the west's most beautiful cut flowers, the scarlet banksia, like most banksias, thrives in the face of coastal winds in the southern tip of Western Australia amongst coastal heath and rocky headlands. The flowers are spectacular but the bush is mostly nondescript out of bloom. It tends to have only a few erect stems, though some forms are bushier. Flowers are short and cylindrical, borne on spikes through the winter months. Leaves are stiff and broad and the plant can be architectural in the right setting.

Size: Height 1.5–4m, spread 1–1.5m.
Care: Almost impossible to grow in the humid eastern states, it resents humid summers. Some success has been obtained apparently by planting in sand laid over limestone rubble. This tends to approximate natural conditions and improve drainage.
Uses: Feature plant, cut flowers, and coastal situations.

HEATH BANKSIA (*Banksia ericifolia*)

The east coast is not as well endowed with beautiful banksias as Western Australia but *Banksia ericifolia* is an exception. It has dense foliage which, as the name suggests, is like the leaves of the introduced heath, fine and lacy. The flowers are borne inside the bush, not on the ends of the branches, giving the effect of decorations on a Christmas tree. These are quite large and usually a gentle orange colour. If anything the bush is a little open. Flowering time is winter to early spring. Larger honeyeaters flock to the flowers.

Size: *Banksia ericifolia* height 5m, spread 4m. 'Giant Candles' height 3.5m.
Care: Well-drained soil in full sun.
Uses: Screening, shrub borders, coastal gardens.
Cultivars: The flowers of the hybrid 'Giant Candles' a cross between this and *B. spinulosa*, are much larger, up to 40cm long, and the colour is a strong ginger or burnt orange. *B. spinulosa* has a denser habit and also contributes its free-flowering habit to the hybrid.

RIVER ROSE (*Bauera rubioides*)

A pretty shrub with dark green leaves and bronze new growth, it's one that is easy to grow though short-lived. There are two colour forms: white and pink and they are always seen in association with water or moist forest areas. Where water is plentiful they adopt a pleasant compact, weeping habit; elsewhere they tend to send out canes which need extensive pruning. They thrive in the dappled sunlight found under the cover of wet sclerophyll forest trees such as blueberry ash or *Angophora costata* though full sun is fine if soil is moist. The dainty, nodding flowers appear in late winter and early spring.

Size: Height 1m, spread 1.5–2m.
Care: Keep moist, prune lightly after flowering and to remove cane-like growths. This should enable the bush to stay compact. Needs replacing after 3 to 4 years or when it becomes woody. Propagate by layering in spring, sowing seed in summer or autumn, or by semi-hardwood cuttings taken in late summer.
Uses: Year-round foliage and winter flowers, shade gardens.
Related species: *B. sessiliflora*, *B. microphylla*.

CALLISTEMON 'REEVE'S PINK'

Along with the grevilleas, the bottlebrushes are the quintessential shrub for the Australian garden. They flower freely, often and generously. While the most popular garden forms have red flowers, nurseries stock a wide range of other colours too. It has quite a dense habit and regular pruning after flowering will encourage this. Flowers mainly appear in spring, with a less spectacular autumn burst.

Size: Height 3m, spread 3m.

Care: Soils and drainage seem not to worry these plants, as they often grow where periodic inundations occur. They do appreciate a regular drenching though when planted in well-drained or dry positions. Light pruning, usually removal of the spent flower head, is essential after flowering. It pays to be cautious and not cut too heavily into hard wood. Prune to an existing leaf bud if overall shaping is needed. Sawfly larvae can defoliate plants in summer. These cling to stems in groups and can be manually controlled. Squashing between a pair of handheld rubber thongs is a good way, or spray with carbaryl.

Uses: Good for screening and colour in the shrub border. Bottlebrushes are bird attracting for nectar-and seed-eating birds such as parrots.

Cultivars: 'Reeve's Pink' is thought to be a chance seedling of *C. citrinus*, a species that produces prolific varietal change. Other pink-hued forms derived from it include 'Angela', 'Pink Champagne' and 'Mauve Mist'.

GERALDTON WAX (*Chamelaucium uncinatum*)

One of the most popular garden shrubs and reliable colour providers in the native garden. It comes from Western Australia and could hardly be called 'native' to most regions. There are several colour variations from white to pink and carmine, and these have been selected for cultivation. It flowers in winter in warm zones and in spring in cooler areas. Fine foliage and plenty of bloom are the chief attraction.

Size: Height 3m, spread up to 4m.

Care: Grow in sandy or gravelly soil with a neutral to acid pH. In areas with heavier soil, raised beds may be useful. Prune after flowering to maintain a good shape and encourage stronger flower production. Can be pruned quite hard but in humid areas may suddenly fail.

Uses: Use as a light screen or a low hedge trimmed to an informal round shape. Use in coastal gardens for salt-resistance. Good for cut flowers.

Cultivars: 'Universtiy', 'Purple Pride' are good purplish forms, 'Album' white, 'Early Pink', 'Bundara Excelsior' pink.

NATIVE FUCHSIA (*Correa reflexa*)

The correas are attractive small shrubs with nectar-rich flowers which attract honeyeaters to the garden. All correas have bell-shaped flowers in red, green, yellow and pink shades. Most flower in winter and early spring. *C. reflexa* has many forms, and has been used as the parent of many hybrids. They are known as native fuchsia in Victoria, and while they have a similar appearance and grow in similar conditions, they are unlikely to replace fuchsias in the exotic garden.

Size: Variable: some forms are upright and may reach 1.5 m, others are low, spreading forms to 50cm and a possible 2m spread.

Care: Needs moist, well-drained and reasonably rich, friable soil and preferably little root competition, as it tends to be starved out by more vigorous plants. It will grow in part shade or sun but often performs well in dappled sunlight. It is salt-resistant and good for coastal gardens. Tolerates mild alkalinity.

Uses: Low informal hedges, border plants, seaside locations, and container plants.

Cultivars: Most named varieties are hybrids, often with *C. reflexa* parentage. *Correa* 'Dusky Bells' is one of the most common correa cultivars. Also 'Marian's Marvel', flowers pink and lime green (*C. backhousiana x C. reflexa*), 'Ivory Bells', white bells.

CRANBROOK BELL (*Darwinia meeboldii*)

Most *Darwinias* are small shrubs, but several are larger, and grafting has allowed many to be grown in more humid gardens of the east coast. The majority of the 40 species occur in Western Australia and the Cranbrook bell is one of them. It comes from heathland at the edge of the Stirling Ranges and needs to be grafted onto a stronger rootstock, usually *D. citriodora* for successful garden use. It has attractive

white bells with red tips and the calyx extends down the petals to give it a very 'Christmassy' appearance. It flowers in spring.
Size: An erect plant to 1.5m.
Care: Plants need part or full sun, good drainage and a cool root run. Sandy soil is preferred. Plant near boulders or sleeper retaining walls where roots can forage in shade. Sometimes attacked by scale. Do not crowd with other plants.
Uses: Use as a low screen or mass it to avoid root competition from other plants.

FERN-LEAF HOP BUSH (*Dodonaea boroniifolia*)

Early settlers around Sydney experimented with food sources and dodonaeas were thought to be useful for brewing beer, hence the common name. The hop bushes are grown not for the flowers (spring), which are insignificant, but for the fruits appearing in summer.
Size: Height 2m, spread 1m.
Care: Easy to grow in well-drained soil and full sun. Propagate from cuttings in autumn. Scale can be a pest in summer. Spray with oil.
Uses: Low screens, grow for summer colour in shrub borders, thickets in the natural garden.
Related species: *D. viscosa* var. *purpurea* has attractive purple foliage.

EMU BUSH (*Eremophila* species)

The emu bushes are small shrubs adapted to arid conditions and have long been used in native gardens especially in the areas of dry summer in Victoria, South and Western Australia. Many species have silver leaves and flower in the colour range of yellow through red and purple.
Size: Generally small shrubs about 1–2m with a similar spread and an open habit.

Above: *E. nivea*

Care: They are short-lived in humid summer zones and need special care to create a dry environment. This can include planting in raised beds, using fast-draining planting mixes and pebble mulching. They need a warm and sunny spot. Many are difficult to strike from cuttings or grow from seed and for this reason the species is probably best for specialist growers.
Uses: They are attractive in the shrub border, provide long-term if not spectacular colour and some are bird attracting. Most are frost hardy.
Related species: *E. nivea* is one of the most attractive with silver leaves and mauve flowers appearing mostly in winter and spring. The spotted emu bush (*E. maculata*) is the most common with yellow, red or purple flowers.

WAX FLOWER (*Eriostemon myoporoides*)

This is one of the most popular of Australian plants and works well in exotic gardens. It has been used extensively in

the courtyard gardens of Parliament House in Canberra. It responds to formal shaping. It flowers in winter and spring with masses of starry white flowers and pink buds.
Size: 1.5–2m tall, spread similar.
Care: Prefers well-drained, humus-rich, neutral soil and regular moisture. Grows well in part shade and in full sun if well watered. Tolerant of moderate frost.
Uses: Formal hedges, garden shrubs, cut flowers, screenings.
Cultivars: *E. myoporoides* 'Profusion' and 'Clearview Apple-Blossom'.

GREVILLEA

There is hardly a garden in Australia that has not contained a grevillea of some type at some time. It is one of the most significant families of plants. Grevilleas range from the large flowered hybrids with a tropical origin to the small flowered forms from the high alpine regions. Many of the latter were amongst the first to be developed for gardens and quite a few have not proved adaptable to warmer climates. The so-called tropical grevilleas, too, are generally not frost hardy and are poorly suited to southern or cool inland climates. Yet it is these that are in the vanguard of garden use. *Grevillea* 'Robyn Gordon' has proved to be one of the most successful of the new breed of grevilleas. It grows just about anywhere, flowers all the time, is dramatic in the garden and birds flock to it — a perfect score.

There are now so many new introductions that it is wise to seek recommendations from reputable and knowledgeable nursery people before making a selection. Local adaptability is too complex to be included in this brief précis, but it can determine whether you will have success or failure with this and many other plants listed. As a rule, it is best to stick with varieties found in the same climatic zone.

Size: Ranges from groundcovers to tall trees.
Care: Well-drained soil, full sun and low-phosphorus soils.
Uses: Bird attracting, year-round and seasonal garden colour, landscaping uses, screening, shrub borders.

DUSTY DAISY BUSH (*Olearia phlogopappa*)

While many in the olearia family are nondescript to ugly, the dusty daisy bush is an exception. It comes from

Tasmania, Victoria and New South Wales and grows best in gardens in the cooler parts of those states where it has become a favourite for native gardens. Colour is variable and includes white, pink, mauve and blue. Flowering is short, confined to a few weeks in spring but a well-maintained bush is entirely covered in 3cm blooms. The leaves are small and grey-green and make an attractive bush when out of flower.

Size: Height 1–2 metre, similar spread.
Care: Grow in well-drained soil in part or filtered sun. It resents alkaline soils. Prune after flowering to prevent the plant becoming leggy.
Uses: Cut flowers, low screens, seaside locations. Flowers are butterfly attracting.

SAGO FLOWER (*Ozothamnus diosmifolius* syn. *Helichrysum diosmifolius*)

The sago flower is little known, but a worthwhile addition to the summer flower garden. The combination of fine, dark needle-like foliage with large white or pink heads of blossom, each about 15–20cm across, is welcome in late spring to early summer when spring flowers have gone dormant. In this respect it flowers at an opportune time and the effect is rather like massed achilleas writ large. It is fast growing and can be short-lived. A single bush can provide a splash of white (a more elegant look than the pink form). Several make a very dramatic statement. Don't underestimate the foliage either. Its bright colour and billowing form are impressive when not blooming.

Size: Height 2–5m, spread 1–3m.
Care: Pruning is essential from an early age, as the branches can take off and become top heavy and leggy. This is hard to correct once stems have hardened, as it sulks when cut into hard wood. Not fussy about soils but needs full sun to flower well. In part shade it can become tall and open. Propagate from cuttings. Water in summer.
Uses: Summer colour in the backs of shrub borders, excellent cut flowers, garden filler.
Cultivars: *O. diosmifolius* 'Pink Cloud' has a longer flowering period and fades from pink to white; 'Cook's Snow White' bushy with white flowers; 'Cook's Salmon Pink' oval salmon buds with white tips; 'Cook's Tall Pink' pink buds; 'Redlands Sandra' upright with cream flowers buds.

FOREST PHEBALIUM (*Phebalium squamulosum*)

This phebalium ranges from south eastern Queensland to southern Victoria, and has many different forms. Flowers are small and star-like, ranging from cream to yellow. They are freely produced in spring and the bush is a colourful addition to an informal Australian plant garden. The buds often have a burnished, silvery or bronze covering before opening and this adds to their appeal.

Size: Common horticultural variety is about 2m high with a 1m spread.

Care: Plants need sharp drainage and a coarse growing medium, as they cannot tolerate waterlogged soil. They are prone to collar rot and root fungus attack. Plant in part shade or full sun. They are tolerant of light frost, low phosphorus fertilisers and seasonal dryness once established. Pruning after flowering improves the shape and extends the life of plants.

Uses: Spring shrub borders, plant collections, containers.

PINK RICE FLOWER (*Pimelea ferruginea*)

One of the most popular and colourful of the Australian plants in common garden use, this rice flower comes from Western Australia's rocky headlands and coastal sand dunes. It can prove tricky in humid parts of the east coast. Flowers often completely cover the bush with pink flowers about 3cm across during a long period in spring. These are produced at the end of branches. It forms a delightfully tight bun with bright green foliage thus making it an attractive plant even out of bloom.

Size: 0.5m–1.5m tall, similar spread, sometimes reaching a spread of 2.5m.

Care: A well-drained sunny position is ideal. Sandy or rubble-filled soil is preferred. This allows roots to find moisture and cooler spots in dry seasons. It also tolerates part shade. It can be prone to dieback and root rot especially if soil is too damp for its liking. Should be pruned after flowering to encourage fresh growth and remove the tendency to legginess.

Uses: Cottage gardens, border edging, low hedges, spot colour in shrub borders, container plants.

Cultivars: 'Bonne Petite' deep pink; 'Magenta Mist' magenta'; 'Pink Bouquet' variegated foliage, deep pink flowers; 'Red' reddish purple flowers.

POMADERRIS (*Pomaderris elliptica*)

It's is a shame this species is not better known, as the pomaderris can put on an eye-catching display in the spring garden. It needs to be grown in groups, though, for full effect. It thrives in coastal districts on the east coast where summers are wet. For many gardeners it is far more reliable than many common springtime plants imported from cooler southern regions, yet it is almost impossible to find in nurseries. Flowers occur in large heads and the large leaves are a soft green with grey–gold overtones. They resemble somewhat the leaves of common exotic cotoneasters. *Pomaderris* is a popular plant with animals, often swarming with butterflies for nectar and as a food plant.

Size: Height 3m, spread 0.5m.

Care: Grow in well-drained, humus-rich soil in full sun. Propagate from cuttings taken in autumn.

Uses: Spring colour, insect attracting, border displays.

PURPLE MINT BUSH (*Prostanthera ovalifolia*)

A worthy and easy to grow mid-spring flowering shrub, the purple mint bush is a very free-flowering plant for a range of conditions. In cooler areas it may delay flowering until summer. It is found in Queensland and New South Wales. Flowers are usually mauve or purple but there are pink and white variations and variegated leaf forms. It is the most commonly grown mint bush and I have found it the most reliable mint bush for the Sydney region, where it seems to like the summer moisture. Other species are not as vigorous or reliably free flowering. Leaves are oval-shaped and release a strong mint fragrance when brushed. It makes a great dense low screen if continually pruned to retain vigour, though I have always preferred to replace it after three to four years in favour of new fresh cuttings. This is not a long-lived plant, but it's fast growing, easy to strike and it takes hard pruning. There is some work being done on grafting to ensure a longer life, but these plants may be difficult to find in commercial nurseries.

Size: Height 2–3m, spread 1–1.5m.
Care: A forest species, it does best in full sun if moisture is maintained, or part shade where soil tends to dry out. Soft tip cuttings taken in summer strike easily, as do semi-hard cuttings in autumn.
Uses: Banks, massed plantings in the shrub border, training as an informal hedge or screen. It deserves to be used structurally not just as a loose naturally grown plant in the bush style garden. Enclosing seating areas or semi-circular plantings are successful ways for it to be used in garden design.

SILVER CASSIA (*Senna artemisioides* syn. *Cassia artemisioides*)

Common in arid inland areas, the silver cassia is a desirable garden plant for its delightful, fine silvery foliage and the contrast of the late winter and early springtime flowers. These, like many sennas, are gold and freely produced. It demands quite heavy pruning after flowering and will usually shoot from hard wood, though if regular maintenance is carried out this should not prove necessary. Left unpruned it becomes an ugly, straggly shrub, as do many of the preceding plants in this chapter. As with them, it is a crime to neglect pruning after flowering.

Size: Can grow to 6m but this is highly undesirable in garden situations.
Care: Prune as above and plant in well-drained soil. Responds to light feeding. Propagate by cuttings or seed sown after soaking in warm water for up to 24 hours.
Uses: Flower borders, cottage gardens, low informal hedges and accent plantings for winter/spring colour.

THOMASIA (*Lysiosepalum involucratum*)

This genus is mainly found in Western Australia and this species is a low shrub, flowering in spring. The flowers are soft and papery and very freely produced. Like many in the genus, the flowers tend to hang down. Plant them in a raised bed or atop a retaining wall at near to eye level to see their full attractiveness. The flowers are pink to pinkish mauve. The plant needs excellent drainage and a dry summer to grow well. In summer rainfall areas it is unreliable to doubtful. Western, southern Australia and parts of inland eastern Australia with a climate approximating the Mediterranean type are best for growing *Thomasia*.

Size: Height 1m, spread 1m.
Care: Good drainage with full to part sun. Winter rains increase the chance of success. Propagate from cuttings.
Uses: Spring shrub borders, cottage gardens, rockery plants.

PAYNE'S THRYPTOMENE (*Thryptomene* 'Payne's Hybrid')

A long-time favourite, many gardeners have tended to let this plant have its head, with disastrous consequences. It becomes very woody very quickly. If pruned heavily during and after flowering in winter and early spring it can be an interesting foliage and border plant. Flowers are not conspicuous, but it will produce lovely sprays of tiny pink flowers on long stems if pruned each September. It requires little other attention at any time of year and the sprays are the ideal filler for cut flower arrangements. The plant is very popular in floristry for this reason. It is thought to be a form of *Thryptomene saxicola*.

Size: Height 1m, spread 1m.
Care: Prune as above, feeding and watering are generally not needed except in severe drought, as it survives on natural rainfall. It grows in full sun or part shade and should be given good drainage or a raised bed. Take cuttings any time from late spring to autumn.
Uses: Borders, cut flowers, garden fillers.
Related species: *T. calycina* and hybrids derived from it. This species from the Grampians grows well in Victoria and higher altitude areas with cooler climates but is extremely poor in areas along the east coast, such as Sydney.

COAST ROSEMARY (*Westringia fruticosa*)

A familiar plant in coast regeneration zones in New South Wales, this plant has been popular in horticulture for many years. It is a versatile little shrub, responding well to pruning and formal treatments as well as to the more informal style of garden. Its major drawback is its tendency to die out for no apparent reason. This is unfortunate when it is used for clipped hedges, as replacing a dead section is always a problem. On the other hand, gardeners have always managed to deal with the same problem when it occurs with *Buxus sempervirens* (with regularity!). It is extremely hardy, particularly in coastal locations, and makes a good informal screen. It has also been used as the understock for grafting mint bushes. Flowers are white or pale grey and appear all year round.
Size: Height 2m, spread up to 4m.
Care: Choose a well-drained site in full sun. Avoid cutting into hard wood when pruning.
Uses: Hedges, screens, formal treatments, coastal buffer.
Cultivars: *W. fruticosa* 'Smokie' has silvery grey leaves; *W. fruticosa* 'Morning Light' has grey leaves with a cream edge.

ACCENT PLANTS

CORDYLINE (*Cordyline stricta*)

A plant for shady moist corners, the cordyline is perfect in a rainforest style garden. There is some variation in flower colour, most being a light purple but occasionally paler. The leaves are strap-like and may be 50–60cm long. It forms small clumps of straight, slender stems. The black seeds are borne in large clusters and are quite striking.
Size: Height up to 3m, with smaller spread.
Care: Moisture and humus-rich soil with regular mulch applied prior to dry periods. It is frost tender and resents long periods of cold weather.
Uses: Clumping in rainforest gardens, mixes well with ferns particularly birds' nest fern. Use as accents in the shady garden and for flower colour. Can be grown in containers without the vigour it has in the ground.
Related species: *C. rubra* has red fruit.

SWAMP LILY WHITE (*Crinum pedunculatum*)

The swamp lily, as the name implies, likes damp conditions but it adapts well to moist garden soils. Grow it for its bold light green leaves which reach 1m in length and measure 10cm at the base. It has 1m flower stems bearing up to 50 fragrant white flowers. These are produced in the warmer months though the plant may flower at any time of year in subtropical and tropical areas. It is found in the Northern Territory, Queensland and northern New South Wales.
Size: Clump grows to about 1m with similar spread.
Care: Plenty of moisture and full sun or shady position. Propagate by offsets taken from the main plant but avoid

lifting as it can sulk. Seeds also germinate readily. Frost tender.
Uses: Water gardens, large scale landscaping, feature plantings and for the bog garden.
Related species: *C. flaccidum*, the Murray lily or Darling lily, white trumpet flowers in spring and summer. Grows in most soils.

GYMEA LILY (*Doryanthes excelsa*)

If this plant did not exist the florists would invent it. The spectacular crown of bright red flowers are mounted atop a spike up to 6m tall. These flowers are rich in nectar and loved by birds. They blend very well with exotic garden plants and are perhaps harder to mix with natives, even though they are a common sight in dry sclerophyll forests around Sydney They were first seen by Banks and Cook aboard the *Endeavour* when it landed in Botany Bay. Surprisingly, the Gymea lily has become a popular landscape plant only in the last decade or so of the twentieth century.
Size: Flower spike can reach 6m with leaves 1–2m long. Spread from 2–2.5m when mature.
Care: Full sun and plenty of room to develop. The plant will tolerate frost but the flower spike can be damaged if a late spring frost occurs. Grow from seed; will flower after 6 to 7 years. It needs full sun to flower well.
Uses: Feature plant for borders and in sunny clearings among trees. A strong architectural plant, it is good for mixed gardens. Useful where a large strap-leafed plant is required as a substitute for agaves, dracaenas and yuccas. Another plus — the leaves are not spiky.
Related species: *D. palmeri*, the spear lily, has orange flowers within dark red bracts on a 3m stem. The stem bears many more flowers than the Gymea lily and is, if anything, more spectacular. The stem is pendant under the weight of the blooms. Found in Queensland and New South Wales.

WARATAH (*Telopea speciosissima*)

One of the world's most spectacular flowers, a large group of flowering waratahs is awe-inspiring. The New South Wales waratah is also an icon of Australian decorative arts with its made-for-art deco styling. It is featured extensively in stained glass, wallpaper, fabric and ceramic designs in the late Victorian age, and was one of painter Margaret Preston's favourite subjects. It is still much loved for advertising logos in its home state. The inflorescence is 15cm across, with deep red bracts and a domed raceme or multitude of tiny scarlet flowers
Size: Ranging from an almost single stemmed bush to a large rounded shrub in deep clay soil with good water supply, it can be 1.5–3m tall. Spread is about 1.5m.
Care: Telopea can be hard to establish, as they need an acid, low fertility soil and perfect drainage. They often grow on sandy ridges with a clay base and access to sub-soil moisture. Good results have been obtained by building up beds to a height of 30–50cm with rocky rubble and poor sandy soil. Waratahs occur naturally where summer rainfall is the normal pattern, so water well in summer, especially for the first few seasons after planting. They can succumb quickly in a sudden dry spell. Avoid applying fertiliser, especially animal manure and chemical fertilisers containing phosphorus. A light dressing of native fertiliser could be applied once well settled in. Mulching is usually adequate.
Uses: Cut flowers, bold garden colour in springtime, accents for foliage plants.
Cultivars: 'Wirrimbirra White', white flowers; 'Brimstone Blush' flowers look pink but have a white style and red perianth; 'Braidwood Brilliant', a cross between *T. speciosissima* and; *T. mongaenensis*, sometimes called the Braidwood waratah, more frost resistant and more adaptable to cultivation; 'Shady Lady', a cross between *T. speciosissima* and *T. oreades*, the Victorian waratah. Flowers are smaller and less well formed due to the impact of the second parent. It grows to 3m and responds to gardens better than the true waratah.

GRASS TREE (*Xanthorrhoea australis*)

This genus is unique to Australia and there is a species for just about every region. The nominated one is found in southern Australia — from South Australia to Tasmania and north to New South Wales. They are slow growing, long-lived and best cultivated from seed. The flowers are carried on long spears about 4–5m tall. They are highly attractive to nectar-feeding birds and insects.

Size: Leaves are tough, spear-like and about 1m long. Plants can reach a height of several metres and spread 1.5–2.5m, depending on age and branching habit.

Care: Select an open, sunny, well-drained position to avoid root rot. Plants taken from the wild under licence are expensive, and have no guarantee of survival. Seedlings are preferable and you can expect a reasonably sized plant within 5 to 7 years. Trunks, however, take many more years to form.

Uses: Architectural and feature plantings for xerophytic (dry climate) landscapes. These plants add interest to a basically green garden of grasses and textural plants, and are particularly useful for entrance gardens when interspersed with sculptural rocks and logs.

Related species: *X. preissii* from Western Australia; *X. malacophylla* from northeast New South Wales; *X. arborea* from Queensland.

PERENNIALS

FLANNEL FLOWER (*Actinotus helianthi*)

The flannel flower bears soft white flowers in spring. It is a short-lived biennial and carpets poor, sandy soil with barely any water-retentive characteristics around Sydney. Cultivation is often difficult, the seeds taking some weeks (sometimes months) to germinate. One way to establish them is to purchase a group of seedlings from a specialist native nursery. These are occasionally available around late spring or early summer. Establish them in a raised bed of loose sandstone rubble. If the ground is rocky and covered with stones, they should self-sow. Good results are also obtained by direct sowing into gravel mulch rather than a prepared bed or seed tray. Seed should be fresh for sowing in autumn or spring.

Size: Plants have a loose habit and grow to 50cm high.

Care: Mulch plants to conserve moisture but avoid overwatering. Take stem cuttings in spring and plant in sharp sand. Sterilise soil and containers. Drench with Bordeaux to prevent damping off. Feed with slow-release fertiliser for natives if plants fail to move.

Uses: Drifts, container plants, specialist plantings. Plants grow well in rockeries where roots can seek shelter and moisture.

KANGAROO PAW (*Anigozanthos* cultivars)

Kangaroo paws have been subject to a great deal of horticultural development and are now very popular here and overseas. New cultivars are a brilliant sight planted in massed displays or in drifts in the cottage garden. There are now so many colours and shades that sophisticated colour coordinating and grading of displays by hue and shade is entirely possible. They originated in Western

Australia but we tend to think of them as desert plants, expecting them to thrive in droughty arid situations. In fact they occur on sand plains with a high water table, so the roots are in reach of water.

Size: New hybrids are classed as small (30–60cm); medium (60–120cm) and tall (1–2m).

Care: In the growing season, they should receive a regular thorough drenching, preferably around the roots. Leaves can be disfigured by black ink disease, this is particularly apparent in the humid conditions of the east coast. Keep plants drier in the dormant winter period. Watering around the base of the plant and avoiding wetting leaves reduces ink disease.

Uses: Landscape planting, containers, cottage gardens and colour bedding.

Cultivars: The 'Bush Gems' series flower for most of the year, though tall varieties are mainly spring and summer flowering. Many are derived from crossing A. flavidus with other species, including A. pulcherrimus, A. rufus, A. preissii and A. humilis.

Small: 'Bush Ranger' (red), 'Bush Illusion' (gold), 'Dwarf Delight (orange), 'Pink Joey' (pink), 'Regal Claw' (orange and red).

Medium: 'Bush Garnet' (purplish red), 'Bush Emerald' (green flowers with red stems), 'Bush Ochre' (orange/gold).

Tall: 'Bush Dawn' (yellow), 'Bush Haze' (yellow with red stems), 'Bush Radiance' (pink), 'Orange Cross' (orange).

BLUE LESCHENAULTIA (*Leschenaultia biloba*)

Few native plants are as free flowering and brilliant as the leschenaultias. They are mat-forming perennials or small lax

shrubs native to Western Australia. *L. biloba* is found around Perth. They need a sandy, very well-drained soil and in other states have been found to be good rockery plants but short-lived.

Size: Up to 60cm, with similar spread.

Care: Avoid watering leaves to prevent humidity building up, and plant where there is good air circulation. Cuttings strike easily; this is the best way to maintain the plant.

Uses: Ideal for rockeries, containers and as a groundcover in raised beds placed in full sun.

Cultivars: *Leschenaultia* 'White Flash' (bi-coloured blue and white).

Related species: *L. formosa* (red), *L. superba* (red-orange).

DARLING PEA (*Swainsona galegifolia*)

A small perennial from arid inland regions in New South Wales, Victoria and Queensland and named for the Darling River along which it grows. Flowers are pea-shaped and range in colour from pink, purple and red to white. These are produced in spring and early summer.

Size: 1m height and spread. Stems are arching.

Care: Prune in winter. Propagate from seed or cuttings and grow in moderately good soil in full sun. Raised beds are needed in areas with a wet summer. It is frost-tender so needs a sheltered spot.

Uses: Rockeries, border plants.

STURT'S DESERT PEA (*Swainsona formosa*)

The floral emblem of South Australia, Sturt's desert pea was formerly known as *Clianthus formosus*. Flower forms vary: some have a scarlet flower and black boss; others are all red or have a plum coloured boss. In cultivation it is usually treated as an annual, but some recent work has concentrated on grafting onto a stronger rootstock to obtain longer-lived plants. In the wild, seeds germinate after heavy rain, which is usually in winter. They grow fast and set seed before summer's heat. Plants may survive a second season with care.

Size: Height 15cm, spread 1m.

Care: Sow seed in autumn for spring or early summer flowering. It is not frost hardy and needs protection. In areas such as Sydney or Brisbane, with wet summers, aim for flowers by November. Seeds need preparation by abrading on sandpaper or soaking in hot water for several hours to break the hard outer covering. Sow directly where it is to flower or in small peat pots, planted without disturbing the roots.

It resents humid conditions but can be grown on the east coast if a dry position under eaves is selected. Growing in deep containers filled with coarse material such as rock, gravel and limestone chips is advisable. It prefers a sandy, fast-draining mix and at least half a day's sun. Plants should not need fertilising. Water as required, probably once a day in summer.

Uses: Groundcover, feature plant, containers, hanging baskets.

FRINGED LILY (*Thysanotus multiflorus*)

All *Thysanotus* have purple flowers which resemble a small native iris or *Patersonia*. It flowers in spring and ranges naturally from South Australia to Victoria to Queensland.

Size: To 30cm and grows in small tufty clumps.

Care: Plant in a sunny, well-drained position. If growing as a container plant, use a coarse, gritty mix.

Uses: Rockeries and cottage gardens. A plant for collectors and specialist growers, but seek it out and plant in small groups flowing from one section of the garden bed to another. They look particularly attractive when allowed to drift through sections of the garden. When used this way, they act as a unifying element. The size of the group can vary and each cluster can be mixed with other species with similar leaf shapes or different types of blue flowers. These plants mulched with gravel have a greater tendency to self-sow and spread than if a conventional mulch is used.

CLIMBERS

FALSE SARSPARILLA (*Hardenbergia violacea*)

This plant may climb or trail over embankments in its original state but there are now so many cultivars that it is easy to choose one for a specific purpose. Some are quite bushy and are sold as cottage or container plants. The flowers are commonly purple but pink and white are known and sold as named varieties. It is a light climber, unlikely to do any damage to structures. The flowering season (late winter to early spring) is generally short but spectacular.

Size: Spread to 2m.

Care: Fertile, humus-rich soil and sun or semi-shade suits it. It prefers moist soil. Frost hardiness varies, but most of the newer cultivars are moderately frost-hardy. Take tip cuttings in spring.

Uses: Light trellises, covering embankments or garden beds. Plant it with other spring-flowering purple plants, such as hovea, or yellow pea-flowers such as goodenia and the climber old man's beard (*Clematis aristata*) for impacting colour effects.

Cultivars: *H.violacea* 'Happy Wanderer' is vigorous and free flowering; 'Rosea' pink flowers; 'Violacea' low mounding habit; 'White Crystal' white flowers late winter.

Related species: *H.comptoniana* from Western Australia

CLIMBING LIGNUM (*Muehlenbeckia adpressa*)

The most common member of this genus is the vigorous New Zealander *M. complexa*. It is useful as a screening plant for a wire fence where it can become so dense with trimming that it looks like a hedge. There are several Australian species and this one has tiny

green leaves and wiry stems, though it tends to be a little more shrub-like than the New Zealand species. It is found in all states except Queensland and the Northern Territory.
Size: Moderately vigorous.
Care: Fertile soil and plentiful water. It is moderately frost hardy.
Uses: Screens, groundcover, hedges and covering old stumps. Could be used on wire frames in containers to create topiary. This plant needs to be trained and regularly trimmed, otherwise it becomes wiry, losing all impact.

WONGA WONGA VINE
(*Pandorea pandorana* 'Snow Bells')

There has been considerable work done to release improved forms of the species plant. This bears trusses of insignificant white flowers with burgundy spots. 'Snow Bells' produces masses of flowers mid-spring. These completely cover the vine with small white flowers.
Size: Can spread from 10–20 m from base.
Care: Prefers sun but will tolerate some shade with reduction in flower production. Grows best in moist, rich soil but is also quite tolerant of periodic dry conditions. Protection from frost is needed.
Uses: A vigorous climber for covering fences, structures and screening unsightly views in a hurry. Good as a nurse plant until the framework of the garden grows up.
Cultivars: *P. pandoreana* 'Golden Showers' has golden flowers blotched russet; 'Rosea' pale pink.
Related species: Bower of beauty vine (*P. jasminoides*) and white cultivar 'Lady Di'.

GUINEA FLOWER (*Hibbertia* species)

One of the most spectacular guinea flowers with a dense mat of starry gold flowers about 2cm across. It is a very desirable garden and container plant but it can be disappointing. Plants may grow fast and furiously for some months, then unexpectedly succumb to root rot, particularly *Phytophthora cinnamoni*. It grows readily from cuttings, so keep a few in reserve as pot plants. It should be tolerant of mild salt spray in coastal gardens.
Size: 15cm high, spread about 30–45cm.
Care: Sandy soil and provide shelter from frost.
Uses: Rockery, border planting, spilling over paths and steps. Try in a hanging basket or over the sides of large containers.
Related species: *H. scandens*, the guinea flower, is the best known, grow it as a climber or groundcover; *H. stricta*, small wiry stems; *H. stellaris*, starry guinea flower, a dwarf shrub and *H. empetrifolia* (pictured).

DRUMSTICKS (*Pycnosorus globosus* Syn. *Craspedia globosa*)

Drumsticks are a perennial plant grown both for foliage and for flowers. It can be treated as an annual and is grown from seed. The leaves are whitish with a silvery sheen and the flowers are borne on long stems suitable for cutting, a fact that gives it some commercial application. It is found from Queensland to Victoria and South Australia.
Size: Flower stems 80cm, the plant reaching about 30–40cm.
Care: Treat as a short-lived perennial or annual. Sow seed in almost any soil in full sun.

Uses: Spot colour in the front row of borders.
Related species: Billy buttons (*P. chrysanthus*) is said to cope with wet soils.

FAN FLOWER (*Scaevola aemula*)

Along with the brachycome hybrids, the fan flower is one of the great groundcover plants for the Australian garden. It spreads along and suckers freely, making it an excellent soil binder. Flowers are blue to mauve and freely produced from spring to summer in both full sun and part shade, though in the latter the flower cover will not be as dense. Many different cultivars are available. It is a reasonably good performer in coastal gardens with some protection from the front line saltspray.

Size: Low groundcover with 2–4m coverage.
Care: Easily grown from cuttings taken in spring or autumn. Sometimes dies back or drops dead in summer, possibly in alternating dry and humid conditions. Prefers good drainage and a humus-rich soil. Prune outer growths to encourage denser growth at the centre of the plant.
Uses: Baskets, urns and other containers, groundcover, driveways and path edges, binding banks.
Cultivars: *S. aemula* 'Purple Fanfare', 'Blue Fandango', 'Mauve Clusters', 'Fandancer', 'Blue Wonder'.

GRASSES AND GRASS-LIKE PLANTS

MAT RUSH (*Lomandra longifolia*)

Grass-like plants can be more successful in the home garden than true grasses. Lomandra has yellow flowers borne on spiky stems from spring to summer. These have a fragrance reminiscent of pineapples, and a long border of them gives a garden a very pleasant perfume.

Size: Height 1m, spread 1.2m.
Care: Plant in full sun to part shade. Reasonably frost hardy if grown in a sheltered position but not good at high altitudes. Unlike grasses, lomandra needs little care except the occasional cutback to keep the lime green foliage fresh. Grasses, on the other hand, need far more regular trimming and are more fire-prone in bush sites.
Uses: Borders, mass planting with other strap-leafed plants, rockeries, foliage and perfume. Tolerant of dry conditions and often used as roadside groundcover.
Related species: *L. confertifolia*, height 50cm, spread 70cm.

COMMON TUSSOCK GRASS (*Poa labillardieri*)

Poa has grey–green leaves and purplish flower heads, which may have an attractive weeping habit. It is ideal grown in clumps in a naturalistic garden. It is a cool-season grass, germinating in autumn and growing through winter. It flowers in spring and is generally past its peak by summer when it can become untidy. Like most grasses, poa is best in the first year of growth. By summer, parts of the centre of the tussock tend to die out, leaving a mass of yellowed straw. It seeds in late summer and autumn.

Size: 30–80cm, flower plumes can be 1m tall.

Care: Grasses can be cut right back in late summer to promote new growth and remove unsightly dead leaves. Most are short-lived and need to be replaced after two years. They are usually replaced from seed, so don't slash until seeds have ripened, but they can become weedy if allowed to self-seed.

Uses: Naturalistic gardens, foliage plants. If using grasses, be bold and plant several different grasses in mass groupings to vary texture, height and spread. Mix spring and summer flowering grasses to avoid an all-over parched earth look. *Themeda triandra* kangaroo grass is summer flowering and stays green for longer periods, especially if leaves are cut back in spring.

CREEPING RUSH (*Restio tetraphyllus*)

A fine plant for bog gardens and watercourses, restio is renowned for its feathery foliage with complementary foliage colours, from rust to lime green. It gives a lift to pond edges. It grows by a creeping rhizome, a useful habit for binding creek banks. It is adapted both to wet conditions and seasonal dryness. It is grown commercially as a filler plant for floristry, but has not crossed over to general garden use.

Size: 1m in height, with similar spread.

Care: Restio prefers a sandy, boggy soil and plenty of water, and should not be allowed to dry out if you want to keep its lush appearance. Propagate by division of the rhizomatous roots.

Uses: In ponds, as a foliage plant and for textural interest and colour in the native garden

Related species: *R. tremulus* from Western Australia.

BAMBOO SPEAR GRASS (*Stipa ramosissima*)

This is a large branching grass with tall leaves which are 1cm wide. It flowers in spring and summer. Seeds form in autumn and are then sown for main growth in winter. It tends to brown off over summer.

Size: Grass to 2m. Flower head to 50cm. Forms tufts about 30cm across.

Care: Grows well in damp conditions in full sun. It is a tufting plant that produces new growth from the side of the plant.

Uses: Massed planting and landscape effects in naturalistic garden styles.

Related species: Feather spear grass (*S. elegantissima*) needs mass planting as foliage is sparse. This is a grass that blends into the background when not in flower. These are tall feathery stems, brown to pink or straw coloured.

RIGHT
Anigozanthos 'Bush Baby'. Kangaroo paws are versatile plants. Use their strap leaves as grass substitutes or plant the flowers to brighten cottage gardens and bold modern planting drifts.

Plant Selection

garden CARE

PLANTING TECHNIQUES

Australian plants can be slow to adjust to new conditions when transplanted from a nursery container. Where possible, choose small tubestock rather than larger, advanced plants.

Tests under field conditions have proved that small plants settle in much quicker than advanced plants. For this reason many nurseries sell their stock in small plastic or reusable metal tubes. These are long and narrow, to encourage the young seedling or cutting to send its roots down to the base of the tube as it would naturally do. The plantlets should be set out in the ground as soon as possible.

Standard growing pots are squatter, with the result that roots head to the side of the container and spiral. They tend to be kept in pots for longer periods than tubes, growing a tighter rootball in the process. When planted out, the roots tend to be slower to spread out into the soil. Good results can still be obtained in well-prepared soil. Only specialist native growers have stock in tubes. Standard pots are more prevalent and better suited to a longer shelf life in the nursery.

PLANTING OUT

Once you have selected plant size, the steps for planting are standard for all plants. The step-by-step approach is the best way to describe the process.

Step 1

Ensure that the soil around the roots is thoroughly wetted before planting. The easiest way to make sure that the potting mix is soaked is to place the pot in a bucket of water. Potted plants sometimes develop dry pockets which are hard to saturate. Leave the pot in water for at least 30 minutes. You will see tiny bubbles escaping — this is simply air in the pot being displaced by moisture. It takes time for the water to soak into the moisture-retentive elements in the potting mix.

ABOVE

A newly planted native garden should allow plenty of room for spreading. These plants have been positioned on a sandy mound covered in mulch.

LEFT

A recently planted cottage garden with kangaroo paws, *Conostylis aculeata* and *Bauera rubioides*.

Step 2

While the pot is soaking, prepare the hole for planting. Loosen the soil around the immediate hole area with a fork or, if soil is hard and compacted or not previously cultivated, a mattock. This enables roots to spread into the surrounding soil. In compacted soil roots tend to stay within the planting hole and the hard soil acts just like the walls of the container the plant has come from.

Step 3

Dig the hole twice as wide as the pot but to the same depth as the container. The soil level in the container should remain level with the surrounding soil when planted out into the ground. Fill the hole with water and allow it to soak into the ground.

Step 4

Break up the soil at the bottom of the hole and remove the plant from the container. If the plant does not come easily from the pot, place your hand over the surface of the pot with the trunk between the second and third fingers. Tap the edge of the pot with a small garden tool or a solid surface and the plant should come away when the pot is turned upside down. Be careful at this stage not to disturb the roots. If the roots are matted and coiled, go to step 5. If not, support the base of the root as you lower it into the hole. Simply cut away the plastic on one side if the plant is in a plastic grow-bag.

Step 5

If roots are coiled at the base, straighten them where possible. If severely coiled, prune roots where they begin to twist. If planted intact, the roots will not be able to secure the plant and will continue to grow in a spiral, eventually strangling the plant.

Step 6

Place plant in the hole and refill soil around the root ball. Tamp the soil lightly with your hand to remove air pockets but take care not to compact the soil.

Step 7

Thoroughly water the plant to settle the soil around the roots.

Step 8

Mulch soil with organic matter or gravel to conserve moisture. In arid climates or if planting during a dry period, ring a low mound of soil about 30cm out from the trunk. This acts as a well, trapping water and directing it to the roots.

PLANTING THE ARID GARDEN

Large parts of Western and South Australia, the Northern Territory and western Queensland contain vast tracts of arid lands where traditional gardens are hard to establish. In an effort to relieve the monotony of brown and grey found in our landscape, many outback gardeners often persist with a bore-watered lawn. But for those willing to try, there are plenty of natives worth trying and a few guidelines to make the task easier.

A thorough site examination will provide information about the landform and water flow. Try to maintain any existing vegetation, as this will aid in the establishment of new plants, offering them shade and protection. Then use the natural drainage patterns for planting. Water tends to flow along the existing slopes, and plants obtain more moisture here in the same way plants in a valley are lusher than those on high ground. You can create shallow depression drains called swales to direct water to or away from specific groups of plants. Water coming off structures or draining from paths can be redirected using swales too. They are often filled with a gravel mulch to prevent them silting up. Group plants according to their water needs and place thirstier ones along these swales.

Choose plants which are known to be drought tolerant or native to your area. Many arid areas follow a Mediterranean pattern of wet winter followed by dry summer. Take advantage of the wetter and cooler conditions of winter to grow delicate annuals and mass displays of perennials and biennials such as Sturt's desert pea. A good shrub and tree cover will help cool the garden and prevent evaporation during the summer months.

FERTILISING

Australian plants can never be planted and then forgotten. Like all plants, they need to be cared for and that includes fertilising and watering, especially during the growing season and in hard times of drought.

On the whole, Australian soils have low nutrient levels and are often sandy and fast draining and therefore easily leached of soil nutrients. Most are low in phosphorus, and plants have evolved to cope with these conditions. The gardener familiar with exotic gardening will need to adjust techniques before embarking on a garden of native plants.

The first issue is that standard garden fertilisers are formulated for phosphorus-tolerant exotics. Phosphorus can be fatal to many Australian plants. Proteaceae have the highest level of intolerance. This includes the Banksia, Telopea, Grevillea, Isopogon and Dryandra genera. These and other plants have developed a way to extract minute amounts of phosphorus from the soil by means of an acid excreted from the roots to dissolve phosphorus. Additional amounts obtained from fertiliser can kill them. Other phosphorus-intolerant natives include *Acacia*, *Baeckia*, *Bauera*, *Boronia*, *Eutaxia*, *Hypocalymma*, *Leschenaultia* and *Pultenea*. So we need to use fertilisers specially formulated for Australian native plants. These are usually labelled as 'native plant food' or 'Australian native plant food'. All are low in phosphorus. If unsure, look at the NPK (nitrogen/phosphorus/potassium) for one with not more than 2 per cent phosphorus. Some are available in the familiar powder form but slow release pellets such as Osmocote® or Nutricote® are other good ways to apply fertiliser. They are released to the plants over a long period and are safe for most native plants.

The second point to consider is the texture of your soil. The qualities of clay and sandy soils vary in the way they are able to deliver nutrients to plants and in their ability to conserve nutrients in the soil. Knowing the textures of the soil you are working with helps you to make informed decisions about your own fertiliser requirements.

Clay soils are richer in nutrients, and many Australian plant gardeners find that there is no need to add fertiliser at all if soil is clay. The natural levels of nutrients are sufficient for healthy and sustained growth. In this case, mulching, which is more soil conditioning than fertilising, maintains soil moisture and temperature and replenishes humus.

Sandy soils are low in nutrients and generally fast draining. Water draining through sand quickly leaches out nutrients, but in nature, organic matter on the surface continually breaks down and replaces nitrogen and potassium. Mulching and replacement of organic matter is needed in the home garden to achieve the same result.

Some organic fertilisers such as blood and bone, cottonseed meal and well-rotted horse or cow manure are good if used in moderation. The evidence suggests that many Australian plants are sensitive to overfeeding and small amounts, more frequently applied, is a good policy. Slow release fertilisers do this for you, releasing nutrients for up to nine months in controlled doses.

If using organic fertilisers, follow the patterns of growth laid down by the seasons. Most plants grow quickly in spring followed by a period of summer dormancy to correspond with dryness and heat. Plants respond to increased temperature and decreased moisture levels by slowing down as a means of survival. When conditions moderate in autumn, growth resumes. Feeding in spring and autumn is therefore recommended. Always soak the soil before applying fertiliser and again afterwards, so that the plant food is washed into the soil. Watering converts fertiliser into a soluble form ready for the roots to absorb. Feeding in the midst of a hot, dry summer, especially in areas with a Mediterranean climate, is essentially wasteful and unnecessary, so wait for milder conditions when rain can dissolve nutrients.

Feed plants when young, but only after the roots have had a chance to establish and break out of the rootball that bound them in the growing container. A light burst of nitrogen and other trace elements during good growing conditions will strengthen their ability to withstand environmental stresses, such as heat and dry conditions.

OPPOSITE

Fertilising a wild garden which uses the existing vegetation as the basis for a garden would be destructive to many plants.

PRUNING TECHNIQUES

One of the worst of the misconceptions about native plants is that they should not be pruned, and should be left in their 'natural' state. In fact, it is arguable that even more than many exotics, natives need pruning to keep them from premature aging and untidiness.

THE BENEFITS OF PRUNING

Australian plants, like all plants, have evolved to regrow when broken, damaged or eaten. Pruning is simply an artificial way of replacing nature's ravages with an ordered system of rejuvenation and revitalisation. Many natives produce copious quantities of seed; this is a means to keep the plants' existence viable in a harsh environment, but it hastens aging. As seed production saps the plant's energy, the plant produces fewer and fewer flowers, hence losing its purpose in life, and older plants are replaced by younger ones. Pruning lengthens the potential lifespan by impeding the aging process. The plant continues to produce vital new growth and plenty of blooms.

HOW TO PRUNE

It is advisable to prune during the growing season, depending on the results and effects you want to produce. The simplest timetable is to prune immediately after flowering, to prevent seed formation, especially on those bushes such as callistemons, leptospermums and melaleucas. These produce unattractive seedpods lasting for many years along increasingly leafless stems. Many native plants flower in late winter and early spring and many plants can be pruned as a single operation by cutting off the spent flower stems immediately after flowering and before new growth commences. This has the effect of encouraging multiple shoots from the old flower point instead of single or widely separated shoots, as seen in bottlebrushes. The resulting plant is tighter, denser and more fully foliaged than the one left unpruned. The extra stems produce more flowers as a result.

Natives sometimes fail to regrow from hard woody branches, especially if they have not previously been pruned, so a cautious approach would be to prune to an existing leaf or plump leaf bud. If bare branches send up new shoots further down the stem, plants can safely be pruned back hard during the growing season, if this is

ABOVE AND BELOW

The dwarf apple *Angophora hispida*, grown as a copsed specimen. With pruning, new growth will develop into a more rounded shape.

desirable, to correct the shaping of the bush. As a general rule, up to one third of the last season's growth can be pruned from branches.

Pruning also maintains plants at manageable size or shape. Pruning to produce a topiary or hedge shape can be done throughout the growing season, starting in spring. Trimming is continued through summer and often into autumn, though if flowers are required of the trained bush, it may be necessary to complete final trimming in January or February to enable wood to mature and produce. The time needed to produce buds for the following season depends on the individual plant, and you will need to observe plants carefully.

Tip pruning prevents shoots becoming long, and encourages new branches to form after the initial post-flowering pruning. Start as soon as the plant goes into the ground by pinching out the growing tips. This encourages side shoots to form, which will produce a bushy plant.

Broken and damaged branches should be pruned to remove jagged edges and produce a clean cut. This heals faster and reduces the chance of disease entering uneven surfaces or pests finding a safe refuge from predators.

PRUNING SOME FAVOURITE PLANTS

New South Wales Christmas bush should be pruned after bracts fade, usually late December or early January, and before new growth starts. They can be pruned into hard wood provided the plant has not become senile or old.

Waratahs are pruned as the flowers begin to fade and before the new shoots appear from the top of the flower. Prune back to 5cm above previous year's growth. Advanced plants can also be severely pruned by cutting back to the lignotuber at ground level. Commercial growers do this approximately once every ten years.

To stimulate flower production on callistemons or bottlebrushes, prune at the base of the flower as it fades. Cutting back beyond this will encourage a denser shape but at the expense of flowers in the short term.

Prostantheras (mint bushes) can be sheared back about one third to remove old flowers.

Grevilleas can be severely pruned back to hard wood and will reshoot provided the plant is healthy and reasonably mature.

REMEMBER

- Be diligent with tip pruning.
- Cut away dead twigs or branches to present plants at their best.
- Prune off dead flowers, especially those on callistemons.
- Prune after flowering to increase flower density and remove unwanted growth, particularly arid area plants which become woody and misshapen.
- Don't tolerate plants that do not perform well, ie are subject to scale, insect attack, fail to flower or do not appear happy where you are growing them.
- Remove and replace plants that are past their use-by date.

LEFT
An example of a standard grevillea. Provided grevilleas are healthy and mature, they will reshoot after being severely pruned back.

MULCHING

Mulching has many functions in a garden. In a country known for its heat and dryness, it is an essential gardening practice. It conserves moisture, maintains an even soil temperature, suppresses weeds and, in the case of organic mulches, adds nutrients to the soil.

While organic mulching is the most common, we can just as easily mulch with inorganic substances such as gravel, stone, blue metal chips, decomposed granite and coarse river sand. Indeed, if you are growing dry climate plants or live in an area prone to bushfire, these are preferable.

LAYING MULCH

Mulch can be applied any time, but early spring and autumn are preferable. If applied too late in autumn in cool areas, mulches can tend to keep soil cool over winter and into spring when it would otherwise be warming up. Mulch applied in summer in hot, dry areas may be too late to take advantage of spring rains and may prevent moisture absorption when rains come towards autumn. Local conditions vary and the latter would not apply to wet summer areas.

If soil is dry, thoroughly soak the area before laying mulch down. If conditions have been dry for some time, it may be necessary to apply a soil wetting agent. Different types can be applied, either in a dry form or as a foliar spray using a watering can or hose end sprayer. These agents break down the surface tension of the soil, which prevents water penetration after rain. Light tilling achieves a similar effect.

Apply a layer of compost, leaf litter or wood chips to a depth of 8–10cm. Make sure when laying it that any organic mulch is not resting against the trunks of trees and shrubs, as this can cause rotting of the trunk and other fungal problems that can prove fatal.

Water thoroughly to moisten the mulch and check that water is penetrating the surface. You should see if the soil is wet if you scrape the mulch from a small area. If dry, lightly break the surface and water deeply.

After two or three months, especially in summer, mulches might need topping up. If conditions have been moist and ideal, the materials may have broken down. Re-cover areas where mulch is thin and water in.

RIGHT
Even plants in arid areas will cope with regular pruning, but mulching ensures that they receive sufficient moisture to sustain the extra leaf cover.

LOW WATER USE

A garden is an aesthetic ideal and relies on plants looking good through good care — this includes watering. Another of the great misconceptions about Australian plants is that they thrive without watering. While it is true that many are tolerant of dry conditions, it is also true that they grow well only when moisture is present.

Plants, whether Australian or from any other part of the globe, may *survive* drought, but they won't *thrive* unless there is a regular and reliable water supply. Desert plants have slightly different needs, as too much water will cause their roots to rot, but even then, many in the wild are subjected to periodic inundation by flood.

Garden watering is, however, one of the major users of our precious water supplies, and authorities are keen to reduce consumption. Planting native plants is one way, but establishing a garden of Australian plants requires regular, deep watering until they are able to withstand the rigours of the climate. Two years is a reasonable time for the average native plant to develop the root system it needs to sustain itself.

Installing a drip irrigation system is the most effective means of delivering water to the roots of young plants where it can be taken up. An added benefit is the reduction of humidity for plants preferring a drier atmosphere. The dripper holes can be plugged and then reused in another area once the plant is well established. After two years, most will be able to thrive on the natural rainfall if proper plant husbandry techniques, such as mulching, are used. Another method is to dig shallow swales across slopes to direct water to needy plants.

In dry periods, you will still need to water; and drippers can supply a deep soaking with little wastage to evaporation. Garden sprinklers are guilty of wastage on two counts. On the one hand they throw water into the air, where it is blown by the wind and washed down paths and into drains and wasted. They also leave a high proportion of their output exposed to evaporation as droplets on leaves or on the soil.

A timer will ensure that water is applied only for the necessary period. For a good soaking using drip irrigation, a period of one to two hours once a fortnight — perhaps more frequently in dry times — is sufficient. When conditions are good, watering may not be needed at all.

Rainforest plants require more water and heavier mulching than plants from dry inland plains or dry sclerophyll forests. Many will also benefit from water droplets on their leaves, as their natural habitat is far more humid than that for the latter plants. Sprinklers are ideal for these plants, but to reduce water use, water in the early evening when the sun has gone down, and add a few water features to the planting area. These can be decorative bowls and large dishes filled with water or ornamental ponds.

ABOVE

Water is directed to roots by gently sloping the ground towards the plants. This device is known as a swale (page 197) and is similar to the contour banks used in agriculture and pastures to force water to flow towards dams.

PROPAGATION

Propagating your own plants is a worthwhile hobby and most methods are relatively easy. It is a good way to increase your stock cheaply and to grow hard-to-find plants, especially indigenous plants rarely stocked by nurseries.

GATHERING SEED

Seed is a simple and economical way to raise plants. Seed is available from commercial suppliers or it can be collected from your own or friends' gardens. Seed needs to be mature before collection; for winter- and spring-flowering plants, expect to harvest seed from early to late summer. Peas are normally ready for collection about December, but are often eaten by caterpillars.

Before either storage or sowing, seed needs to be cleaned and prepared. Seeds contained within fleshy fruits should be dried and the outer covering removed. A fine sieve will remove the covering from most dried seed. Banksia seeds should be placed in a warm oven to open the capsules.

In your records, include an identification label and note where seed was collected and the date, if storing.

RAISING SEED

Some seeds need to be prepared before planting. Any member of the Fabaceae or pea family including acacia, senna, bossaia and chorizema needs to be treated to break open the hard covering or *testa* surrounding the actual seed. With larger seeds, rub them on sandpaper to abrade the coating, but with smaller seeds, it is better to place seeds in a cup and pour boiling water over them. The seeds are ready when the covering softens and swells. This may require overnight soaking.

Some seeds need smoke treatment before successful germination. Fire, or more particularly smoke, triggers the germination process for many plants, including many of the well-known Western Australian plants such as *Leschenaultia*, *Anigozanthos*, *Verticordia* and *Pimelea*. King's Park Botanical Gardens have pioneered the use of a solution of smoked water containing the chemicals found in smoke to simulate the effect of fire. This is now being marketed and has proved a boon to home gardeners. Ask your local nursery or use the contact details in the resource list on page 215.

SOWING

Sow seed in a prepared seed-raising mix in a seed tray or in smaller pots. Avoid sowing seed thickly — mix very fine seed with builders' sand for more even distribution. Sowing too deep is one of the commonest causes of failure, especially with fine seed; in most cases, pressing into the surface of the mix is sufficient. Always ensure that seeds remain moist once sown. Fine misting with a spray bottle or bottom soaking are ideal watering methods for small seed.

When seed germinates, it should be 'pricked out' when the first true leaf forms. Seedlings are very tender at this stage and need careful handling. They can often be lifted with the tip of a pencil if very small, and even though it is a fiddly process, it produces healthier seedlings with strong root formation. To transplant, use a dibble or pointed stick to make a deep hole in the new container and carefully allow the roots to fall. Back fill, ensuring the roots remain in the downward position.

A fungal disease called damping off sometimes affects seedlings. To prevent it, a precautionary spray with Bordeaux mixture is recommended.

CUTTINGS

Unlike seed, cuttings can be obtained at most times of the year. Cuttings have the advantage of producing a clone of the original plant, unlike seeds, where an enormous amount of variation can occur.

Stem cuttings prove successful for a large proportion of Australian shrubs. The best part of the plant to use is a tip cutting from 5–10cm long. The actual length of the cutting will depend on the distance between the internodes; the longer the distance, the longer the cutting.

Make the cut just below the node with a sharp knife or secateurs. The cut must be clean, so ensure that your tools are freshly sharpened before use. It's not a bad idea to wipe the blade with methylated spirits if taking cuttings from a range of plants, to prevent possible spread of fungal diseases.

Remove leaves and any flower buds from the bottom two-thirds. Cut large leaves in half or by two thirds to reduce moisture loss through transpiration.

Place cuttings in a pot containing equal parts coarse river sand, perlite and peat moss. No nutrients are needed at this stage but drainage and moisture retention are essential — the two latter ingredients achieve this aim. If perlite is not available, an equal amount of sand and peat or a peat-substitute can be used.

Soft tip cutttings are often taken in spring for shrubs such as prostanthera or at any time for herbaceous plants such as brachycome daisies, climbing plants or *Plectranthus argentatus*. These cuttings may need a glass or plastic cover to prevent their drying out. Place the containers in a warm, shaded place. If placed where sunlight strikes the transparent cover, the young cuttings can cook.

Semi hardwood cuttings are taken from woody shrubs such as *Grevillea*, *Callistemon*, *Waratah* and *Thryptomene*. This wood grew as fresh growth in spring and hardens over the following season. For instance, tips that grew well in spring would be ready early to mid-summer.

DIVISION

As with exotic perennials, many Australian perennials can be divided. Brachycomes, scaevolas and native violets that spread either by stolons or suckering shoots can be divided at any time. Kangaroo paws should be lifted and divided in autumn. Cut the leaves back to 5–10cm above ground level and replant in a prepared bed.

ABOVE

Flower buds of *Eucalyptus caesia*. Many keen collectors gather seed before it is ripe. These flower buds will not be ready to pick as seed capsules for many months. They should be large, plump and greyer in colour. Viable seed is found only when the capsule is matured.

PESTS AND DISEASES

THE CLEAN GARDEN
One of the outstanding motivations for growing Australian plants is their attractiveness to native birds and insects, which are enticed by a plentiful supply of food. Nectar attracts insects (and some birds and mammals) and insects attract even more birds to feast on them. Fortunately, native gardens seem less prone to insect and fungal attack than those composed almost entirely of exotics. Exotics imported many of their own pests when they arrived, and the problem for us is that their natural predators did not arrive with them, so the impact of pests is more severe. This is one of the defining benefits of the native plant garden. Insects have evolved to feed on native plants but they are subject to natural and organic controls. Our birds, animals and beneficial insects are the natural predators, and can cope with the clean up. Using chemical agents can often be a last resort and generally best avoided.

Many gardeners are unduly worried about any change in the appearance of their garden plants. Their first assumption is often that it must be due to an insect pest or a disease, and they reach for the spray gun. But many changes, such as the appearance of rust-coloured spores on staghorns or birds' nest ferns, are due to natural causes and require no treatment. Generally, the more you spray, the more you need to spray, and this is particularly true with gardens of Australian plants.

Diagnosis
The first step in dealing with pests and diseases is diagnosis, knowing what is a problem and identifying it as accurately as possible. Lenticels on banksia trunks, leaf spots and marks, spores on ferns, scribbly gum marks, lignotubers and epicormic buds on eucalypts are all naturally occurring, non-harmful and definitely not pests. Natural marks are usually regular and evenly distributed, while marks caused by pests and diseases are irregular, so look for variations and abnormal marks or colourings in leaves.

As part of your diagnosis, any changes in the way you may have cared for or maintained a plant or the garden as a whole should be remembered. Drying out caused by extreme heat or wind, disruption to regular watering regimes, animals fouling plants, poor nutrition or excess fertilising are all possible causes of changes in leaf colour and condition. Only when you have exhausted these as possible causes should you assume that there may be a pest problem.

Consider
- Plant's age and size. The character of leaves, trunk and bark in older plants often changes and over-mature plants are also more susceptible to disease and insects, as their immune system breaks down with age.
- Location of the problem. Is it all over or limited in spread? If the 'problem' is evenly distributed, it may be a natural appearance of the plant, but if it is isolated to one section it is more likely to be pest- or disease-related.
- Severity of the problem. A severe attack may seriously weaken a plant, but a healthy plant usually fights back and resists attack. The amber secretion on many trees is a natural method used by plants to smother insect attack. It is a good indicator of the extent of any infestation.
- Appearance of the problem. Note how it manifests itself. Look for leaf texture, colour, marks, trunk and stem punctures, weakened stems, pattern of leaf chewing. A thorough search will show up much of the above and you can make an assessment of how it is affecting the plant's growth.

Narrow the diagnosis to define the problem
A proper diagnosis requires you to be fastidious in examining the plant systematically and thoroughly. Look under leaves and on top; check the leaf axils, again top and bottom, for the presence of insects or irregularities, and inspect stems for fissions, tears, cuts or holes. Look for sawdust, caterpillar frass (droppings), webs, black marks or silvering of leaves. If signs of caterpillar damage (such as chewed leaves and black wastes) are apparent, but a thorough inspection fails to find them, look in the top layers of the soil. Some rest by day in litter or under the bark of trees, only emerging at dusk.

Garden pests are varied and if you learn to recognise the categories and the most common symptoms, solutions are easier to find. Roughly, problems fall into two categories: fungal disease or insect attack.

Fungal diseases are divided into root rot or leaf and stem diseases. Root problems are the harder to diagnose, obviously, because the problem is out of sight and the symptoms may not appear until the disease has taken hold. Leaf and stem diseases include rust, powdery mildew and ink disease.

Garden Care

Insect attack is most simply divided into leaf-eating, boring or sapsucking pests. Understanding whether a problem is caused by one or the other, is half the solution. In general, sapsuckers are harder to shift and more likely to require the use of chemicals.

Sapsuckers are a varied and common group and include leafminers, thrips, aphids, lerps, mealy bugs, mites, nematodes, psyllids and scale. Caterpillars, grasshoppers and some beetle larvae are the main leaf-eating pests, though snails and slugs can also do damage. Borers are mostly beetles and moth larvae.

BENEFICIAL INSECTS

Not all insects are bad. Many are natural controllers of pest species and should be encouraged. Spraying is undiscriminating and kills the ones you need to keep as well as the ones you don't, so avoid using chemicals except in the most extreme infestations. Even then it is worth going over the tree or bush to remove any beneficial insects where possible. Gardeners and garden books can become obsessive about controlling insects so it's worth remembering these friendly ones and emphasising their importance to good garden management. Too often they are added on as an afterthought.

The best known are the ladybirds, which eat aphids or larvae of mites. The one exception is the 26- or 28-spotted ladybird, which is a leaf eater. It is bigger than most other ladybirds and the colour is duller.

Lacewings are a common but little-recognised insect. Their name comes from the variations on their opaque wings. They have a voracious appetite for hoverflies, praying mantis, leaf-eating caterpillars, assassin bugs and predatory mites.

FUNGAL DISEASES

Root fungi (*Armillaria mellea*)

Sometimes known as mushroom root rot due to the strong mushroomy smell of an infected area, this fungus commonly attacks native trees as well as commercial fruit trees. Plants under stress are more susceptible. Large trees such as figs and other street trees in public places subjected to root compaction either by foot traffic or car parking are particularly at risk. Roots infected with the fungus are covered with white threads. Brown or yellow toadstools appear in humid autumn weather — these are another indicator of its existence.

Fungi may indicate the presence of *Armillaria* root rot.

Wilting occurs on trees infected with root rot.

The New Native Garden

Native and exotic grasses can be affected by damping off.

• Control — remove and burn off infected stumps.
• Chemical — soil may need to be fumigated with methyl bromide, a dangerous chemical that is only applied by skilled operators with a licence from state departments of agriculture.

Phytophthora cinnamomi

Infection is often seen as dying off of tip growth and failure to put on any new growth. The fungus attacks the small feeder roots and spreads to other roots slowly and systematically. Larger plants usually die from secondary causes such as drought, fire or frost, due to the weakening and depletion of the root system. It is usually spread in water flowing from one infected plant to another. Young plants may wilt and die with little warning.

• Control — a raised bed can control drainage; lime and dolomite are thought to inhibit the fungus. Some experts have suggested adding a layer of limestone chips under the soil of susceptible plants. These include species from the sand plains of Western Australia, *Angophora costata* and many eucalypts.
• Chemical — drench soil with Fongarid ® (1 gram per litre of water).

Pythium spp.

Pythium or damping off generally affects the roots of grasses and is the cause of damping off in seedlings. It can kill seedlings before they emerge or after the first leaf stage. Grass may develop dead patches in wet weather. Poorly drained soil is a common cause of damping off. *Phytophthora* may also be responsible.

• Control - avoid overwatering, especially in humid weather, and avoid feeding with high-nitrogen fertilisers when plants or grasses are young. Improve drainage.
• Chemical — drench soil with Fongarid® or copper oxychloride.

Rhizoctonia spp.

Mat plants that hug the ground are most susceptible. The centre of the plant dies and a thin web of fungal mycelia are apparent. The roots beneath these patches are also rotten. *Leschenaultia formosa* and *Scleranthus biflorus* are worst affected.

• Control — spray with benomyl (Benlate®).

LEAF AND STEM DISEASES

Ink disease

Ink disease occurs on kangaroo paws (*Anigozanthos* species) particularly *A. manglesii*, the floral emblem of Western Australia. If severe, all the leaves are blackened and the plant dies within two years.

• Control — water from the ground and avoid wetting leaves. Cut out infected and dead leaves. Choose cultivars with resistance to the disease.
• Chemical — there is no complete control, but spraying with mancozeb helps reduce incidence.

Powdery mildew

Powdery mildew is found in warm, humid conditions and affects the leaves of eucalyptus seedlings. Powdery spots appear on leaves and may spread to cover the entire leaf.

• Control — spray with benomyl (Benlate®) or lime sulphur. Do not use the latter in hot weather or if plants are in dry soil as it can burn leaves.

Rust

Rusts are more common on exotic plants, but some have recently been reported on native plants. Rust appears as brown blotches on the leaves, often on the undersides.

• Control — spray with zineb or sulphur.

Garden Care

Ink disease on kangaroo paw leaves.　　Powdery mildew.　　Sooty mould results from insect attack.

Sooty mould

Sooty mould is an unsightly secondary fungus which grows on the honeydew secretions of mealy bugs, aphids and psyllids. It affects the leaf's role in photosynthesis. Once the insect which causes the honeydew is removed, sooty mould generally disappears. This is assisted if you can remove the ants which nurse the insects.

• Control — destroy the above insects and hose leaves with a jet of water.

LEFT
This example of rust on a bean leaf shows the tell-tale rust-coloured lumps associated with this fungus.

SAPSUCKERS
Aphids

Aphids are not a great problem on native plants, but they can sometimes be seen on the flower spikes of orchids and on the stems of native daisies, *Sollya* and *Pandorea* species. The sap is sucked from soft stems of new growth and flower buds, weakening the plant and interfering with reproduction if found in large numbers. They reproduce rapidly and are often attended by ants. These feed on honeydew secreted by the aphids and discourage natural predators from controlling the pests. Aphids like temperate conditions and are not seen in hot, dry weather or in very cold or wet conditions.

• Control — ladybirds, wasps, hoverflies. Wasps and lacewings feed on colonies of aphids. Severe localised colonies can be wiped off with the fingers or hosed off with a hard jet of water. In the latter case, they may return.

• Chemical — spray with dimethoate (Rogor®).

Leafminers

This is a name given to the larvae of many different insects including sawflies, wasps, flies or moths. The larvae burrow under leaves, producing tunnels which often end in a small blister. The larvae can be traced and are usually visible as a small raised lump within the 'mined' leaf. They can be killed manually, but this is a tedious job. An alternative is to remove the infected leaves and destroy them.

The New Native Garden

Aphids are sap-sucking insects.

Psyllids on the underside of eucalypt leaves.

Look for leaf miner tunnels in natives that are similar to these, on cinerarias.

• Chemical control consists of spraying with a systemic insecticide such as dimethoate.
• Plants affected are *Acacia* species (especially *A. podalyriifolia*), *Eucalyptus* spp., *Lomatia* spp. and *Acmena* species.

Lerps and psyllids

The insect is called a psyllid, and the outer waxy covering is called the lerp. Psyllids are part of the sap-sucking Hemiptera family, which includes scale, aphids and mealy bugs. The adults are winged insects which lay eggs on leaves. The larvae build a protective cover, the lerp, and feed on the leaf, causing unsightly bumps, particularly in *Eucalyptus* and *Syzygium* species. Severe infestations can completely defoliate some ornamental *Ficus* species.
• Control — the problem is usually controlled by natural predators such as birds and insects.
• Chemical — spray with dimethoate (Rogor®) or maldison.

Mealy bugs

Mealy bugs are white insects covered with a cottony substance. They congregate where leaf stalks join the stem or on roots where ants have built tunnels they can move along. They often appear in colonies. Like aphids, they are nursed by ants, which carry the eggs to new locations and deter natural predators. They are a major pest of container plants both indoors and in greenhouses and bush houses. They attack ferns, *Araucaria* spp., palms and soft-stemmed plants.

• Control — outdoors they are controlled by predators unless stressed.
• Chemical — spray with white oil alone (20ml per litre of water), dimethoate and white oil combined, fenthion or omethoate.

Mites

Mites are tiny insects related to ticks and spiders. They can cause deformation of stems or severe leaf damage and curling. Some spread viruses and others secrete growth regulators which can produce galls or a phenomena called 'witches' brooms', an abnormality of flattened, distorted leaves best described by the name. They can become resistant to insecticides and biological control has been developed for some species, notably the two-spotted mite. Mites attack many native rainforest plants. Two-spotted mite attacks waratah, hoya and banksia. They are more common in hot, dry weather.
• Control — lacewings, ladybirds and predatory aphids feed on mites but insecticides kill these beneficial insects as well as the mites. Hose leaves in dry weather to discourage them.
• Chemical — spray with dimethoate or difocol applied to the underside of leaves.

Scale

Scales are a serious problem of Australian plants. Scales are either hard or soft. There are hundreds of indigenous scales

Garden Care

Adult thrips are often hard to see.

White wax scale commonly attacks wattles, tea trees and boronias.

Two-spotted mites cause a mottled, yellowing effect on leaves.

plus many that have been introduced. Most produce a waxy covering, ranging in colour from white to pink or brown. Different species attack different plants, especially wattles and tea trees, members of the Mimosaceae and Myrtaceae families respectively. *Pittosporum undulatum* and boronias are often affected. The treatment is roughly the same no matter what the species. As they do with other members of the order Hemiptera, ants cultivate and protect the scale insect, so control of ants is paramount. Scales produce honeydew, which can lead to sooty mould on leaves and stems. If severe, this reduces photosynthesis.

• Control — for low-level scale attack, use a toothbrush dipped in white oil solution and scrub off waxy coatings. Spray white oil on large plants extensively covered by scale. White oil is a relatively safe control made from oil blended with water. It prevents the wax adhering to stems and leaves.

Spittlebugs

Spittlebugs are related to scale but produce a frothy substance like spittle around the nymphs. They feed on *Eucalyptus, Acacia, Baeckea, Casuarina* and *Callistemon* species.

• Control — wash off insects and spittle with a hose.

Thrips

Thrips are tiny insects that are often not noticed by gardeners, and they can cause serious problems, such as bud drop and leaf damage. You are more likely to see the insects' droppings sticking to the leaf. Thrips eat by rasping and sucking juices from the surface of the leaf, destroying the leaf's ability to photosynthesise sunlight. Different thrips feed on different plants. Natives affected by thrips include: New South Wales Christmas bush (*Ceratopetalum gummiferum*) — damage to flower; calyx falls before changing colour.

Moreton Bay fig and other species of *Ficus* — sucking causes leaves to curl and drop off.

Bottlebrushes (*Callistemon* spp) — unsightly damage to leaf, preventing transpiration; deformed flowers.

• Control — thrips are most apparent during dry weather and can often be controlled by hosing leaves regularly to increase humidity. On large plants hosing is often the only effective control.

• Chemical — spray with dimethoate or maldison if other measures fail.

NEMATODES – LEAF-EATING INSECTS

Caterpillars

Caterpillars are usually the larvae of moths and butterflies, though sawflies are a type of wasp and the larvae look like black lepidopterous caterpillars.

• Control — controlling them can be difficult, as most need to come into direct contact with an insecticide. Most

The New Native Garden

Larvae of the longicorn beetle tunnel into healthy wood.

Like most of their kind, steel blue sawflies cluster on stems or trunks.

Callistemon sawfly skeletonise leaves.

butterfly larvae cause little damage, but there are some exceptions. Organically, the biological control, *Bacillus thuringiensis* (B.t) found in the preparation Dipel®, is a natural bacterium that kills many lepidoptera larvae. It causes a stomach disease in caterpillars which kills them. It is best if sprayed so it comes into contact with the larvae. Spray the underside of leaves as well as the top.

• Chemical — one should be cautious when using chemicals on caterpillars as many insecticides are ineffective. Carbaryl is a good drenching spray for caterpillar control. Systemic insecticides are rarely used for these larvae and there is rarely much point in using one of the more potent systemic poisons on them.

Teatree webbing caterpillars
Cluster-feeding caterpillars, the tea-tree webbing caterpillars shelter by day in a web between stems. The web can be removed but it is wise to lay a sheet of paper below, as the larvae often drop to the ground when the web is disturbed. Spraying can be difficult as the threads hinder effective contact with the caterpillars. A wetting agent such as white oil helps insecticide stick to larvae. Use gloves to drag webs out of branches. Infestation is often more severe in shade or where the bush provides dense cover. Several species have the same webbing habit and may attack baeckea, melaleuca, thryptomene and kunzea as well as leptospermum.

Processionary caterpillars
These hairy caterpillars belong to several different families and can cause major defoliation. Some people are susceptible to skin irritations after touching them. They appear most commonly on white cedar (*Melia azederach*) and acacias in arid zones. They are the larvae of a rather plain moth (*Ochrogaster lunifer*). They get their name from the habit of travelling in single file along the branches. They shelter in bags (made up of their silken threads) during daylight, feeding only at night, and this habit makes them relatively easy to eliminate. Remove shelters during the day when they are filled with caterpillars or, alternatively, wrap a piece of sacking near the base of the trunk. Caterpillars will rest there and can be destroyed by spraying or squashing.

Cup moth
Cup moths feed on the leaves of *Eucalyptus* spp. and can cause serious defoliation. They have spines at both ends of the body and are brightly coloured. These spines inflict a painful sting, which can be alleviated or neutralised by dabbing ammonia on the wounded area. These insects do not normally appear in large numbers. If they do, treat it as an indicator that the tree could be under severe stress from another cause. Examples include poor drainage, drought or chemical imbalance in the soil.
• Control — Dipel® will control small infestations, but use carbaryl or maldison for bigger problems.

Garden Care

Tea tree web moths leave unsightly nests.

Saunders case moth is a solitary insect and rarely damages trees.

The larvae of hawk moths are large but not likely to require control.

Case moths

Case moths construct a twig-encrusted woven bag around them as protection. They feed on a range of native trees including *Eucalyptus* species. The female moth is wingless, living within the case for all its life. No control is necessary.

Sawflies

Sawflies of different species attack *Callitris*, *Callistemon* and *Angophora* species. They are a clustering larvae and feed by swarming on a localised area, causing severe damage by completely defoliating branches. When disturbed they raise both ends threateningly and exude a pungent liquid which is not hazardous. The rear 'spine' does not contain a sting, as is sometimes thought. Control by clipping off an eaten growing tip containing a cluster of caterpillars, then squash or spray the caterpillars.

Kurrajong leaf roller

The larvae of these insects form a shelter by webbing several leaves together, creating a series of unsightly paper bag-like nests all over the tree. They feed at night and rest by day. Larvae are apt to fall if their shelter is disturbed, so a sheet needs to be placed underneath to catch them. Members of the *Brachychiton* family, including Illawarra flame trees and kurrajongs, are favoured. Spray with carbaryl or omethoate (Folimat®).

Citrus butterfly

There are three types of swallowtail butterfly that feed on these exotic citrus and native species: *Eremocitrus glauca*, *Microcitrus australasica* and *Eriostemon myoporoides*. They are the small dingy swallowtail (*Papilio anactus*), the canopus butterfly (*P. canopus*), found near Darwin and coastal parts of Western Australia and Northern Territory, and the orchard butterfly (*P. aegeus aegeus*). None of these beautiful butterflies should be destroyed. They rarely cause damage and if found on small natives relocating them onto larger citrus is the solution.

Emperor gum moth

This is one of the world's largest and most beautiful moths. It often feeds on *Eucalyptus* spp. but rarely causes serious damage. If found on a young tree, relocate the caterpillar to a larger one.

Double-headed hawk moth

This moth feeds on members of the Proteaceae such as *Persoonias*, *Grevilleas* and *Banksias*. Again, it does little damage except in localised areas of the bush and should not be harmed.

Grasshoppers

Grashoppers can cause severe damage in summer. Some of the swarming species can wreak havoc over large areas, but

The handsome emperor gum moth is becoming rare due to insect control.

The adult longicorn beetle produces larvae that bore into trees.

solitary species are less destructive. Control them by picking off individuals or spraying with carbaryl in the early morning, while insects are still inactive.

Beetles

The larvae of beetles often feed on roots or on the wood of trees and shrubs. The latter are known as wood borers and can cause severe damage. They can also allow fungal infections to take hold on the damaged wood.

Longicorn beetles and weevils are the two types of wood borers most responsible for damage to plants. Their activity is usually seen as sawdust on the ground or a raised web-like substance with sawdust on the trunk.

Acacias and eucalypts are the most commonly affected plants, though Proteaceae (eg banksias, waratahs and grevilleas) and Myrtaceae (eg leptospermum, melaleuca, eucalyptus and callistemon) are also prone to borer attack.

Control by injecting active holes with carbaryl or an alcohol such as methylated spirits. A thin wire poked into the hole may help extract the larva. Keep plants healthy by proper feeding and adequate watering. Stressed plants are more prone to attack, as most healthy trees have their own defense mechanisms. In the case of healthy angophoras and eucalypts, this often takes the form of swamping the intruding larva with a sticky substance known as amber. Large amounts indicate a tree under stress and a severe infestation.

RESOURCE LIST

BOTANICAL GARDENS

Australian National Botanic Gardens
Clunies Ross Street, Black Mountain
ACT 2601
Postal address: GPO Box 1777
Ph: (02) 6250 9450 Fax: (02) 62509599
E-mail: general enquiries: murray@anbg.gov.au
Website is http://www.anbg.gov.au/anbg/

Mount Annan Botanic Garden
Mount Annan Drive, Mount Annan, NSW 2567
Ph: 02-4648 2477 Fax: 02-4648 2465
(Native seeds available by mail order.)
Website is:
http://www.rbgsyd.gov.au/RBG/Annan/annan.html

King's Park and Botanic Garden
Fraser Avenue, West Perth, WA 6005
Ph: (08) 9480 3600 Fax: (08) 9322 5064
(Some native seeds available.)
Email postmaster@kpbg.wa.gov.au
Website is http://www.kpbg.wa.gov.au/index.html

The Olive Pink Botanic Garden
Tuncks Road, Alice Springs, NT 0871
Postal address: PO Box 8644
An arid area botanical garden with over 300 Central Australian species.
Ph: (08) 8952 2154 Fax: (08) 8953 5522
E-mail: opbg@topend.com.au.
Website is http://alice.topend.com.au/~opbg/

Illawarra Grevillea Park
Bulli Showground, Pacific Highway, Bulli
(Turn at the Woonona-Bulli Sports Club, just south of Slacky Creek).
Website is:
http://www-personal.usyd.edu.au/~markz/grevillea/

GARDENS TO VISIT
The Australian Open Garden Scheme lists gardens containing Australian plants open to the public on specified days. The OGS Guidebook is released each August.

Society for Growing Australian Plants
The Society for Growing Australian Plants (SGAP) has chapters in each state and several regional and specialist groups. National website is http://farrer.riv.csu.edu.au/ASGAP/

SGAP ACT Region
P.O. Box 217, Civic Square, ACT 2608
Ph: (02) 6251 1501
Website is http://jcsmr.anu.edu.au/~gfq213/sgap

Australian Plants Society NSW
P.O. Box 744, Blacktown, NSW 2148
Ph: (02) 9621 3437 Fax: (02) 9676 7603
Email: sgap@ozemail.com.au
Website is http://www.ozemail.com.au/~sgap/scontact.htm

SGAP Queensland Region
PO Box 586, Fortitude Valley, Qld 4006
Website is:
http://www.gu.edu.au:81/uls/sgap/SGAPhome.html

Wildflower Society of Western Australia
PO Box 64, Nedlands, WA 6909
Website is http://www.ozemail.com.au/~wildflowers/

SGAP South Australia
PO Box 304, Unley, SA 5061
Website is http://members.iweb.net.au/~sgap/

SGAP Tasmanian Region
420 Brightwater Road, Howden, Tas 7054
Website is:
http://www.trump.net.au/~joroco/sgaptas-index.htm

SGAP Victorian Region
3/17 Pine Crescent, Boronia, Vic 3155
Website is http://home.vicnet.net.au/~sgapvic

PLANTS BY MAIL

The Digger's Club
105 Latrobe Parade, Dromana Victoria 3936.
Postal address: PO Box 300, Dromana).
Email: info@diggers.com.au

Yates and Mr. Fothergill's (available from most major nurseries) both have good ranges of native annuals including everlastings and Swan River daisies. Yates website is http://yates.com.au/

For information on Richmond birdwing vines:
Email Sue.Scott@sqld.helix.csiro.au
Website is http://www.nor.com.au/environment/species/birdwing/gardening.html

WILDLIFE RESOURCES

Care of Australian Wildlife by Erna Walraven, New Holland

Living with Wildlife by Eva Murray, Reed Books.

If you need help for injured animals contact your local wildlife authority, (National Parks or Conservation Department) or the RSPCA. They will provide contact details of local shelters. In NSW, contact the Wildlife Information and Rescue Service (WIRES), PO Box 260, Forestville 2087
Ph: (02) 9975 1633/1643.

ACKNOWLEDGEMENTS

We wish to thank the following people and organisations for their help with this book:

Australia's Open Garden Scheme; Michael Bates of Bates Landscaping Services; Chris Bennetts of Ishi Buki; The Royal Botanic Gardens at Mt Annan, Mt Tomah and the Australian National Botanic Gardens; Robert Boyle Landscape Design; Carol Brennan, Hot Dot Designs; Don and Marea Burke; Paul Chambers of Australian Native Landscapes Co. U.S.A.; Gregg Chapman of Faulkner & Chapman Landscape Design; Michael Cooke of Avant Garden; Tamaria and Ian Cox; Andrew Davies Landscapes; Brian Donges; Norah Elliot; John England; Gordon Ford; Peter Fudge of Garden Impressions; Jean Galliet; Graeme Greenhalgh of Tropic of Sydney; Joanne Green Landscape Design; Jo Hambrett; Bev Hanson; Eliza Heap of Art for Gardens; Margaret & Bill Henderson; Pat Hersey; Jeff Howes; Elspeth & Gary Jacobs; Barry Jarrott Landscape Design; Mr Don Lange, Director Community Relations, Olympic Management Centre, Homebush, Sydney; Chris Larkin; Professor Ron Laura; Henri Lekeu; Betty Maloney; Rhonda & Lorelle Mercer; Peter Nixon Garden Design; Andrew O'Sullivan Associates Landscapes; Sue & David Plath; Brian Preston; Diana Pringle; Rast Bros. Nursery; Beverley Read; Gordon Rowland of Indigenous Landscape Design Associates; Phillip Samios, Marketing Manager, Joint House Department, Parliament House, Canberra; Don Sands, CSIRO; Craig Scott of East Coast Flower Farm; The Society for Growing Aust. Plants; Roger Stone Landscape Design; Paul Thompson Landscape Design; Nina & Lou Tudor; Jean Villani; Vision Graphics film processing; Bobbie Waterman & George Stent; Jeremy Winer of Marsupial Landscapes; Michael Wright Garden Design.

PICTURE CREDITS

t = top   c = centre   b = bottom   l = left   r = right

NSW = New South Wales, Vic = Victoria, WA = Western Australia, Qld = Queensland, Tas - Tasmania

Designers featured

Jonathan Allin, The Sacred Holdings, NSW, 122
Michael Bates, Bates Landscaping Services, NSW, back cover *t r*, 66, 73, 74, 77, 147, 162–163
Robert Boyle Landscape Design, Vic, 23, 144, 145 *t*, 151
Don Burke, NSW, 55 *t & b r*, 79 *t r*, 117–119, 148 *r*, 163, 196 *t*
Paul Chambers, Australian Native Landscapes Co., USA. 80 *l*, 81, 202, 203
Gregg Chapman, Faulkner & Chapman Landscape Design, Vic, 67 *l*, 80 *r*, 108, 109, 111, 145 *c*, 154 *b l*, 160 *l*, 165 *t*
Michael Cooke, Avant Garden, NSW, 31, 70
Andrew Davies Landscapes, NSW, 146
Brian Donges, NSW, 143 *t r*
Peter Fudge, Garden Impressions, NSW, half-title page, back cover *l*, 121, 123
Good Manors Landscaping, NSW, 2, 83, 124, 125, 126, 127 (original design)
Graham Greenhalgh, Tropic of Sydney, NSW, 138 *r*, 139 *t*
Joanne Green Landscape Design, NSW 61, 68
Eliza Heap, Art for Gardens & Katisma Landscapes, NSW, 156
Barry Jarrott Landscape Design, NSW, 2, 83, 124, 125, 126, 127 (replanting)
Henri Lekeu, NSW, 75, 82
Darryl Mappin, Qld, 72 *b*
Peter Nixon Garden Design, NSW, 85
Andrew O'Sullivan & Associates Landscapes, NSW, 75, 79 *b*, 82, 152, 153
Brian Preston, NSW, 21
Diana Pringle, NSW, 161
Beverley Road, Good Garden Sense, NSW, 164 *t*
Gordon Rowland, Indigenous Landscape, NSW, 76, 159 *r*
Roger Stone Landscape Design, Vic, 14–15, 86–87, 100, 102, 103, 141 *t l & r*
Richard Stutchbury, NSW, 148 *l*
Paul Thompson Landscape Design, Vic, 59, 136–137, 138 *l*, 141 *b l*, 145 *b*, 149 *l & r*, 150, 154 *t l*
Jeremy Winer, Marsupial Landscapes, NW, 160 *r*
Michael Wright Garden Design, Vic, back cover *b r*, 49 *t l*

Locations featured

The Australian National Botanic Gardens, Canberra, 164 *b*
Blue Courtyard, Olympic Management Centre, Homebush, Sydney, NSW, 72 *t*
Bridgewater Quest Apartments, Qld, 142 *r*
Butler garden, NSW, 159 *l*
Cox garden, NSW, 65
East Coast Flower Farm, NSW, endpapers, back cover inset, 32–33, 166–167, 174–175, 193
John England garden, Qld, 72 *b*, 78
The Everglades, NSW, 19
Fülling garden, Vic, 162 *l*
The Gallery & Gardens LLC, Hawaii, 79 *t l*
Jean Galliet garden, Vic, 139 *b*
Hanson garden, Vic, 27, 63, 104, 107, 157 *r*
Henderson garden, Canberra, 165 *b*
High Trees, NSW, 55 *t l*, 68, 143 *b l*
Howes garden, NSW, 128, 129, 131, 196 *b*
Jacob garden, Vic, 30, 50–51, 194–195
Joint House Department, Parliament House, Canberra, 67 *r*, 69
Joyce garden, Vic, 59, 136–137, 138 *l*, 145 *b*, 149 *r*, 150
Kings Park, WA, 64 *l*
Larkin garden, Vic, 14–15, 86–87, 100, 102–103
Laura garden, NSW, 92, 93, 95
Betty Maloney garden, NSW, 24, 55 *b l*, 96–98, 132–135, 140
Mercer garden, NSW, 112, 115
Mt Tomah Botanic Gardens, NSW, 141 *b r*
The Royal Botanic Gardens, Mt Annan, NSW, 88, 143 *b r*
Seddon garden, WA, 62
St Anthony's Creek, NSW, 10
Tudor garden, NSW, 84
Waterfall Cottage, NSW, 56, 168
Wyadra Falls garden, NSW, 158 *l*
Yanderra, NSW, 17

Artists featured

Chris Bennetts, Ishi Buki, NSW, 154 *t r & b r*, 158 *r*
Carol Brennan, Hot Dot Designs, NSW, 154 *b r*
Rudi Jass, Vic, 156
Rural Design, Tas, 157 *l*

Additional photography

Nan Barbour, 207 *t*
Anthony Healy, 210 *l*
Lansdowne Publishing (Reg Morrison & Ray Joyce), 207 *b*, 208–209, 210 *c & r*, 211–214
Don Sands, CSIRO, 171

INDEX

accent plants, 29
annuals, 90
arid gardens, 31, 80–2, 197
artworks, 154–7
Australian Open Garden Scheme, 215
Australian plants
    history of white discovery, 10–12
    as national symbols, 13

balance, 20, 146
birds, 132, 134, 135, 172–3
blended gardens, 83–5, 126
bog gardens, 112–15
borders, 93–5, 147
botanical gardens, 215
boundaries, 142
bush garden style, 52, 57–8
bushland, 54
butterfly gardens, 170–1

children, gardens for, 148, 152
climbing plants, 30
colour, 35
    blues, 39
    contemporary garden design, 71
    contrasts, 35
    copper tones, 45
    courtyard gardens, 75
    creams, 42
    discords, 35
    greens, 41, 116
    harmony, 35
    mauves, 39
    oranges, 46–7
    pinks, 36
    reds, 36
    silver, 40
    whites, 42
    yellows, 46–7
columnar plants, 30
containers, 164–5
contemporary garden design, 71–4, 125–7
cottage gardens, 62–4, 93–5
courtyard gardens, 75–8
    naturalistic style, 129–31
curves, 61

desert landscape, 53
design, see also site analysis
    for gardens next to bushland, 54
    preliminary, 25
    principles, 18, 20–1
    process, 16–17
diseases, 206, 207–9

drainage, 26

entrances, 142

fences, 142, 143
fertilising, 198
formal gardens, 66–70, 71, 120–7
frogs, 169
fungal diseases, 206, 207–8

garden art, 154–7
garden style
    definition, 52
    types, 52–3
gardens
    near bushland, 54
    to visit, 215
gates, 142
grasses, 116
gravel 'beach' gardens, 105–7
groves, 148–51

harmony, 59
hedges, 121–3, 142, 143, 147

informal style mixed with formal style, 126
irrigation, 203

Japanese garden design, 102

lawns, 105
leaf-eating insects, 211–14
levels, 20
lines
    created by paths, 138
    formal gardens, 21, 67, 120
    of sight, 20–1
lizards, 168–9

mail order plants, 216
meadow gardens, 89–91
mixed borders, 93–5
movement, 18
mulching, 202

natural landscapes, 52–3
naturalistic style, 57–61

orchids, 96–9, 132
outdoor living concept, 23

paths, 138–40
patterns, 21
perspective, 102
pests, 206, 209–14

planning, 24–5
planting
    around pools, 144–5
    techniques, 196–7
plants, choosing, 28–31
playground areas, 153
ponds, 160, 169
pool planting, 144–5
possums, 169–70
propagation, 204
pruning techniques, 200–1
pyramidal plants, 30

rainforest gardens, 57, 132–5
raised beds, 27, 108–11
repetition, 21, 146–7
Rock Lily gardens, 96–9

sandpits, 152, 153
sapsuckers, 209–11
scale, 102
seaside plants, 31
shade-loving plants, 31
shapes, 21
site analysis, 22
Society for Growing Australian Plants (SGAP), 13, 215
soil, 26–7
space
    creating illusion of, 101–2
    principle, 18
spreading plants, 30
steps, 140–1
stroll garden, 103
surprise, 18
symmetry, 67

tapestry gardens, see blended gardens
texture, 48
touch, 48
tree ferns, 116
tropical gardens, 78–9

urban gardens, 75–8

visual links, 60

Walling, Edna, 13, 18, 67
walls, 108–9
water bowls, 158, 159
water features, 125, 144–5, 158–61
watering, 203
Wildflower Society of Western Australia, 215
wildlife, 132, 134, 168–73
woodland garden, 116–19

PLANT INDEX

Acacia, 31, 57, 81, 171, 172, 173, 198, 204, 211, 212, 214
    A. baileyana, 171
    A. baileyana 'Purpurea', 39
    A. boormanii, 173
    A. cognata 'Lime Magik', 147
    A. dealbata, 171
    A. decurrens, 171
    A. drummondii, 95
    A. glaucoptera, 45
    A. howittii, 147
    A. iteaphylla, 147
    A. longifolia, 171
    A. podalyriifolia, 40, 171
    A. ulicifolia, 173
Acer palmatum, 125
Acmena smithii, 171
Actinotus helianthi, 42, 187
Agathis robusta, 59
Agonis, 173
    A. flexuosa, 147
    A. flexuosa 'Jervis Bay Afterdark', 36, 71, 147
Alloxylon, 173
    A. pinnatum syn. *Oreocallis pinnata*, 60
Alocasia brisbanensis syn. *A. macrorrhizos*, 113, 115
Alphitonia excelsa, 60
Alpina coerulea, 41
Alyogne huegelii, 37
Angophora, 213
    A. costata, 10, 34, 61, 150
    A. hispida, 200
Anigozanthos, 34, 187, 204
    A. costata, 34
    A. manglesii, 41, 208
    A. 'Bush Dawn', 34, 47, 55
    A. 'Bush Emerald', 41
    A. 'Bush Gem', 62
    A. 'Bush Gold', 64
    A. 'Bush Haze', 125, 127
    A. 'Bush Illusion', 64
    A. 'Bush Ranger', 95
    A. 'Bush Twilight', 64
    A. 'Pink Joey', 125
    A. 'Red Ranger', 125
Araucaria, 13, 59, 210
Aristolochia elegans, 171
Asclepia, 170
Asplenium
    A. bulbiferum, 55
    A. nidus, 132, 134, 135
Athrotaxis cupressoides, 59
Austromyrtus dulcis, 78, 120, 123

Bacon-and-eggs, 12
Baeckea, 198, 211
    B. gunniana, 113
    B. linifolia, 60
    B. linifolia 'Clarence River', 60
    B. virgata, 123
    B. virgata 'Clarence River', 172
    B. virgata 'Nana', 30, 63, 143
Bamboo Spear Grass, 23, 192
Banksia, 30, 31, 45, 48, 54, 99, 149, 172, 173, 198, 204, 210, 213, 214
    B. coccinea, 179
    B. ericifolia, 45, 46, 105, 107, 17
    B. integrifolia, 149, 176
    B. menziesii, 47
    B. prionotes, 46
    B. robur, 31, 45, 113, 115, 125
    B. serrata, 96
    B. serrata 'Austraflora Pygmy Possum', 30
    B. spinulosa 'Coastal Cushion', 30
    B. 'Giant Candles', 46, 47, 143
Bauera, 198
    B. rubioides, 45, 113, 179, 196
Berberis thunbergii 'Atopurpurea Nana', 123
Biennial, 197
Billy Buttons, 55, 89
Bird of Paradise, 126
Birds' Nest Fern, 78, 85, 132, 134, 135
Black Bean, 173
Black Wattle, 171
Blackboy, 173
Blandfordia nobilis, 113
Blechnum
    B. cartilagineum, 107
    B. fluviatile, 113
    B. nudum, 113
    B. wattsii, 113
Blue Lace Flower, 62
Blue Leschenaultia, 39, 188
Blueberry Ash, 60, 177
Bonsai, 155
Boronia, 13, 48, 145, 198, 211
    B. denticulata, 108, 111
    B. mollis 'Lorne Pride', 29, 30
Bossaia, 204
Bottlebrush, 36, 83, 113, 147, 173, 200, 201
Bower Wattle, 147
Bracelet Honey Myrtle, 173
Brachychiton, 213
    B. acerifolium, 60, 171
    B. populneus, 60, 171
    Brachycome, 34, 42, 62, 63, 90, 129
    B. iberidifolia, 90
    B. multifida, 90, 111, 131
    B. multifida alba, 63
    B. multifida 'Break of Day', 111
    B. 'Bush Gems', 62

Bracteantha, 63, 85, 89, 90
    B. bracteata, 89
    B. bracteata 'Cockatoo', 39, 47, 95
    B. bracteata 'Dargan Hill Monarch', 39
    B. bracteata 'Diamond Head', 64
Broad Leaf Geebung, 173
Buckinghamia celsissima, 78
Bunya Pine, 13, 59
    Buxus, 66, 121
    B. sempervirens, 120, 121

Cabbage Tree Palm, 13
Callistemon, 29, 45, 85, 147, 171, 172, 173, 200, 201, 205, 211, 213, 214
    C. citrinus, 113
    C. pinifolius, 41
    C. salignus, 125
    C. sieberi, 113
    C. subulatus, 113
    C. 'Reeve's Pink', 179
Callitris, 13, 59, 172, 173, 213
    C. collumellaris, 30
    C. rhomboidea, 30
Calytrix, 13
Camphor Laurel, 17
Canberra Grass, 34, 41, 113
Cassia brewsteri, 78
Castonospermum australe, 173
Casuarina, 45, 59, 172, 173, 211
Cat's Whiskers, 78
Cattleya, 96
Celery Top Pine, 59
Ceratopetalum
    C. gummiferum, 12, 173, 176, 211
    C. gummiferum 'Magenta Star', 36
Cercis siliquastrum, 105, 107
Chamelaucium uncinatum, 93, 95, 120, 123, 173, 180
Chinese Star Jasmine, 120
Chorizema, 63, 204
    cordatum, 24, 46, 47, 95, 131
Chrysocephalum apiculatum, 55, 89
Cinnamonum oliveri, 17
Clematis aristata, 30
Climbing Lignum, 189
Club Rush, 173
Coast Banksia, 40, 149, 176
Coast Rosemary, 115, 185
Coast Teatree, 173
Common Tussock Grass, 23, 191
Conostylis aculeata, 196
Convolvulus sabatius, 111
Cootamundra Wattle, 39, 142, 171
Cordyline, 185
    C. australis, 108, 111

C. rubra, 78
C. stricta, 85, 96, 101, 134, 135, 185
Correa, 30, 36, 41, 126, 173
C. reflexa, 180
Corymbia, 171
Cranbrook Bell, 180
Creeping Rush, 113, 192
Crinum pedunculatum, 115, 125, 142, 185
Cunjevoi, 113, 115
Cupressus, 66
Cyathea cooperi, 79, 116, 132, 134
Cymbidium, 96
Cypress Pine, 59

Daisy, 131
Daisy Bush, 37
Dampiera, 147
D. linearis, 64
D. purpurea, 27, 29
Danthonia, 173
Dark Red Kangaroo Paw, 127
Darling Pea, 188
Darwinia, 36
D. citridora, 69
D. meeboldii, 180
Dendrobium
D. kingianum, 96, 99, 129, 131
D. speciosum, 96, 99, 129, 131
D. X delicatum, 99
Dianella, 113, 116
D. caerulea, 119
D. tasmanica, 119
Dianthus, 84
Dicksonia antarctica, 113, 116
Dietes bicolor, 125
Dillwynia, 36, 45
D. sericea, 12
Dodonaea, 171
D. boroniifolia, 181
D. viscosa var. *purpurea*, 36
Doodia aspera, 107, 113, 134, 135
Doryanthes, 142
D. excelsa, 36, 41, 85, 131, 185
Drumsticks, 190
Dryandra, 198
Dusty Daisy Bush, 182
Dutchman's Pipe, 171
Dwarf Apple, 200
Dwarf Kangaroo Paw, 64
Dwarf Lillypilly, 63, 145

Elaeocarpus, 171
E. reticulatus, 177
E. reticulatus 'Prima Donna', 177
Elkhorn, 78

Elm, 60
Emu Bush, 181
Epacris, 36
E. lanuginosa, 45
E. longifolia, 45
E. reclinata, 113
Eremocitrus glauca, 213
Eremophila, 57, 181
E. nivea, 93, 95
Eriostemon, 13, 99
E. australasius, 37, 55
E. buxifolius, 27
E. myoporoides, 66, 69, 142, 145, 181, 213
Eucalyptus, 45, 52, 60, 95, 149, 171, 173, 210, 211, 212, 213, 214
E. caesia, 40, 147, 176, 205
E. erythrocorys, 47, 177
E. haemastoma, 45, 125, 149
E. leucoxylon, 177
E. maculata, 40
E. melliodora, 10
E. papuana, 81
E. punctata, 149
Eutaxia, 198
Exotic Candy-tuft, 63
Exotic Santolina, 123

False Sarsparilla, 189
Fan Flower, 191
Fern-leaf Hop Bush, 181
Ficus, 171, 173
Fig, 171, 173
Flannel Flower, 42, 187
Flax Lily, 116
Flowering Gum, 36
Forest Phebalium, 183
Fringed Lily, 189

Gardenia, 121, 126
G. florida, 120
Gazania, 84
Geebung, 173
Geraldon Wax, 93, 95, 120, 123, 173, 180
Ghania, 171
Ghost Gum, 81
Golden Penda, 78
Gompholobium, 46
Goodenia
G. humilis, 113
G. lanata, 113
Goodia lotifolia, 173
Graptophyllum excelsum, 123
Grass Tree, 41, 48, 55, 71, 75, 82, 83, 126, 142, 173, 187
Grevillea, 13, 29, 36, 47, 60, 63, 78, 80, 85, 93, 95, 131, 147, 171, 172, 173, 182, 198, 201, 205,

213, 214
G. biternata, 42
G. buxifolia, 12
G. hookeriana, 30
G. robusta, 60
G. thelemanniana, 30
G. 'Bronze Rambler', 30, 64
G. 'Ivanhoe', 30
G. 'Pink Pearl', 95
G. 'Robyn Gordon', 29, 145
G. 'Royal Mantle', 30
G. 'Superb', 115
Grey Gum, 149
Grey Spider Flower, 12
Gungurru, 176
Gymea Lily, 36, 41, 85, 129, 131, 142, 186

Hakea, 45, 60, 173
H. leucoptera, 173
Happy Wanderer, 30
Hardenbergia, 30
H. violacea, 189
Heath Banksia, 45, 179
Hebe, 126
H. 'Blue Gem', 125, 126
Helichrysum, 89, 90
H. petiolare, 31
H. ramosissimum, 55
Helipterum, 89
H. roseum, 91
Hibbertia, 64, 101
H. empetrifolia, 30
H. stellaris, 101, 190
Honey Bracelet Myrtle, 149
Hoop Pine, 13, 59
Hovea, 63
Hoya, 210
Hymenosporum flavum, 177
Hypocalymma, 198

Illawarra Flame Tree, 60, 171, 213
Illyarie, 47, 177
Isopogon, 173, 198
Ivory Curl Tree, 78

Japanese Maple, 125
Judas Tree, 105, 107
Juncus, 173
J. pauciflorus, 113

Kalanchoë, 84
Kangaroo Grass, 40, 48, 89, 126
Kangaroo Paw, 34, 46, 47, 55, 62, 64, 83, 126, 172, 187, 196, 205, 208
Kauri Pine, 13, 59

Index

Kennedia, 80, 126
    K. prostrata, 30, 64
    K. rubicunda, 30
King Fern, 113
King Orchid, 99, 129, 131
Kunzea, 172, 173
    K. capitata, 113, 172
Kurrajong, 60, 171, 213

Large Flowered Thomasia, 184
Lavender, 63, 85, 123
Leichhardt Bean, 78
Lemon-scented Tea-tree, 173
Leptospermum, 31, 54, 57, 147, 171, 200, 214
    L. flavescens, 173
    L. laevigatum, 173
    L. lanigerum, 113
    L. rotundifolium 'Lavender Queen', 101
    L. rubrum 'Nana', 123
    L. scoparium, 113
    L. scoparium 'Red Damask', 143
    L. 'Cardwell', 93
    L. 'Rudolph', 71
Leschenaultia, 39, 62, 198, 204
    L. biloba, 64, 188
    L. formosa, 64, 208
Leucodendron, 85
Leucophyta brownii, 123
Leucospermum, 85
Lillypilly, 30, 41, 63, 83, 85, 120, 121, 122, 145, 173
Lily, 116
Liquidamber, 60
Lomandra, 85, 115, 116, 129, 173
    longifolia, 23, 55, 131, 191
Lomatia, 116
Lonicera, 121

Macrozamia, 58
Magenta Star, 36
Mangle's Everlasting, 90
Maple, 60
Mat Rush, 55, 131, 191
Melaleuca, 31, 57, 60, 61, 85, 171, 172, 173, 200, 214
    M. armillaris, 113, 149, 173
    M. armillaris 'Green Globe', 123
    M. bracteata, 113
    M. bracteata 'Golden Gem', 41, 120, 123
    M. bracteata 'Revolution Gold', 41
    M. bracteata 'Revolution Green', 41
    M. diosmifolia, 41
    M. incana, 40, 48
    M. linariifolia, 95
    M. linariifolia 'Seafoam', 42
    M. quinquenervia, 113

    M. styphelioides, 113, 173
Melia
    M. azedarach, 101, 212
    M. azedarach var. *australasica*, 60, 84, 178
Microcitrus australasica, 213
Midyim, 78
Milkweed, 170
Mint Bush, 36, 63, 145, 201
Moreton Bay Fig, 13
Muehlenbeckia adpressa, 189
Murraya paniculata, 66

Native Buttercups, 89
Native Cypress, 172, 173
Native Frangipani, 177
Native Fuchsia, 173, 180
Native Ginger, 41
Native Grass, 45, 116
Native Hibiscus, 37
Native Rhodendron, 85
Native Tibouchina, 78
New South Wales Christmas Bell, 113
New South Wales Christmas Bush, 12, 150, 173, 176, 201, 211
Norfolk Island Pine, 13
Nothofagus
    N. gunnii, 60
    N. moorei, 60

Olearia, 13, 63
    O. phlogopappa, 13, 37, 182
Oliver's Sassafras, 17
Orthosiphon aristatus, 78
Orthrosantus
    O. laxus, 39
    O. multiforus, 111
Ozothamnus
    O. diosmifolius, 147
    O. diosmifolius syn. *Helichrysum diosmifolius*, 182

Palms, 60, 78, 132, 210
Pandanus spiralis, 173
Pandorea, 80
    P. jasminoides, 30
    P. pandorana, 30, 66
    P. pandorana 'Snow Bells', 190
Paper Daisy, 62
Pararistolochia
    P. laheyana, 171
    P. praevenosa, 171
Patersonia, 129
    P. glabrata, 39, 101
Payne's Thryptomene, 131, 184
Pea, 204

Pencil pine, 59
Pennisetum alopecuroides, 36
Persoonia, 60, 173, 213
    P. levis, 173
    P. pinifolia, 173
Phebalium, 145
    P. lamprophyllum, 42
    P. squamulosum, 183
Phyla nodiflora, 113
Phyllocladus, 59
    P. aspleniifolius, 59
Pimelea, 171, 204
    P. ferruginea, 183
    P. nivea, 40
Pink Rice Flower, 183
Pink Wax Flower, 37
Pittosporum, 145
Plane tree, 60
Plectranthus
    P. argentatus, 40, 48, 71, 205
Poa Grass, 129, 173
Poa labillardieri, 23, 40, 191
Podocarpus, 59
    P. elatus, 122
Pomaderris, 145, 183
    P. elliptica, 183
Pratia concolor, 42
Prickley Moses Wattle, 173
Prickly Paperbark, 173
Prostanthera, 201, 205
    P. lasianthos, 108, 111
    P. magnifica, 36, 64
    P. ovalifolia, 76, 111, 183
    P. rotundifolia, 108, 111
Prunus cerasifera 'Pissardii', 85
Pultenea, 198
Purple Mint Bush, 183
Pycnosorus globosus syn. *Craspedia globosas*, 190

Queensland Bottle Tree, 143
Queensland Firewheel Tree, 60, 173, 178
Queensland Wattle, 171

Raise Grass Tree, 75
Ranunculus rivularis, 113
Rasp Fern, 113, 134, 135
Red Ash, 60
Red Cap Gum, 177
Red Cedar, 60
Restio, 45, 116, 147, 165
    R. tetraphyllus, 45, 47, 48, 113, 192
Rhagodia
    R. crassifolia, 123
    R. nutans, 123
    R. spinescens, 123
Rhodanthe, 36, 89, 91
    R. appaceus, 89
    R. chlorocephala ssp. *rosea*, 63, 90, 91

R. manglesii, 36, 90
Rhododendron, 60
   R. lochiae, 78, 85
Riberry, 60
Richmond birdwing vines, 171, 216
River Rose, 113, 179
Rock Lily, 96, 99, 131
Rosy Everlasting, 90
Rottnest Island Daisy, 62
Rush, 173

Sago Bush, 147
Sago Flower, 182
Sago Palm, 82
Scaevola, 34, 63, 101, 108, 147, 171
   S. aemula, 39, 101, 111, 191
   S. aemula 'Purple Fanfare', 39
Scarlet Banksia, 179
Schoenia
   S. filifolia, 47, 89
   S. filifolia ssp. *subulifolia*, 64, 90
Scirpus 'Fairy Lights', 173
Scleranthus, 101, 147
   S. biflorus, 34, 41, 103, 113, 208
Screw Palm, 173
Scribbly Gum, 149
Sedum, 84
Senna, 57, 204
   S. artemisioides syn. *Cassia artemisioides*, 184
She Oak, 173
Showy Everlasting Daisy, 36, 47, 89, 90
Silky Oak, 60
Silver Bells, 90
Silver Cassia, 184
Silver Needlewood, 173
Snow-in-summer, 84

Snowy Everlasting Daisy, 47, 64, 89, 90
Snowy Pimelea, 40
Snowy River Wattle, 173
Sollya, 80
South African Protea, 85
Spanish Iris, 125
Staghorn, 78
Starry Guinea Flower, 190
Stenocarpus sinuatus, 60, 173, 177, 178
Sticky Wattle, 147
Stipa ramosissima, 23, 192
Stoloniferous, 113
Strawflower, 34, 47, 62, 83, 90, 168
Sturt's Desert Pea, 57, 62, 80, 81, 188, 197
Swainsona
   S. formosa, 188
   S. galegifolia, 188
Swamp Banksia, 31, 45, 113, 115, 125
Swamp Fox Grass, 36
Swamp Lily, 142
Swamp Lily White, 185
Swan River Daisy, 62, 90
Swordgrass, 116
Sydney Golden Wattle, 171
Syzygium, 30, 52, 121, 142, 173, 210
   S. australe 'Blaze', 120, 121, 122
   S. australe 'Bush Christmas', 121, 122
   S. australe 'Lilliput', 120, 121, 122
   S. australe 'Tiny Trev', 120, 121
   S. luehmannii, 60
   S. paniculatum, 122

Tea-tree, 64, 143, 211
Telopea, 198
   T. speciosissima, 186
   T. speciosissima 'Wirrimbirra White', 42
   T. 'Shady Lady', 48

Themeda
   T. australis, 171
   T. triandra, 40, 48, 89
Thomasia
   T. grandiflora, 184
   T. pygmaea, 101
Thryptomene, 160, 205
   T. 'Payne's Hybrid', 41, 76, 131, 184
Thysanotus multiflorus, 189
Todea barbara, 113
Toona ciliata syn. *T. australis*, 60
Trachymene caeruleus, 62
Tree Waratah, 173

Verticordia, 173, 204
Viola
   V. betonicifolia, 113
   V. hederacea, 113

Waratah, 85, 186, 201, 205, 210, 214
Wattle, 173, 211
Wax Flower, 181
Westringia, 31, 116, 119, 126, 145
   W. fruticosa, 66, 69, 115, 125, 185
   W. fruticosa 'Hedge', 125
   W. fruticosa 'Wynyabbie Gem', 111, 123
White Cedar, 60, 84, 178, 212
White Ironbark, 177
White Waratah, 42
Wonga Wonga Vine, 190

Xanthorrhoea, 71, 75, 173
   X. australis, 41, 55, 187
Xanthostemon chrysanthus, 78

Yellow Box, 10
Yellow Gum, 177

Page 6
Most eremophilas are desert plants but they adapt to a range of habitats provided soil is well drained. *Eremophila nivea* is one of the most useful decorative shrubs for the native or blended garden.

Endnotes

1. *Watkin Tench 1788*, edited by Tim Flannery, Text Publishing, 1996, p 70.
2. Ibid, p 231.
3. Quoted p 34, *Cherish the Earth*, from 'Lectures on the Horticulture of NSW' by Thomas Shepherd, W. M. M'Garvie, 1835 and 'Lectures on Landscape Gardening in Australia' by Thomas Shepherd, Sydney, W. M. M'Garvie, 1836.
4. Ibid, p 43.
5. Ibid, p 69.
6. Thomas D. Church, *Gardens are for People*, University of California Press, reprinted 1995, p32
7. Ibid, p 32.

Published in Australia by
New Holland Publishers (Australia) Pty Ltd
Sydney • Auckland • London • Cape Town

14 Aquatic Drive Frenchs Forest NSW 2086 Australia
218 Lake Road Northcote Auckland New Zealand
86 Edgeware Road london W2 2EA United Kingdom
80 McKenzie Street Cape Town 8001 South Africa

First published in 1999 by Lansdowne Publishing Pty Ltd
Reprinted in 2000 and 2001 by New Holland Publishers (Australia) Pty Ltd

Copyright © 1999 in text: Paul Urquhart
Copyright © 1999 in photographs: Leigh Clapp, except where listed on p.217
Copyright © 1999 concept and design: New Holland Publishers (Australia) Pty Ltd

All rights reserved. No part of this publication may be reproduced, stored in a retrieval system or transmitted, in any form or by any means, electronic, mechanical, photocopying, recording or otherwise, without the prior written permission of the publishers and copyright holders.

National Library of Australia Cataloguing-in-Publication Data:

Urquhart, Paul, 1952–.
The new native garden: designing with Australian plants.

Includes index.
ISBN 1 86436 749 0.

1. Native plant gardening — Australia. 2. Landscape gardening — Australia.
I. Clapp, Leigh. II. Title.

635.95194

Commissioned by Deborah Nixon
Designer: Robyn Latimer
Production Manager: Sally Stokes
Project Coordinator: Kate Merrifield
Editor: Susan Tomnay
Illustrations by Jeff Lang
Typeset in Cantoria and Avant Garde
Printer: Imago Productions